David Brooks

BACKWARD AND UPWARD:

The New Conservative Writing

David Brooks, formerly Op-Ed editor of the
Wall Street Journal, is now senior editor of the
Standard. He lives in Washington, D.C.

D1056373

BACKWARD AND UPWARD:

The New Conservative Writing

BACKWARD AND UPWARD:

The New Conservative Writing

EDITED AND WITH AN INTRODUCTION BY

David Brooks

VINTAGE BOOKS • A DIVISION OF RANDOM HOUSE, INC. • NEW YORK

A VINTAGE ORIGINAL, JANUARY 1996
First edition
Copyright © 1995 by David Brooks

Grateful acknowledgment is made to the following for permission to reprint previously published material:

Regnery Publishing, Inc.: Excerpts from *The Conservative Mind* by Russell Kirk (Washington, D.C.: Regnery Publishing, Inc., 1953). Reprinted by permission of Regnery Publishing, Inc.

Warner Bros. Publications U.S. Inc.: Excerpt from "How's Your Romance" by Cole Porter, copyright © 1932 (renewed) by Warner Bros. Inc.; excerpt from "I'm Throwing a Ball Tonight" by Cole Porter, copyright © 1936 (renewed) by Chappell & Co. (ASCAP); excerpt from "Night and Day" by Cole Porter, copyright © 1932 (renewed) by Warner Bros. Inc. All rights reserved. Reprinted by permission of Warner Bros. Publications U.S. Inc., Miami, FL 33014.

Library of Congress Cataloging-in-Publication Data
Backward and upward : the new conservative writing / edited and with an introduction by David Brooks.
p.   cm.
ISBN 0-679-76654-5 (pbk.)
1. United States—Politics and government—1993–   2. Conservatism—United States.   I. Brooks, David (David Benjamin)
E885.B33   1996
973.929—dc20   95-23867
CIP

Pages 327-330 constitute an extension of this copyright page.

Printed in the United States of America
10 9 8 7 6 5 4 3 2 1

Talk of the ways of spreading a wholesome Conservatism throughout this country: give painful lectures, distribute weary tracts (and perhaps it is just as well—you may be able to give an argumentative answer to a few objections, you may diffuse a distinct notion of the dignified dullness of politics); but as far as communicating and establishing your creed are concerned—try a little pleasure. The way to keep up old customs is, to enjoy old customs; the way to be satisfied with the present state of things is, to enjoy that state of things. Over the 'Cavalier' mind this world passes with a thrill of delight; there is an exultation in a daily event, zest in the 'regular thing,' joy at an old feast.

—*Walter Bagehot, 1876*

Contents

CONTENTS

Introduction

I PUT UP A GOOD FIGHT, struggling vainly like a hooked fish. But the twenty-second time the photographer from *The New York Times Magazine* asked me to cross my arms in front of my chest, I gave in. Of the hundred or so he snapped, that was the photograph they decided to publish.

It was a romantic notion, hoping that I could be the first conservative in the history of glossy magazines to be shown with his arms not folded across his chest. But the weight of the cliché was too strong; conservatives are always shown that way. Sometimes, as in a *New York Times* shot of Bill Kristol, the photographer can make the chin jut forward, mouth grim—Mussolini-style. A *GQ* story showed four conservatives, including Bob Tyrrell and the Heritage Foundation's Ed Feulner, and they all had their arms crossed. Those pictures were stark black-and-white, and the subjects' expressions were so severe and unforgiving that they looked like the town fathers of old Salem during the incineration of an especially blasphemous witch. Baby-faced Ralph Reed of the Christian Coalition got the arms-crossed treatment from *Newsweek,* but Reed can hold a smile, so they could only make him look smug.

In my case, the photographer from the *Times Magazine* was a tattooed young man, in a soiled T-shirt. He stuck me in a dark hallway and put the camera on a tripod about a foot and a half off the ground. The lens was kept open about thirty seconds for each shot, and while I had to remain stock-still, mouth clenched, the photographer darted around shining a flashlight in my face at odd angles. I thought I ended up looking like a serial killer, but my friends thought child-molester.

In the melodrama of American politics, conservatives are the heavies. We are the stern ones, the thin-lipped ones. Even when we are complimented, it's with phrases appropriate to a dangerous villain. A piece on the *Wall Street Journal*'s editorial page in *New York* magazine was headlined SMART, FEROCIOUS AND VERY, VERY POWERFUL, as if the page's editor were Lex Luthor. The cliché headline for a story about conservatives is THUNDER ON THE RIGHT, suggesting a stampede in Adam Smith neckties. The driving force behind the '94 election was said to be Angry White Males; a spirit of meanness was abroad in the land.

Well, I've been around conservatives, and "angry" is the wrong word to describe them. Lately "giddy" might be more accurate. "Tipsy" is sometimes appropriate. "Obnoxious" is not to be missed. But most intriguing is "hefty."

It used to be that liberalism, and the labor movement in particular, boasted the public figures who looked like former high-school linebackers. But now as one surveys the field of 1990s-style conservative leaders—Rush Limbaugh, Bill Bennett, Newt Gingrich, Bill Kristol, Ed Crane of the CATO Institute, and Ed Feulner of Heritage—one can't help noticing the bulk. Trend-spotters label it Hefty Chic, the emergence of people not cut from the Brooks Brothers cloth, with robust appetites—who are not strangers to big steaks and a mug of beer.

These days, conservatives are as likely to draw inspiration from Falstaff as from Savanarola. Which is not to say that every contributor to this anthology of new conservative writing is fat. I judge people by the content of their character, not the quantity of their skin surface. But modern conservative writing (as opposed to politics) is low on puritanism. Conservatives are still moralists, but they are merry moralists.

In the pages that follow, James Bowman defends violence on TV, Florence King praises the sophisticated insult, and Danielle Crittenden makes the case for heavy drug use in the delivery room. Joe Queenan ridicules the antismoking brigades (a big conservative cause—not because there are a lot of conservative cigarette smokers, but rather because it is necessary to demonstrate that life has a spiritual element, and everything cannot be reduced to the question, Will it help you live longer). John Podhoretz celebrates Washington, D.C., and the parties one finds there. Richard Brookhiser celebrates the clever life, as lived by Cole Porter.

Look at contemporary conservative heroes. P. J. O'Rourke celebrates fast cars, hard liquor, and adventurous sex, and he is now the favorite speaker on the conservative dinner circuit (two of his talks are included in the pages that follow). The *American Spectator* draws inspiration from H. L. Mencken and publishes an American Saloon Series, paying homage to great bars across the globe. The *National Review* has run a few special sections devoted to pleasure (though, to be fair, in the first one they left out sex). Allan Bloom, one of the most misunderstood conservatives, wrote two magnificent books in defense of eros. Dana Rohrabacher, a former Reagan speechwriter and now a staunch conservative congressman, is one of several notable conservative surfers. Judge Alex Kozinski is a Nintendo aficionado and snowboarder. John Buckley, former spokesman for Jack Kemp, began his career as rock critic for the now defunct *Soho News,* while Danny Wattenberg, a writer for conservative magazines, began his as a punk rocker.

Imagine someone who personifies the modern improprieties. He would be a bombastic red-meat-eating, cigar-smoking, overweight white male with unrelenting views and a mischievous sense of humor. That's Rush Limbaugh (our very own Falstaff).

The temperance impulse certainly isn't absent from the Right—politicians still must pay homage to it, and any sensible person respects bourgeois puritanism, given the alternative of nihilistic relativism. But there is also a new conservative personality that is urbane, self-assured (rather than defensive), cosmopolitan, and diverse in race and gender.

The essays in this book have to be seen in context of the history of the conservative movement. The story of modern American conservatism is an exodus story. In 1950 Lionel Trilling famously noted, with some justice, that there were no conservative ideas in general circulation. Then came the founding of the *National Review,* which in its inaugural editorial announced that conservatism's duty was to stand athwart history yelling stop. Whittaker Chambers felt that in leaving communism for conservatism, he was jumping from history's winning side to the losing one. Conservatives of that era toyed with the idea of "The Remnant," a small band of civilized people who would harbor ancient civilities while the rest of humanity sunk into depravity.

Political movements that perceive themselves in the wilderness often demonstrate courage, clarity, and brilliance, but they do not emanate good cheer. Conservatism in that era was primarily rural and Western, alienated from the urban engines of culture. It was often a movement of farm boys in small towns, solitary readers of Hayek, Oakeshott, Burke, or Rand. A young Fred Thompson passed the time as a night clerk at his local motel in Tennessee reading Russell Kirk's *The Conservative Mind.* (Mr. Thompson was elected to the U. S. Senate in 1994.) Conservatives felt themselves overrun by a liberal establishment that was bigger, better connected, and importantly, socially prestigious. Only William F. Buckley could match the social skills and sophistication of the leading liberals in, say, the Kennedy camp: Schlesinger, Galbraith, Sorenson.

In a recent piece in *Commentary,* Reagan administration official Charles Horner described how conservatives even in the 1980s had, to borrow a phrase from the Left, internalized their own oppression. Depending on public esteem for career success, they found themselves adapting to the cultural arbiters, the people around the *Washington Post* and the networks. That meant subtly differentiating themselves from the primitives who were Reaganite "ideologues." The pressure was intense to demonstrate that one knew which fork to use.

Even in the 1980s, conservatism was a political moon, its course determined by the gravitational pull of the mother planet, liberalism. *National Review* editor John O'Sullivan posited "O'Sullivan's Law": that any institution that is not explicitly conservative turns liberal over time. He could cite the Ford and Rockefeller Foundations, *Time* magazine, and other institutions to illustrate the pull to the Left. Meanwhile, Erwin Glikes, the great publisher of Robert Bork, George Will, Allan Bloom, and other best-selling conservative authors developed a theory on how to sell conservative books. According to his protégé, Adam Bellow, Glikes felt that conservatives do not buy books on the basis of rave reviews in conservative organs. It is necessary first to outrage the liberal press. Conservative book buyers will then purchase a book in order to buy into their side of the controversy. The theory nicely illustrates how many conservatives found themselves dependent on the agenda of their opponents.

Recently, it has been hard for conservatives to perceive of themselves in wilderness terms, as individuals bravely out of step with the times. First came the fall of Communism, which vindicated the cold warriors and the Hayekian critiques of economic planning. Those of us who hung around the Soviet Union during its final days learned, to our delight, that there the beautiful people were conservative. Everything hip Muscovites loved—Ronald Reagan, Margaret Thatcher, the products of Philip Morris—hip Americans detested. Traveling there the conservative found himself on the side of the angels.

Then came the 1994 congressional elections, which swept not only Republicans into power (which by itself would have been as much fun as a chastity ball) but self-described conservative revolutionaries. That vote reminded us that elections are not just political turning points; they are also cultural events. In November 1994 the conservative movement left the Sinai and completed its exodus into Jerusalem. The end of the wilderness era brings political benefits. The conservative agenda now dominates national politics. But the more important transformation is psychological. Modern conservatives no longer feel that liberals are arbiters of how they, conservatives, are doing. Liberalism is no longer the mother planet.

Since the election, we have two establishments in this country: a conservative political establishment headquartered in Washington and another less politically cohesive establishment headquartered in New York, and expanding out to the university campuses. It is very hard to satisfy the success criteria for both. If you are in the arts community and look to New York tastes, it will be hard to get funding from a federal agency that must answer to Congress. If you are a politician who gets standing ovations at the Heritage Foundation conferences, it is unlikely that you will be profiled positively in *Vanity Fair* or the *New Yorker.*

It transpires that one establishment doesn't rise by tearing down the old one; it simply builds new institutions on green field sites, and once the establishment attains political power, everybody else has to pay attention. The conservatives never succeeded in having much of a voice at elite universities, but they did invent dozens and dozens of think tanks for academics in exile. They haven't managed to crack onto the news staffs of large newspapers or into the network news divisions, but they did revive talk radio, and they do well on cable, as well as in the print forum that was invented in the 1970s, Op-Ed pages. The quintessential institutional shift came after the 1994 election, when Harvard's John F. Kennedy School of Government was forced to cancel the series of seminars it had traditionally held for incoming congressmen. That year congressmen decided to attend Heritage Foundation seminars.

No longer are political conflicts primarily between Southern and Western outsider/conservatives versus East Coast urban liberals. The typical political conflict now is something like the Bork hearings, in which well-educated liberal activists and journalists go up against well-educated conservative theoreticians. The people who staff the new conservative think tanks, the media organs, the new conservative charities and foundations, are not usually rural. They live in New York and Washington. Moreover, as conservative ideas become more compelling, new sorts of people identify themselves as conservative. I maintain, only half-facetiously, that you can't have a creative intellectual movement in this country unless you've got some Jews, gays, and blacks on your side. Today there are many Jewish conservatives, there is a group of gays on the right, mostly in libertarian circles, and a growing and impressive group of black intellectuals whose ideas often coincide with conservative beliefs. In addition, there has been a strong infusion of Irish Catholics (Peggy Noonan comes to mind) whose parents were Democrats to the bone.

Today many conservatives are ambivalent about their new establishmentarian status, fearing that the halls of power will change them as much as they will change the halls of power. They are half barbarians, still with a taste for bomb-throwing; while at the same time they are learning how to create a governing philosophy. They are intellectuals, yet they still rail against the intellectual elite, media heavyweights who still crusade against the media. Some still engage in the pleasures of resentment and whining, while at the same time no longer feeling so threatened by, say, *The New York Times*. Newt Gingrich and *Wall Street Journal* editor Robert Bartley are perfect examples of people who are in touch with the establishment, and who frequently travel in elite circles yet who remain fundamentally aloof and genuinely radical.

The new establishmentarianism has affected the tone of conservative writing. This is no trivial thing; sometimes how a person holds his beliefs is as important as the beliefs he holds. There is more cheerfulness and self-assurance on the Right. People there are happy with the flow of history and so are less given over to resentment and grievance. Conservative writers are more likely to be attuned with and approving of popular culture. There has been an increased concern with happiness, pleasure, and even sensuality. Charles Murray wrote a book on happiness, which has a cultlike following. At least two conservative writers, James Bowman and Philip Terzian, have written to praise the MTV show *Beavis and Butt-head.*

Many people have trouble reconciling these sorts of views with the very real conservative admiration for the Victorian virtues. But remember what bits of Victorianism are being celebrated. There are perhaps some conservatives who long for the Victorianism of calling cards, corsets, Anglos running society, and clothed sex. But for most conservatives, the admirable aspect of Victorianism is the robust, manly stuff: Gordon at Khartoum, railroads across the continents, muscular Christianity, friendly societies, and what Shirley Robin Letwin called the vigorous virtues: merit, self-sufficiency, adventurousness, and a sense of high aspiration.

"One of the cardinal differences between the mid-Victorians and ourselves," Walter Houghton wrote in his classic *The Victorian Frame of Mind,* "lies not in their optimism and our pessimism, but in the much greater faith they had in the power of the human will." That was a world pre-Freud and pre-Marx, when a person's fate was not determined by his race, class, or gender. Willpower was thought to matter preeminently. And, indeed, the running assumption of much conservative social policy these days is that people are to be treated as captains of their own fate, not the victims of social forces so huge that only government can ameliorate them.

At one point, Goethe's Faust says that he hopes "to open to the millions living space/not danger proof but free to run their race." That sentence captures the spirit of most of the pieces in this book, and a large chunk of modern conservatism. American conservatism seeks to open up space so that individuals can be free to exercise and develop good character.

That means pushing back the government, which in its well-intentioned desire to minimize risk and suffering can on occasion suffocate character. In his piece "A Nation of Cowards" Jeffrey R. Snyder argues that gun control laws stunt courage and independence. George Gilder condemns the financial puritanism that shackles large dynamic individuals such as Michael Milken.

But opening up living space also means pruning the new form of social puritanism, which now leads to psychological restrictions on what can be said and thought, what can be eaten and imbibed. Everything in liberalism gets wrapped up in a prissy etiquette (even eating an ice cream now is connected to helping the rain forest). This is suffocating to the growth of robust individualism and antithetical to the vigorous virtues. Tone down exuberance, diminish individual aspirations in the name of egalitarianism, and you undo a person. In this anthology, Kay S. Hymowitz stands up for love and romance, against those who want to expose the most magical human relationships to the glare of "frank and open discussions." Lisa Schiffren explores the persnickety rules that supposedly combat sexual harassment. In "Darkness in Massachusetts," Dorothy Rabinowitz exposes the ugly side of this secular puritanism—social workers who see oppression in inequality and end up sending teachers to jail on trumped-up charges of sex abuse.

It is hard to run your race when you are cemented together with everyone else who shares your race, gender, or sexual orientation. Several authors celebrate individual character by making fun of those who reduce everything to group identity. Christina Hoff Sommers in "Sister Soldiers" makes fun of those who think their uterus determines their destiny, and Andrew Ferguson does it for the men's movement, led by men who define themselves by the fact that they have penises.

In a recent essay, William Kristol wrote that the "agenda of American conservatism can be defined as the construction (or reconstruction) of a politics of liberty and a sociology of virtue." That sounds like half fun—the liberty part—and half church—the virtue part. But in reality the two are complementary. At least they are if virtue is seen not as the property of scolds but as a code for people who are free to run their race. Leo Strauss once observed that the meaning of the word "virtue" had shifted. Whereas in classical times it had meant "manly vigor," by the nineteenth century it had come to mean "female chastity." It's time we created a new meaning, based on individualism, vigor, and high ambition.

What conservatism can point out is that virtue cannot be developed in a country in which people are constantly asking government to do things for them, and where social standards are designed to tame, pacify, and stifle.

A few years ago, while living in northern Europe, I came across a phenomenon that represented everything conservatism should mobilize to refute. A group of sadists and masochists formed an organization to lobby for tighter regulations for their brothels. They wanted special fire-fighting apparatus, as it would take people who are handcuffed or tied up longer to leave a burning building. The group advised that wire cutters should also be at hand in fireboxes. This really is the apotheosis of the welfare state mentality. They wanted government to sanction their underground behavior and then to domesticate it through regulation.

In a world run by conservatives, perverts won't demean themselves further by becoming lobbyists. And when people go out and want to do something bad, they'll enjoy the badness of it; they won't plead with anybody to tell them that they are respectable.

BACKWARD AND UPWARD:

The New Conservative Writing

Part 1

PIETIES

Knock Me Out with a Truck

Danielle Crittenden

ONE DAY, shortly after my daughter was born, I got into a conversation with a woman in a doctor's waiting room. The woman looked to be in her mid-fifties and had the poodlish, apricot hair color and shaped nails of so many aging Manhattan receptionists. It came out that, yes, she was in fact a receptionist, but for a "birthing center" on Madison Avenue. I looked at her quizzically, because she bore none of the traits I associate with women who work at birthing centers, namely a WHALES FOR PEACE T-shirt and the dazed air of someone who spends too much time meditating in uncomfortable positions.

"Where'd you have your baby?" she asked.

"Mount Sinai," I said.

To my surprise, she chuckled approvingly. "Honey, you went to the right place."

I lowered my magazine. She leaned forward and asked, "Did you take any drugs?"

"Only as many as they were willing to give me," I conceded. "Unfortunately, there was a limit."

She chuckled again, nodded her head and said, confidentially, "When I had my kids—and I've had five of 'em, you understand—I said to the doctor, 'Look, knock me out with a truck, okay? I don't want to feel a *thing*. . . .'"

"But these ladies," she went on, "they come in wanting it 'all natural' like. I don't want to tell you the number of times we've had to send them away in ambulances. And the screams! I hear them all the time coming up through the ventilator. One time a lady wanted to

3

take a shower—can you imagine taking a shower while you're in labor?—and the baby falls out, splat, right there on the tiled floor. The lady says—get this—'Oooh look, I've had a water birth. . . .'

"And then," she said, her Queens accent growing more vigorous, "there was the time when one of the midwives got pregnant. You know, none of these midwives ever seem to have kids of their own but they're happy to tell other ladies how to have babies. Anyway, so this midwife has her baby. She comes back to work, and I say, 'So, honey, how did those breathing exercises work?' and you know what she says? She says, 'Those breathing exercises don't work shit.'

"I don't know why they do it," she said, clucking her tongue. "Five kids—Yeesh. I say: knock me out with a truck."

STATISTICALLY, we're having a baby boom, the biggest since the early 1960s, and consequently, the "correct" way to give birth is much discussed. The emphasis in books on the topic is on planning the event itself: on what kind of birth *experience* the mother wants to have. Will it be in a hospital or a birth center, a swimming pool or a double bed? Would Great Aunt Gladys feel snubbed if she wasn't invited to watch? What sort of music should be playing—and will it be taped, or a live band? Will the new arrival be toasted with champagne or San Pellegrino?

When it comes to the actual delivery, it is felt that ideally, barring medical complication, a woman should try to give birth "naturally," or without anesthetics. This, most of the authors argue, provides the ultimate "birth experience" for the mother, who can participate in and control the birth in a way she can't if she is tanked up on Demerol and hooked up to high-tech machines in the brusque, impersonal environment of a hospital delivery room. A popular expert on "natural birth," Sheila Kitzinger writes in her book *Homebirth: The Essential Guide to Giving Birth Outside the Hospital*:

Women who feel that they can retain control over them during the birth, who understand the options available, and are consulted about what they prefer, are much more likely to experience birth as satisfying than those who are merely at the receiving end of care. . . . When birth is disempowering, a woman feels degraded, abused and mutilated.

Even the last sensible expert on the planet, Dr. Spock, has come around to the "natural" alternative. "Most women who have had this experience consider it the most moving and creative experience of their lives," he writes. And in a hospital, where everything is taken care of "so completely," a mother may experience "a feeling underneath of being somewhat ignorant and useless."

All of which may be true—unless we remember that we are not talking about the staging of a wedding or a cocktail party, but a very serious medical event that, until recently, claimed a huge number of mothers' and babies' lives. Giving birth used to be a very natural way to die, and that is why the best thing you can say about modern medicine is that it has made birth a very unnatural experience.

DURING MY LAST few months of pregnancy, my husband and I dutifully attended a course recommended by the hospital (it seemed funny to take a class for it, but then, what area of life isn't now taught at The Learning Annex?). Our "birth instructor," a petite, enthusiastic woman named Jane, spent most of the five weeks of class time giving the women lessons on how to achieve a kind of Zen-like placidity through the most horrendous contractions, while teaching the husbands to behave like aerobic instructors, keeping time with the contractions by shouting supportively, "That's it, three more, two more, come on now, *one big push!*" She used a bag of helpful props—a plastic uterus, a sock, a stuffed doll—to demonstrate the normal birth process; and screened a graphic and discomfiting video about births that go wrong: cesarean sections, methods of extracting babies in emergencies (hooks, vacuums, forceps), etc. Throughout the course we spent much time discussing our personal feelings about being pregnant, during which the men were prodded to contribute ("My husband loves my body right now, don't you Hon? *Hon?*").

On the topic of what Jane called "medicated" versus "unmedicated" birth, she tried to be an agnostic. Each way was presented as equally good and valid, depending upon the woman's preference. She herself had given birth twice, both times with drugs, a fact she was a bit sheepish about. She had no choice—there were medical complications—but if there hadn't been, she said, she would have preferred to do it "unmedicated."

In retrospect, following my own "birth experience," I realized how ridiculous it was that she should present the two methods of birth so neutrally. She dwelled only upon the complications that could result from having drugs—but never upon the risks of not taking the drugs. And as for all that time spent practicing panting like a dog, what Jane also never told us was that if you decide to take the drugs (administered through an epidural), all of these exercises are for naught: as if you were taught emergency drills for crossing the Atlantic by ship, when all along you planned to fly. The half-class that Jane spent discussing medication, she fell into the antihospital rhetoric that, up to that point, I'd only come across in books like Ms. Kitzinger's: There were terrible dangers associated with the epidural, yet the doctors and nurses would always try to force them on you anyway, like street pushers, without informing you of the risks. Once the mother accepted the epidural, she became helpless, a "patient." As patients we would be "confined" to our room and bed, and hooked up to ominous, controlling machines that went *ping*. We would no longer be able to *experience* the birth.

Instead, she urged us to stay at home in labor for as long as possible, "listening to classical music, sipping herbal tea," while our husbands fanned us and massaged our lower backs with tennis balls. Only when we could no longer bear it should we turn up at the delivery room, and if we *had* to resort to an epidural, we "shouldn't feel bad about it, because not all women can handle the pain." But if we paid attention to her breathing exercises, we shouldn't need it.

When our evening came, and my husband and I turned up at Mount Sinai, contractions five minutes apart and beginning to render me speechless, the nurse informed me I'd probably be another seven hours or so in labor.

"You can stay here," she said cheerfully, "or you can go home and come back."

"What happens if I stay here?" I asked her suspiciously.

"Well, you can have the epidural, and wait—or you can walk around, or do whatever you want."

The "birthing room" was like a miniature hotel suite, with a large comfortable bed, a television set, an armchair, and flowered wallpaper.

"You mean," I asked, the situation dawning on me, "I can have the epidural *now,* and lie here and watch television with my husband, feeling *absolutely no pain*—or go home in agony, and do stupid breathing exercises, and count away the hours until I can finally be rushed back here?"

She smiled. "That's about it."

My husband and I opted for the rerun of *Born Free* on the hospital's movie channel. Every so often he'd check the machine I was attached to—the one that measures the size of the contractions—and say, laughingly, "Ooh, Danielle, that was *enormous.* You would have hated that one."

And so when it came time to push I was rested for the hardest part. The baby was born without complication. Had there been any, the emergency room was on the floor above. I was already anesthetized should I have needed a cesarean at the last minute. My doctor said proudly, "We can have that baby out of there if necessary, from start to finish, in *thirty seconds.*"

THE FASHION for giving birth "naturally" arose, unsurprisingly, from ideological considerations, not medical ones: it is another wayward child of the feminist movement of the early seventies. As Ms. Kitzinger puts it: "Decisions about where to give birth should spring from realistic risk assessment and from your own inner values. Any woman who decides that birth without a hospital is right for her in a society that is hostile to freedom in childbirth takes responsibility for weighing up the risks, and also expresses the courage of human beings to resist autocracy, dogma and the power of the medical system. Her decision is based on deeply held values."

But while it's true that "natural" childbirth, outside of a hospital, does advocate a kind of extreme female machismo (I guess the male equivalent is being man enough for "natural" prostate surgery), still, if logic prevailed, you would think the feminist position would be exactly the opposite: just as the pill "liberated" women sexually, giving them control over their reproductive system, so has the epidural "liberated" women from the horrific pain of childbirth; and the technology available in a hospital has virtually eliminated the risk of death to mother or child. Certainly those early pioneers of childbirth, like Elisabeth Bennett, upon whom was performed the first reported cesarean in America in 1792, would have preferred a modern hospital to her kitchen. During labor, Mrs. Bennett was discovered to have a contracted pelvis:

> An operating table was devised from two planks laid across a couple of barrels. Elisabeth was given a large dose of Laudanum—the closest the eighteenth century would come to anesthesia—and placed on a board with a Negro woman on each side to hold her. As witnesses reported later, "Dr Bennett, with one quick stroke of the knife laid open the abdomen and uterus." He enlarged the opening in the uterus with his hands and lifted out the baby girl and the placenta. Elisabeth's sister, who was present, took the baby, and the doctor, remarking, "This shall be the last one," reached in again and removed both ovaries. Then with the same strong linen thread that Elisabeth used to make . . . shirts, he sewed up the wound." (Nancy Caldwell Sorel, *Ever since Eve: Personal Reflexions on Childbirth.* Oxford University Press, 1984.)

Ms. Kitzinger claims, however, that the "cultural definition" of birth, as seen by modern male obstetricians, is a "potentially pathological process" and an "illness." What she calls romantically the "woman's way" is instead to see birth as a "social event." While hospitals are "alien territory to the woman," offering a "bureaucratic, hierarchal system of care" in which a "woman is separated from those close to her," "woman's way," on the other hand, offers an "informal system of care, with other women of the neighbourhood and family" in a "home or other familiar surrounding." As for those male obstetricians, there is often "class distinction" between them and their patients, they foster a "dominant-subordinate relationship" under which "care is depersonalized," there is "little emotional support," but rather "threatening and often punitive behaviour, e.g. commanding, scolding, warning." They have "little cultural awareness of rituals, beliefs, social behaviours, values" and either ignore the "spiritual aspects of birth" or treat them as "embarrassing." Further, "information about health, disease and degree of risk is kept secret." But women caregivers offer an "equal relationship," "strong emotional support," "verbal and non-verbal encouragement," and use "familiar language and imagery." They are aware of all the "spiritual and cultural significance of birth."

So why do women persist in going to hospitals?

Because giving birth, especially for the first time, can be a terrifying experience. From the moment a woman discovers she is pregnant, she has a sense of losing control—not to the male medical establishment—but to the baby inside her, who now feeds off of her, distorts her figure, and who will, eventually, have to get out of her somehow. A woman does not lose control of her "birth experience" in a hospital; rather, the technology available, and her doctor's expertise, hands the woman back a measure of control over her body and its health should the baby decide to emerge, say, backwards.

Because, as Ms. Kitzinger acknowledges in a small notation, while women "caregivers" in birthing centers or home births have many "comfort skills, e.g. massage, hot and cold compresses, holding," they also have "few resources to handle complicated, obstructed labour."

Now it's true that complicated and obstructed labors account for a small percentage of births, and there are many ways today—compared to Mrs. Bennett's time—to screen out high-risk women in advance and send them to the hospital. Ms. Kitzinger could even argue that it would make economic sense for the most low-risk, or "normal" births to take place outside of the costly hospital system. The trouble is, the many potential complications of a so-called low-risk, "normal" pregnancy don't tend to happen until the very last stages of labor. And then there is an ambulance to be called. And the ride to the hospital from the birthing center or the home. And in New York at least, there is always the factor of traffic, which seems (like the timing of births) to follow no pattern, and can be jammed even at 2 A.M. It is not, as my doctor boasted, a matter of getting that baby out in thirty seconds. It could be thirty *minutes*.

Neither is giving birth at home or in a birth center today any more "natural" than giving birth at a hospital. If all things go well, it might be nicer, and less "institutionalized" to give birth at home or in a cozy center, but let's not call it "natural." All people in attendance have washed their hands. The instruments, and everything else that comes in contact with the mother, are sterilized. Hearts and pulses are monitored. The mother is not giving birth by herself in a thicket, or in the veld, or squatting behind a bush (although maybe this is a movement that's coming). The difference between this birth and a hospital birth is simply that the woman is doing it without access to drugs, and is at more risk to herself and the baby than if she were in a hospital.

W E TAKE RISKS everyday, like crossing the street for instance," insists a midwife at the Childbearing Center in Manhattan, the very first birth center (established 1975) in the United States. It is considered the preeminent center and is now located in a mansion on the Upper East Side. A group of us, on an initiation tour, were sitting in one of the old great rooms, stripped of its ornament except for the dentil molding. We'd just watched a video about giving birth in a birthing center much like this one. The mother in the video was a paragon of calm throughout, breathing deeply, even managing a serene smile at the end. I thought, admiringly, this woman could withstand anything—torture by the North Koreans—anything. The baby was born, and the camera faded out on mother and father, together in the big bed, clutching their new son. A narrator reassured us that this scene of family intimacy was common at a center and would be undisturbed: there were no hospital orderlies waiting to snatch the baby away from its mother, no bureaucrat demanding that forms be filled out, no noisy nurseries and bright lights.

We were all a bit choked up. No question, this was birth as it should be.

Then a woman, fiftyish, wearing sensible brown shoes, a tweed suit, and her graying hair cut efficiently short, strode into the room followed by the midwife in a lab coat and carrying a clipboard. The elder woman, apparently the matriarch of the center, outlined—in that chirpy, officious way of another generation of women, one that survived a war—all the benefits of giving birth in the center. It was cheaper, homier, and yet as sophisticated as you could get outside a regular hospital.

"We're here," she said, "because we love the natural birth experience. We don't like the hospital-imposed limits."

It is probably right that when this woman, along with others, established the center in 1975, giving birth in a hospital was a more brusque, impersonal business than it is now. And through the advocacy of people like her, hospitals loosened up somewhat and, in my case, papered the walls, put up a television, and let husbands in. Some of the New York hospitals even accommodate midwives.

"Sometimes," she went on, "a hospital can be inhumane. But we get good results with our pain techniques. You will not be pinned down to a bed. *We* treat birth as a normal process."

I asked her about risk, and she replied that up to three hundred births a year took place at the center, and of those, only 8 percent (or as many as twenty-four) had to be transferred, in emergency, to the nearby hospital. At this point the midwife cut in and assured me how unlikely this was, how much could be foreseen in advance, and how it was only seven minutes to the hospital (traffic permitting, after an average eleven-minute wait for the ambulance): how, in the end, one must be "willing to take the risk—and maybe that's not for you." She shrugged. "It's not for everybody. You have to decide."

Then we were led downstairs to the birthing rooms, in the basement of the mansion. You had to reach them by way of an old, chugging elevator, the kind that waits a few seconds after the doors close, then lurches, and takes half a minute to descend one story. The other women crammed into the elevator with me all glanced at each other during that first lurch, and one giggled.

"Can you imagine if . . . ," she started to say, before the doors thunked open.

The rooms below were much the same as the one I'd had at Mount Sinai, only without the emergency floor above. There was that flowered wallpaper again, and lamps, and television sets, and armchairs. Instead of the electrically powered, reclining and disassembling bed I'd had in the hospital, there were ordinary double beds, done up in pretty sheets.

The only benefit of this setting, that I could see, was that unlike in the hospital, you could leave within twelve hours—you weren't checked in for the mandatory two days. And there was a nicer waiting room for the family. On the other hand, you *had* to leave after twelve hours. There were no nurses around to change your sheets, bring you things, or take care of the baby for you when you needed to sleep. I thought, yes, this is all very nice, but if there is the *slightest* hint of something going wrong, I want teams of doctors swooping down on me, with every sort of high-tech, pinging contraption they have, and I want that baby out of there, intact, the right shade of pink, breathing, screaming. And if I look back on this experience as not the perfect Martha Stewart kind of birth experience, so what? I'm alive. The baby's alive. My child has not been deprived of oxygen because I wanted guitars, flower petals, the local homeless woman, and my extended family in attendance at the birth.

The real reason to give birth here instead of in a hospital would be that you agreed with the staff that the aesthetics of a birth are more important, ultimately, than the safety.

As I left the center to walk back home, I remembered that woman I met in the doctor's office; I smiled and thought, *Yeesh, knock me out with a truck.*

My Wife as Attorney General

Mark Helprin

Dear Mr. President:

I WRITE IN REGARD to inquiries I have received concerning the appointment of my wife, Lisa Kennedy Helprin, to the post of attorney general of the United States.

There is no question that she possesses the essential qualification for being the nation's chief law enforcement official: She is a woman. I realize that these are changing times and that I may be seen by some as counter-diverse, but I would not marry anyone but a woman. Not only was it courageous of you to allow your wife to require that the attorney general be of the correct sex, it was, of course, politically astute. Certainly no one can question either the moral or the intellectual basis of your decision.

It follows as day follows night that because women, who are the majority, are an oppressed minority, the attorney general should be a woman. Although reactionary elements will infer somehow that this means that the attorney general cannot be a man, this negative way of looking at the question is purely gratuitous. In affirmative actions one need not consider the negative, just as in facing the budget and investment deficits one must advocate more and less spending simultaneously and as equal moral imperatives.

In the interest of full disclosure, however, I feel that I must point out that my wife does not believe this. She thinks, on the contrary, that she is capable of achievement without reference to her sex, and that to fall back upon it as a method of selection is meaningless given that in this country approximately half of the population is female. She does have certain blind spots, and I recommend that during the interview you refrain from suggesting to her that she is a victim, for if you do you may feel afterward that, indeed, it is not she who is the victim.

In regard to the next most important qualification, never having hired an illegal alien, she has a perfect record. Shortly after the birth of our first child, she left the practice of law for the sole purpose of taking care of the baby. After the first baby came yet another, and after almost eight years she has yet to resume her career. That is a potential political problem, I agree, but the fact is that she and I believe that our children are more important than her career. We also believe that our children are more important than my career. And we believe as well that our children are more important than your career, which is one of the reasons that we did not vote for you.

Still, some things are of fundamental importance, and the fact remains that not only has she never hired an illegal alien; the occasional baby-sitters that we have engaged are the reason for a complete dossier—a record of federal and state taxes and workers' compensation levies that we have paid, all documented with proofs of mailing and the Byzantine notations that lawyers make upon the copies of documents they can prove they mailed. We expect that in your administration the girth of such dossiers will swell, but in the Darwinian years of Republican rule they grew only to a thickness of about two inches.

With reference to the third critical qualification, although she is ethnically a woman my wife has never trained as a Playboy bunny. Nor, I might add, in regard to my role as a potential political spouse, have I. Have you questioned the other members of your administration about this dangerous pitfall? Were I you, I would quickly telephone both Donna Shalala and Lloyd Bentsen.

I am happy to inform you that, in keeping with your recent standards for the appointment of attorneys general, she has absolutely no experience with criminal law or enforcement. She is an alumna of the Wall Street firm Chadbourne, Parke, Whiteside, and Wolff, and was for years a corporate attorney with Chase Manhattan Bank. Probably her graduate law degree in taxation will be more pertinent to the activities of your administration than would have been practice in putting the heat on criminals.

The press can be neutralized on this point simply by stressing that on-the-job training is likely to be available given the incestuous involvements of the secretaries of commerce and the treasury, and the reluctance of your chief economic coordinator to take leave of his friends. You might further point out that in an administration based upon goodness you never have to say good-bye, but you always have to say you're sorry.

Lastly, politics. My wife comes from a Democratic family and was raised in Brookline, Massachusetts. She looks terrific in a suit. In heels she's taller than you are and will make feminists feel great as she peers over your head during the swearing-in. Be grateful for the fact that she's a Republican. That may cost you some points before she takes office, but then you can be assured that she will fry the special prosecutor in his own oil, which can only be good for you. In fact, not only can she bake like Hillary; she has a number of recipes for Lawrence Walsh that she's been wanting to try. She won't tell me exactly what they are, but I peeked and I know that they begin with plucking, eviscerating, and deboning.

Some fine points, perhaps obstacles, remain, such as the fact that she is not comfortable with Hillary Rodham Clinton's role in all this, pointing out that the First Lady was neither elected, appointed, nor confirmed, and that, like Princess Di, she cannot be removed except in a Götterdämmerung. In fact, my wife points out that the lack of accountability that attaches to the First Lady, and that is now being fused with new powers, has, shall we say, the flavor of the special prosecutor.

Still, my wife has three names, too, although your wife seems only recently to have come by her three names. This sudden change, coincident with the assumption of unprecedented power, sounds very much like the granting—or, rather, the taking—of a title. The press followed its instruction with exactitude, and the transformation was wrought overnight. Suddenly, Hillary Clinton became Hillary Rodham Clinton. It sounds very English, doesn't it? And as if Dan Quayle had said, "From now on, I will be known as J. Danforth Quayle," and the press had obeyed without the slightest sarcasm. What will she be next? Percy, Duke of Etheridge? Toinette, Duchess of the Maldives?

I know this is a digression, but think of the further potential in your administration: Leon, County of Panetta; Mickey, Trade Lion of Los Angeles; Donna, Woman of Shalala; Robert Keep-in-Touch Rubin; Lloyd King of Breakfasts Bentsen; Les Money for the Military Aspin; Warren Turn-the-Other-Cheek Christopher; and Albert, Prince of the Rain Forest. Royal pretensions are as healthy for a new presidency as childhood diseases are for children—they help to build immunity for later assaults. Do you remember President Nixon's dressing of the White House guard detachment in Merry Widow hats? It gave him strength for what was to come later.

Mr. President, as Europe slides toward war you are Churchillian to make homosexual rights the centerpiece of your national security policy. As the nation reels under the assault of street criminals, you are right to focus on nannies and bunnies. As your predecessor's budget deal proved, a tax increase will stimulate any faltering economy. You know that, and I know that. And the American people know, as you do, that we need a lot more red tape.

We have to have the courage to change America, and you cannot fail. You have done great service to your nation and, not least of all, to your party. And you have honored the memory of previous Democratic presidents, for during just your first few weeks in office, you have made Jimmy Carter look like Abraham Lincoln.

Unfortunately, my wife is unenthusiastic about these things, and the bottom line, sir, is that she is stubborn and enigmatic. When I try to focus her attention on the post that she may be asked to fill, she smiles patiently and says, "Wait for Kemp." What could she possibly mean by that? Believe it or not, I don't think she'll be available. But do not despair. Have you considered Whoopi Goldberg? She may not be qualified in the old way, but as long as the attorney general is a woman, must she be a lawyer, too?

Sexual Politics, the Real Thing

Lisa Schiffren

TWO SUNDAYS AGO, I stumbled to the door to retrieve my *Washington Post* and, like most Washingtonians, scanned the headlines to see what was happening—a local euphemism meaning, "What politician has been caught doing something outrageous or disgraceful?" I didn't expect much, since transitions are dry periods for scandals, but habit is strong and, anyway, my search was rewarded.

The front-page headline screamed that several women had accused newly reelected Senator Bob Packwood of Oregon of making unwanted sexual advances to many women. I read on with the nonpartisan schadenfreude that all lowly Washington staffers reserve for the troubles of the mighty. The article sparked a few entirely personal observations.

This was no everyday scandal, like Congress's bounced checks or eavesdropping on political appointees. Unwanted sexual advances are, of course, sexual harassment, the hottest scandal category of the moment.

Nor was this the same old sexual harassment we've heard about continuously from the Thomas-Hill hearings through the election. The article called the allegations a genuine paradox, because the senator has, by feminist standards, an excellent record on "women's issues."

This paradox was so complicated that I didn't quite get it, so I skimmed the rest of the article, more than a full page of descriptions of various women's complaints that he had lunged at or grabbed them in inappropriate circumstances. Surrounding these allegations were testaments to his advocacy of abortion rights, hiring of women for important jobs, and devotion to pet feminist causes. Senator Packwood has been an exemplar of that quaint breed, the socially liberal Republican. ACCUSATIONS RUN COUNTER TO RECORD, stated the headline.

Could this possibly mean that it is considered inconsistent (therefore paradoxical, even hypocritical) for liberals, who believe in unfettered sexual autonomy, especially for women, to make overtures to women who might not reciprocate? Evidently so. I guess I had missed this important sociolinguistic evolution. Last I'd heard it was only hypocrisy when conservatives, who talk about morality, favor "family values," and oppose abortion, were found to have personal interests in sex beyond marriage.

Perhaps there were other new paradoxes I had missed. Indeed, close study of the reporting on the Packwood story has revealed several worth noting, just in time for the forthcoming Senate ethics investigation.

1. The greatest paradox involves the politically driven inversion of morality. Men who profess traditional moral views on sexual issues, who believe that sexual liberty is bad and committed monogamy good, that abortion is sinful, that women deserve respect, which is shown by treating them like ladies, even if that means forgoing an amount of familiarity and comfort, are considered condescending, insensitive, and therefore "evil." Because they are evil, it is said to follow that they would be sexually predatory toward the women with whom they worked.

2. On the other hand, men who advocate abortion rights and absolute sexual equality are considered virtuous. This despite the fact that these feminist achievements make intimate relations more convenient for men, by releasing them from traditional obligations and considerations toward women. Nonetheless, it is considered paradoxical to find these new men treating women insensitively.

3. Though political correctness requires that men support all demands for sexual freedom but forgo any personal benefits from the

ensuing sexual free market, that old moral failure—womanizing—is, paradoxically, no longer a vice. We have many impressive Democratic leaders who are known to be virtuosos in the art of seduction. Yet they have not been held to public account by feminists.

Until recently we had a definition of sexual harassment that included some obvious use of power to obtain sex. That would include threats of firing, promises of promotion, and professional retribution. But sensitivities have evolved. In Senator Packwood's case, all of the complainants alleged that he made inappropriate, sometimes physical advances at them, but that when they said no firmly, he accepted it. Though they felt uncomfortable, there were no ramifications in their professional lives—no threats of firing, no vengeful behavior.

So our paradox here is that those of our public men who have mastered the art of seduction, and thereby slept with and discarded many women, are blameless. The inept, the less attractive and therefore unsuccessful, however, are guilty of the new crime—sexual harassment.

This is more than a paradox: It is a new standard. Unwanted sexual advances will get you disqualified from high office. Wanted sexual advances will get you—sex.

4. So far our paradoxes have concerned male behavior. But women are capable of paradoxical—or is it hypocritical?—behavior as well. Despite longtime rumors of Senator Packwood's foibles, prominent feminists had assiduously cultivated the proabortion alliance, tacitly covering for him. Is it merely a coincidence that they are now willing to throw him overboard just when liberal Republicans are no longer needed—when we've elected a Democratic president for the first time in twelve years, who, with a Democratic Senate majority, promises to approve long-thwarted feminist demands? It will be interesting to see what standard the feminists will demand of the Clinton administration.

5. Speaking of our new leadership, one last paradox. Only a month ago, the liberal women's groups, the Democratic party and the mainstream media were victoriously staunch in refusing to allow the "character issue"—especially the womanizing question—to play any

role in the election. Now they want it to be a defining standard for officeholders.

Soon a great many Democratic luminaries will be sent to Capitol Hill to be confirmed for high office. I suppose I'd better keep reading the papers, because their careers may also include a paradox or two.

America's New Man

Andrew Ferguson

IT'S EARLY Saturday morning and Chuck is getting down in his body. Chuck is overweight. His jeans are cinched a good distance below his waist, down where his stomach descends into his pubic bone. His jeans have been ironed. The crease brushes the top of his Nikes, which look brand-new. Chuck is getting a divorce, his third. Too, he's a drunk, as he told me last night, or rather a recovering alcoholic, also a sex addict. These are the two addictions he has so far been able to acknowledge and process through. He is worried there might be more. Plus his life is littered with codependencies.

All of which led him inexorably to the First International Men's Conference: A Journey Toward Conscious Manhood in the basement exhibition hall of the Stouffer Arboretum Hotel in Austin, but none of which he's thinking about at the moment, for the moment is the place where he is now, it's all there is in fact, and Chuck is trying to experience just this moment by listening to his body. A speaker with a microphone at the front of the hall is guiding the experience. Chuck rolls his head loosely on his shoulders. He bends his knees, rises and falls on the balls of his feet, pushing himself downward, lower and lower onto the indoor-outdoor carpeting, past the cigarette burns and the flattened wads of gum, deeper and deeper into his body. All around him are other men, more than seven hundred of them, dressed in Dockers and Izod shirts, some in T-shirts and running shorts, each trying to listen to his own body, too, while at the same time listening to the speaker at the podium.

The speaker is Shepherd Bliss, a pioneer in the men's movement and an acknowledged expert in bodywork. "Feel the weight of your hands," Dr. Bliss says softly, and Chuck swings his arms gorilla-fashion, palms facing backward. "Root your body to the ground with your proud serpent's tail," says Dr. Bliss. Chuck pushes his skinny bottom outward behind him. The room is as silent as eternity. "Let the fullness of your bellies relax," says Dr. Bliss. "Feel the pride in your belly." Chuck thrusts the arc of his stomach outward, straining the buttons on his oxford cloth shirt. "This is the great bow of a male pelvis," Dr. Bliss says. "Now let go!" His voice is a thunderous whisper over the PA, and from the back of the silent swaying group comes a high keening sound, then a sob from somewhere else, and Chuck begins to sniffle. It is only in the last year or so that he has learned to cry. Someone in the exhibition hall calls out for his dad. Chuck's sniffle descends from his nasal passages into his throat, and as his throat chokes up the sniffle is squeezed deeper, into his chest cavity and then down into his pelvis, and then suddenly it shoots back up, opening his throat, and his face contorts and turns upward, and from deep in his body comes a yowl: "*Yeeeeiiii!*" The leader falls silent while the mewling and yowling and keening fill the room. "Listen!" says Dr. Bliss. "Hear the sounds of men!"

HARKEN TO THE SOUNDS of men, of men made new! Whimpers, sobs, shuddering grunts from the solar plexus, high-pitched beseeching whines for the mom and dad who did you dirt—these are the sounds of men today, drowning out the beer-belly belching and ulcerated gurgling and hapless farting and midnight snorting and locker-room scratch-scratch that have been the signature noises of men in the past.

Take it from Robert Bly, a poet who once won an award, and from Bill Moyers, his PBS flack whose "A Gathering of Men" runs like a tape loop on public television stations. Take it from 20/20 and *Newsweek* and *The New York Times;* take it from *Fortune* and *USA Today:* The men's movement is "sweeping the country," scooping up bricklayers and accountants, lumberjacks and corporate attorneys as it rolls through every village and hamlet, leaving sobbing men transformed in its wake, more sensitive, more in touch with the inner child, more resistant to the oppression of a heartless culture. Take it from Victoria Rich Communications, the public relations firm wisely hired by the sponsors of the conference in Austin:

> All across the country, men are coming together to explore the meaning of being a man in the '90s. Members of the rapidly growing men's movement, a phenomenon already totaling more than 100,000 predominantly professional men, are searching for and finding the courage—in the company of other men—to look deep within themselves for answers to difficult questions about their manhood.

All across the country . . . rapidly growing . . . a phenomenon! But all is not well. Leaders of the movement—the seminar holders, book writers, newsletter publishers, videotape lecturers, drum makers, and mail-order cataloguers—are getting a little annoyed. Not every press account has shown the same respect as *Newsweek* and Moyers and 20/20: Some have focused on the "externalities" of their movement, the drums, the chanting, the feathered headdresses, the American Indian affectations, the pseudo-orgiastic dancing, to the exclusion of the substantive issue, which is, let's face it, to explore a deep masculinity that does not oppress women, children, or other men. And it's undeniable. Each of these outward signs has by now been used for target practice by every freelance satirist and cheap-shot artist in the country.

For the purposes of this account, then, let's stipulate that the drums are fine. The chanting is perfectly okay. The feathers—they look fabulous. Really. And the dancing is no fruitier than what you'd find at a Tri Delt Oktoberfest in Champaign-Urbana. But the movement leaders should honor the showman's cliché that all publicity is good publicity. Every Jay Leno wisecrack and smart-ass piece in *Esquire* reinforces the notion that the men's movement actually exists. And the notion, however implausible, is an undoubted moneymaker. Men's movement leaders can get annoyed if they want, but they're getting annoyed all the way to the bank.

The Men's Conference in Austin was, as its title suggests, the world's first, "an important next step in the further development of the men's movement"—the words of the conference chairman, Marvin Allen. Marvin is a slight, bearded man with an understated Texas accent, if such a thing is possible, and an uncertain manner that suggests he might at any moment have to break off conversation and dive into a foxhole. His bio describes him succinctly as "director of the Texas Men's Institute, founder and creator of the Texas Wildman Gatherings, psychotherapist, writer, and national lecturer on men's issues." He is also, let it be stressed, an operator of great gifts. This conference was more than his idea: it was his monument. But the practical limits of his leadership were painfully evident, too. Where, one wondered, was Robert Bly, the movement's Grand Wizard? It was a question that would not be resolved until conference's end.

THE SITING OF THE CONFERENCE was auspicious, not to say inevitable. Austin is one of those American cities—like Eugene, Santa Fe, Boulder, St. Paul, Taos—with a sufficient supply of men in ponytails and women in wraparound skirts to sustain any trend, no matter how preposterous, until *Newsweek* can get around to putting it on its cover. Stroll down Sixth Street in Austin or Telegraph Avenue in Berkeley and you'll find the Hare Krishna temple across the street from the Rolfing Center, around the corner from the Yogananda Society, and down the block from the Institute for Spiritual Rebirth, which is in the old est headquarters. Add to these now the local Men's Center. Every progressive town has one.

Any such movement must take its life from a story, not a metaphysics exactly, but a shared belief accounting for how things are. Distilled to its essence by Bly and his colleagues, the men's movement's myth, like so many others, postulates a dreamy ideal world in the faraway past, a long-ago estrangement from paradise, and the possibility of return. The movement's Eden, in which fathers nurtured sons and taught them intimacy and emotional resilience through a community of tribal elders, was shattered by the Industrial Revolution, which dragged men away from their sons into the workplace. Dad devoted himself to the daily grind, neglected the kids, and often resorted to the bottle and such vulgar pursuits as Sunday afternoon NFL games.

The result, says the movement, is plain to see: grief, rage, disorientation, dysfunction, this last a portmanteau borrowed from a sister (brother?) movement led by specialists in "codependency." The commonest figure cited by movement leaders is that 96 percent of American families are dysfunctional, providing an almost bottomless pool of potential subscribers to newsletters, purchasers of audiotapes, buyers of drums, and attendees of men's conferences. The key is to become conscious of oppression, which can take time. Most of the New Men are middle-aged. "In your twenties you buy into the American Dream, that if you get married and buy the station wagon and get a job, everything will be okay," Marvin Allen says. "By your late thirties, you learn that the Dream is a fraud." And the New Men are not only middle-aged but white. I saw two blacks attending the conference, but a gathering of men's leaders is snowier than David Duke's campaign staff. "We heard of one man of color who did seminars in men's work," Marvin Allen said, explaining the conference's complexion. "We couldn't find him. I think he's up in Canada someplace."

BUT UNDER THE SKIN, of course, all men are, well, *men,* equally capable of grasping the insidious dynamics of oppression. "They gave white men the semblance of power," another movement leader, John Lee, told *Newsweek.* "We'll let you run the country, but in the meantime, stop feeling, stop talking and continue swallowing your pain and your hurt and keep dying younger than you need to be dying." *Newsweek* followed this sobering thought with a recitation of mortality rates for American men. But the referent for *they* is of course left unidentified.

The methods for overcoming dysfunction—the conveyances for a return to that faraway ideal community of men—were also on display in Austin. There is the drumming, first and foremost (and I'll try to mention it only this once). My acquaintance Chuck bought his drum for $400, an octagonal affair based on a design borrowed, the drum maker told him, from the Indian tribes of the Great Plains. All weekend he walked around the hotel, clutching at it like Linus's blanket. For three mornings straight Chuck and several hundred other men gathered in the Stouffer's basement exhibition hall for a heaving hair-raising session, the boom-boom shaking through the walls and ceiling and up into the hotel's nine-story atrium while the tourists and the businessmen hurried through. Inside the exhibition hall the noise was deafening.

Why drum? One of the movement leaders put that question to an assembly of the New Men one evening. "It goes boom!" hollered one. "It grounds me!" "It clears a space for my healing!" "It connects me to something primal!" And: "It's naughty!" In a word! All the affected civility, the weak-kneed you-betcha-boss, sorry-honey-I-didn't-mean-it deference, the subservience and subjugation of true selfhood, the *sucking up,* that has been so fastidiously pressed upon us by . . . by *them* . . . well, drumming strips it away, sends it streaming out into the world with the great sonic thunderstrike of those $400 drums. "It doesn't work so well when you do it alone," Chuck told me regretfully. But with hundreds of other men! The crescendo and then the final *whump!* leave an unearthly silence. Nobody should deny the effect such concentrated drumming can have deep in a listener's body, especially at 8:30 A.M. after a couple of cups of coffee.

After drumming there's bodywork, the thrusting outward of bellies and fannies, and the swinging of arms and rolling of heads in utter silence, inevitably inducing the sobs that rise from deep in the body. Then the New Men might chant the ancient ancestor chants—"Grandfathers we are calling come come." It creates the healing space, the place for safety. It connects them to the Old Men, not the workadaddy drones the New Men once were but the primal men of the forest, for the old men too chanted, locked man to man and arm in arm in thatched huts or under the great wide sky in that ideal world before . . . *they* invented the lathe and the division of labor and Caterpillar tractors and spreadsheets and the machine-shop torture devices to which . . . *they* strapped men in order to divorce them from feeling.

After chanting a movement leader will take the microphone and recite poetry in the emphatic, hyperdramatic sonorities made famous by Bly. Each poem is greeted with a cry of "Ho!"—another signature sound of the movement, an ancient Indian phrase, the men have been advised, that translates roughly as "Right on." And stories are told, primal stories of dragons slain and treasures found, while the men ease themselves onto the indoor-outdoor carpeting, sitting cross-legged in the attitude American kindergartners once called Indian style. All that's missing in this carefully orchestrated sequence is for an elderly woman to pass around cookies and milk before nap time.

Drumming and bodywork and chanting and storytelling and then each morning the men dispersed to workshops. The choices were daunting: Does one forgo "Manhood in the Making" in favor of "Incorporating Gestalt Therapy and the Men's Movement in Working with Men"? Could "Healing Each Other's Wounds: Straight Men & Gay Men in Dialogue" possibly be more enlightening than "Warrior's Journey Home: Healing Men's Codependency and Addictions"?

Regardless of the advertised subject matter, all movement workshops center on a common activity, which is *talk.* New Men cannot talk enough. A gathering of New Men is more than a gabfest, more than a talkathon; it is a flood of words, confessions, preachments of pain and explications of anger, tales of villainous victimization told not just in workshops but in the hotel atrium, at the urinals in the men's rooms, over Diet Cokes in the hotel bar, while having a smoke on the verandah overlooking the arboretum. Passing two men in a hallway you might hear: "Getting fired was the first chance I had to create a space for my grieving." Talk unlocks the treasure chest of self-dramatization. It is the means whereby your tiny simpering grievances—the sarcasms of a coworker, the smirks of an ex-wife— are refined into a narrative with twists and turns and climaxes and delicious denouements. The day Dad missed your football game becomes a hero's tale, and the hero is—Yes! Talking about yourself (*What was I feeling at that moment? What do I feel now while I think about what I was feeling then?*) is the most delirious of intoxicants, and for the New Men it is the one addiction that dare not speak its name.

That scumbag of a boss! That bitch of a wife! Mom just stood there, while Dad—don't even ask. (You don't have to ask.) If the New Man is the Luke Skywalker of the epic, Dad is the Darth Vader, always, his heavy bronchial breathing rumbling beneath every tale a New Man tells.

"PEOPLE SAY I'M blaming it all on my Dad," said John Lee, during his workshop "At My Father's Wedding." "I'm not blamin' anything on my Dad. I blame it on this fuckin' culture." A very important point, a bow to logic—after all, if you blame Dad for everything, you embark on an endless regression, since Dad can blame his dad, who was in turn screwed up by his dad, and so on, stretching backward into the primordial soup of victimization. It's far tidier to blame the culture. Unfortunately, in John Lee's most famous book—*The Flying Boy,* which launched him into men's movement superstardom and engendered a mini-industry of videotapes ("Grieving: A Key to Healing") and follow-up books and audiotapes ("Saying Goodbye to Mom and Dad") and lecture tours that fly the boy from Eugene to Chapel Hill and all points in between—he does indeed blame Dad for everything, and damn the endless regression. Of course Dad figured prominently as well in his workshop, held in one of the larger meeting rooms of the Stouffer, in deference to his superstar status.

"My father ain't here," Lee began in his Alabama drawl. "Is yours? My father would think this was funny. And basically what I have to say to my dad is: Fuck you."

"Ho!" said the New Men.

"He'd say, look son, it wasn't that bad. What the hell are you doing spending all this money doing this for? I put a fuckin' roof over your—"

"Head!" shouted the men.

"And fuckin' clothes on your—"

"Back!" shouted the men.

"And fuckin' food on yer fuckin'—"

"Table!"

Laughs! Cheers! Dad always said that! John knows!

But soon the hilarity was over. There was work to do, stuff to process through. It is one of the ironies in a movement that disparages the nine-to-five grind that all this delicious self-absorption is called "work" (but still delicious!). John himself admitted that he and his girlfriend "had been working our asses off" with a Gestalt therapist to process through some of the "stuff" that was threatening their relationship.

"Tell me about your fathers, you all know about my father," Lee said, and they did—*The Flying Boy* is in its fifteenth printing (and soon to be a major motion picture, according to the publisher). "But I must ask you this—make your comments short and succinct, so we can all talk."

Good luck, fellows! It was an impossible request. One lucky guy from Lubbock jumped in first: "My dad—I feel a real need to reconnect with the other men here because it was just like his hyperreligiosity that I just couldn't work through when he'd come to me and . . ." Good luck John! But it is not for nothing that John Lee is a superstar, a workshop sultan. He vacuumed the fog of logorrhea that was gathering in the center of the room by cutting the fellow off. He instead suggested the men break up into little groups, according to what kind of Dad they had.

"All you with passive fathers, leave your seats and come up to the front of the room. I tell you, the passive father is one of the most abusive kinds of father there is. He just won't do it. 'Dad,' you say, 'I want to talk about masturbation,' and it's like, 'Argh, I ain't gonna listen to ya.' Like that. You know?"

"Ho!"

"Critical fathers—really abusive—you all come up here."

"What about if your father was passive until he drank?" asked one of the men.

"Over here," said John authoritatively. "If you had a dad who just wasn't fuckin' there, just a disappearing dad, you all get here in the center." People with aggressive dads were put over by the windows. A number of the men had questions about what kind of dad they had, and they inquired at great length. "What if your dad wasn't exactly invisible; it was that *you* were just sort of invisible, he wouldn't notice you unless sometimes—like there was once . . ." John put him with the disappearing dads.

A mountain, a Matterhorn, an *Everest* of grievances! They dissolved and poured out in tears and sometimes in gut-wrenching field hollers. One fellow had to sit all by himself, because he said his dad was okay. This brought John up short. Momentarily. "We'll talk about this dad later. Because let me tell you," John said, full of pity, "this dad—this one who did a pretty good job—this dad is the toughest of all. We've got some work to do."

Meaning: Let's talk. "My dad never taught me how to be intimate with a woman," one man said.

"The men's movement will teach you," John reassured him. "It's going to take some time. You better be in it for the long haul."

One fellow's dad refused to go out to brunch with him. "Ho!" said the other men. Nobody's dad would talk the way the New Men wanted him to talk. They wanted to talk about their feelings; Dad wanted to watch football or read the paper or, worse, go to work.

But there comes a point when talking must cease and another kind of work be done. The last half hour was given over to a guided meditation. The men let their heads fall as the lights in the room went down and they were told to envision Dad in their mind's eye. John's voice was quiet. "Tell your dad good-bye. Good-bye, Dad. I gotta letcha go. Dad left you. Now you leave him. Gotta letcha go." The sniffles began in the darkened room, and then the keening, and the mewling, and then a loud "Daddy!" And then another: "Bastard!"

When the lights came back up the workshop was over, men wiped their eyes. There had been some healing here. John announced, as an afterthought, that he would be happy to see everyone that afternoon—at a "book-signing thing" for himself.

"Ah," sighed the man next to me as we gathered our things to go. "It's amazing what ten minutes of crying can do. I feel supergreat."

I T IS VITAL that people who talk as much as the New Men never be embarrassed by anything they say; embarrassment would cramp the enthusiasm for talk, especially the talk about the subject of the day (week, year, lifetime!), which is of course *me*. Of necessity no word is too hackneyed, no sentiment too overdone, to be employed in the task of further expressing as precisely and affectionately as possible how the men's movement man might be feeling about himself at any given moment. "I've gotten better at getting in touch with my feelings," one New Man actually said one afternoon, "which is important to me, because I'm a people person."

We were all sitting in a big circle—a powwow!—out in the forested office park that abuts the Austin Stouffer. We had signed up, and paid $12, for a "ropes course," in which all fifteen of us "would discover self-empowerment, joy, and hope." Our guide was Steve, who told me he was a "certified wilderness therapeutic counselor." "We use wilderness as a modality for bringing up issues and processing through them," he explained.

This requires some heavy unblocking, and of course lots of talk. We started by forming a tight knot of men, a New Age scrum, with arms crisscrossed and interlaced, and then tried to untie ourselves and expand into a large circle without letting go of one another's arms. In such close contact you realize again, with considerable force, that men are hairy creatures, often neglectful of the rudiments of hygiene, and as I felt legs rolling over the back of my neck and heads bobbing next to my thighs I wondered, not for the first time that weekend, why anyone would strive to come into closer contact with this gender.

But we did it! And this was the beginning of our coming together. So we all unlocked and sat down and talked about what we had just done several seconds before. "Some people took charge. Other people just laid back," said Larry from Dayton. "I think I was taking charge too much, and this is a problem for me, one of the things I have to honor and work through. I run a small construction company, and one of the guys at work is always telling me . . ."

"Yes," said Steve, interrupting, aware that we only had three hours to complete our ropes course. "Anyone else?"

"You probably noticed what I did with my arms," said my acquaintance Chuck. "That's a Marine Corps thing. I can't get that monkey off my back."

"Honor it," said Steve, consolingly. "Then you can start the processing through."

"I guess there's a lot of work ahead of me," Chuck admitted glumly.

"Be careful not to go up into your head too often," said the counselor. "Try to stay down in your body more."

The men were led to perform other tasks, most of them involving similarly close body contact, from which I demurred. Each exercise was followed by glowing self-appraisals, startling in their detail. The coming together grew tighter. We were a group of men, relying on one another, as men, with great enthusiasm and encouragement. We began to resemble a team on *Family Feud,* with lots of clapping and commenting and hopping up and down.

After one exercise, as we sat in a circle on the ground, Larry from Dayton told us that he was feeling better. "You can see how I stood back there for a while, let somebody else take over," he said. "I've always got this stuff: 'I gotta do it.'"

"Ho!" said a couple of men.

"Did everybody hear Larry?" Steve said. "Is that old male? 'I gotta do it, I gotta earn the money, I gotta succeed, I gotta pay the bills.' We're getting rid of that. That's what this conference is all about."

Larry looked modestly at the ground, from which he had just torn up several square inches of turf.

"I want to honor Larry," Steve said, as everyone applauded. ("Good answer!") "He just made himself very vulnerable here. I want to celebrate that." The drama, the little revelations, the climax, the delicious denouement—all for Larry!

"Ho!" the men shouted.

"It's like that song," Larry said, stretching out the exquisite moment as long as possible. "'Why can't I just let someone else be strong?'"

See what I mean? A businessman from Dayton, near tears, quotes a line from "Have You Never Been Mellow," by Olivia Newton-John, and more than a dozen men answer with the Indian word for "Right on." Unembarrassable.

THERE WERE MANY movement leaders at the conference: the Big Dogs of the New Age, Pooh-Bahs among men; the conference brochures offered brief bios of each. Beautiful Pointed Arrow "is following a vision of creating sound chambers around the world used in chanting for world peace." Rich Armington is a "Certified Bioenergetic Therapist"; Gaya Erlandson is a "Certified Imago Relationship Therapist." Coyote is "a ceremonialist in private practice in New Mexico," presumably uncertified. Stephen Johnson's "public work is in the areas of co-creativity and the development of an integrated, spiritually centered brotherhood of men who serve in planetary stewardship."

Among the rank and file, the spiritually centered brotherhood seems to be coming along quite nicely. The following colloquy, which I witnessed during one of the workshops, is exemplary of the decorum that obtains among the New Men:

WORKSHOP LEADER: You mentioned your gayness. I want to thank you for that.

MAN: Well, thank *you*. It's liberating to have that honored.

LEADER: You're welcome. But really, thank you. I do honor it.

MAN: Thank you.

LEADER: And I think that for us as men, it's important for us to celebrate it, even. So thanks for that.

MAN: Thank you.

LEADER: No, thank *you*.

MAN: No, no . . .

The Alphonse-and-Gaston deference can get a bit suffocating, so I'm happy to report that among the Big Dogs themselves the relationship is more Tom and Jerry.

By any measure the Biggest of the Big Dogs in the men's movement is Robert Bly, and for many participants his absence from the conference was puzzling and hurtful, although not, as one leader told me, "fully negating": Like a gathering of Trekkies without William Shatner, or even George Takei, the men at the conference soldiered through, vaguely aware that their experience lacked the validation of a hero's presence.

Bly had of course been invited, but had declined. On Friday morning, he faxed to many movement leaders a letter denouncing

Marvin Allen as a media hound, a sensationalizer, who was using the conference to further his own career. It was too early in the movement's growth, Bly wrote, to coalesce, much less to do so in a Stouffer hotel in full view of the press. Bly demanded moreover that the letter be read to a plenary session of the New Men at the Austin gathering.

Ignoring the wise counsel of his PR advisers, Allen decided not to read the letter to his fellow men, but word of it spread, from workshop to workshop, in hushed tones between chants and drum-banging, throughout the weekend. A rift! A cynic less advanced in the grieving process might suggest that it's easy for Bly to disparage Marvin as a press hound, now that PBS and countless fawning profiles in the slick magazines have made him a millionaire, but for the New Men the breach was hard to fathom. How could Robert Bly, who had told the world of the Wildman within, himself an Adult Child of an Alcoholic, the poet who had won an award, a man who was so . . . so *there,* how could he be wrong about Allen? But then who could doubt the good faith, the *thereness,* of Marvin Allen, originator of the Wildman weekend, founder of Austin Men's Center, not to mention the revered Texas Men's Institute, the self-effacing leader featured in *Fortune* and *Newsweek* and *The New York Times Magazine*?

"There's some pain," Chuck told me. "This conference was a chance to create a space of safety, of healing. To see this bickering between two men we all love and respect . . . obviously, there are some wounds there. But I honor them both." This was Sunday morning, right before the closing session. All seven hundred of the New Men gathered in the ballroom just off the lobby for a particularly frenetic session of drumming, a bit of bodywork, and a reading from D. H. Lawrence. Then Marvin Allen climbed the stage.

He looked more fretful than usual. A few minutes before, unknown to most of the men, in the empty exhibition hall one floor below, Marvin and his conference cochair Allen Maurer had got in a shouting match with Shepherd Bliss, the bodywork expert. Bliss insisted Bly's letter be read. Marvin demurred. It got ugly. When Maurer tried to defend his cochairman, Bliss turned on him. "From what I can see," Bliss said, "you are acting as a codependent protector for Marvin!"

Devastated, the chairmen offered Bliss the podium to read the letter to the men in the ballroom, after which poor Marvin, his reedy voice faltering, took the microphone. "I've known Robert Bly for four years," Marvin said. "And in those years I've learned a lot about Robert Bly that I could share with you right now, but I won't." An even lower blow! Innuendo, betrayal, secrets among men for whom there can be no secrets! Hollers rose from the floor, say-it-ain't-so protests, the rumble of drums—war drums!—began to build, until a man popped up from the front row and grabbed the microphone from Allen.

This fellow, plump and balding, had spoken earlier in the conference, identifying himself as a "recovering Presbyterian minister," and had apologized to the men "for all the ministers in the world and the damage they've done to you." He carried, I mean to say, a good deal of moral authority.

"I know Robert Bly," said the minister, "and I know Marvin Allen, and I tell you that what they think of each other is beside the point. This is the new church. We're the healthiest group of men on this planet, but that doesn't mean we aren't still fucked up. Bly still has a lot of work to do, so does Marvin Allen. Bly's fucked up and"—he pointed to Marvin trembling on the podium—"he's fucked up. I'm fucked up. You're fucked up. The point is, we're all fucked up!"

Ho! Another revelation, a peak experience. The drums began again, uniting them in an unbreakable bond of fuckedupness, and there was chanting, and Shepherd Bliss told the men to telescope their necks like turtles and feel the fullness of their bellies, letting go of all the stuff that sometimes comes up when you do menswork. Coyote, the ceremonialist, lit a peace pipe in closing, and smoked it right there at the podium, honoring all the fathers who have gone before, back to the earliest days, long before the invention of fire regulations and the posting of no-smoking signs in hotel ballrooms.

Marvin regained the microphone for a final word. "When you go back to the real world—you know, the one that isn't really real, where you can't be yourself—I hope you can take some of this with you."

AND SO THEY TRUDGED OUT OF THE BALLROOM, through the vast hotel atrium, hugging and sobbing, taking, by the look of it, much with them: a new drum from Drums for Modern Man, Inc., perhaps, or an extra copy, this one autographed, of *The Flying Boy,* maybe a smudge stick of sage ($4.00) or several audiotapes from Sounds True cassettes ($12.95), the new edition of *Is It Love or Is It Addiction?,* meditation cushions for bottoms made weary from hours of self-exploration, packets of incense, bongers for self-massage, thuribles painted in sacred Aztec symbols, Indian feathers . . .

If the men's movement didn't exist, the purveyors of all these goods would have to invent it—Say's law applies to self-empowerment, too. But the men's movement doesn't exist in any definable sense, and certainly not as we have been led to believe. I had my own peak experience during one of the conference's plenary sessions, when John Lee asked how many of the seven-hundred-plus New Men gathered before him had been in a Twelve Step program—AA, for example, or Cocaine Abusers Anonymous. A forest of hands shot up. Lee said it was about 80 percent of the participants; my own informal polling put the figure at closer to 90 percent. A large industry has long been in place to proffer salves to these unhappy people: The men's movement is for those who have gone from one to the next, from Twelve Step to Rebirthing to est to Holistic Healing. It provides them with a new gimmick, yet another excuse for thinking about, studying, exploring, investigating, dwelling on . . . *me.*

They share certain characteristics. All, clearly, have way too much time on their hands. Many of the men I spoke with had been divorced twice or more. "It's beginning to dawn on me what's so odd here," a woman journalist told me one evening. "There are no—I mean *no*—good-looking men here." New Men tend to be paunchy, with much facial hair to compensate for the diminishing crop up top. Calling the Austin gathering of men the First International Losers' Conference would have been unkind but more accurate. One morning I attended a workshop, "The Healing Power of Relationships," led by an affable husband-and-wife team from Southern California, Jim Sniechowski and Judith Sherven, who have become the

Regis and Kathie Lee of the movement. Amid the wisdom—"Most of you already know this stuff," Jim told them: "It's just a matter of organizing it in such a way that it speaks to what a relationship can be rather than what it is"—Judith asked a question, "How many of you are in a place where you can never, ever please a woman, sexually or otherwise?" The unanimous "Ho!" almost blew out the windows.

IT IS OF COURSE in the interests of *Newsweek,* with fifty-two covers to fill a year, and of Bill Moyers, constantly polishing his reputation as America's chronicler, and of Bly and Marvin Allen and Shepherd Bliss and the rest of the workshop holders and marketers of grief to persuade us that the movement really is rolling through every city and suburb, even where men stay married and like their kids and tolerate their jobs and have pleasant conversations, once in a while, with their parents. The claim isn't true, but we should remember that less outlandish propositions have sometimes proved self-fulfilling. The sales success of such movement bibles as Bly's *Iron John* and Sam Keen's *Fire in the Belly* is an ominous sign. Is it possible that the men's movement can swell outward from the ranks of the balding and sodden and pudgy and sexually inept, to overtake the well-coiffed, employed, and reasonably fit middle-class American male? Could this rock on which American prosperity has been built, this hardworking, self-denying model of rectitude and enterprise at last succumb to the siren song of self-flattery and indulgence, and come to believe that he too is oppressed and wounded and desperately needful of expensive healing?

Sure.

Sister Soldiers

Christina Hoff Sommers

THE HYATT REGENCY in Austin, Texas, is a pleasant hotel, but not all of the five hundred participants in this year's National Women's Studies Association (NWSA) Conference were happy with it. One woman from a well-known Southern college complained about the weddings held there throughout the weekend. "Why have they put us in a setting where *that* sort of thing is going on?" she demanded.

Dissatisfaction was a conference motif. The keynote speaker, Annette Kolodny, a feminist literary scholar and until recently dean of the humanities faculty at the University of Arizona, opened the proceedings with a brief history of the "narratives of pain" within the NWSA. She reported that ten years ago the organization "almost came apart over outcries by our lesbian sisters that we had failed adequately to listen to their many voices." Five years ago sisters in the Jewish Caucus had wept at their own "sense of invisibility." Three years later the Disability Caucus threatened to quit, and the next year the women of color walked out. A pernicious bigotry, Kolodny confessed, persisted in the NWSA. "Our litanies of outrage . . . overcame our fragile consensus of shared commitment, and the center would no longer hold."

At past conferences oppressed women accused other women of oppressing them. Participants met in groups defined by their grievances and healing needs: Jewish Women, Jewish Lesbians, Asian-American Women, African-American Women, Old Women, Disabled Women, Fat Women, Women Whose Sexuality Is in Transition. None of the groups proved stable: the fat group polarized into gay and straight factions, and the Jewish women discovered that they were deeply divided: some accepted being Jewish; others were seeking to recover from it. This year concern extended to "marginalized" allergy groups. Participants were sent advance notice not to bring perfumes, dry-cleaned clothing, hair spray, or other dangerous irritants to the conference out of concern for allergic sisters. Hyperconcern is now the norm: at the first National Lesbian Convention in Atlanta flash cameras were outlawed—they might bring on epileptic fits.

Eleanor Smeal, the former president of the National Organization for Women (NOW), was scheduled to be the first speaker on the NWSA "Empowerment Panel," but her plane had been held up in Memphis. To pass the time, we were introduced to an array of panelists who were touted as being experienced in conflict resolution. One woman was introduced as a member of the Mohawk nation who "facilitates antibias training." Another, who had training as a holistic health practitioner, headed workshops that "creatively optimize human capacity."

Still no Smeal. A panelist named Angela took the mike to tell about "ouch experiences." An "ouch" is when you experience racism, sexism, classism, homophobia, ableism, ageism, or lookism. One of Angela's biggest ouches came after her lesbian support group splintered into two factions, black and white. Tension then developed in her black group between those whose lovers were black and those whose lovers were white. "Those of us in the group who had white lovers were immediately targeted. . . . It turned into a horrible mess. . . . I ended up leaving that group for self-protection."

A weary Eleanor Smeal finally arrived and was pressed into service. She confided that she was feeling discouraged about the feminist movement. "We need totally new concepts. . . . In many ways it's not working. It is so depressing. . . . We are leaving . . . the next generation [in a] mess." Smeal's liveliest moment came when she attacked "liberal males on the campus," saying, "They have kept us apart. They have marginalized our programs. We need fighting madness." Still, Smeal's talk was a downer, and the moderator hastened to raise our spirits: "What we want to do now is to dwell for a minute in success. . . . Think about the fact that we have been so successful in transforming the curriculum. . . ." It was soon time for a song.

We are sisters in a circle.
We are sisters in a struggle.
Sisters one and all.
We are colors of the rainbow.
Sisters one and all.

As it happened, I did have a real sister (in the unexciting biological sense) with me at the conference. Louise and I were relieved when the proceedings were interrupted by a coffee break. Half-and-half was available—though perhaps not for long. The ecofeminist caucus has been pushing to eliminate all meat, fish, eggs, and dairy products at NWSA events. As the break ended, Phyllis, the panelist from the Mohawk nation, holding two little puppets, a dog and a teddy bear, came round to inform us, "Teddy and his friend say it's time to go back inside."

Inside, Phyllis led us in some healing exercises.

Let us take a moment to give ourselves a big hug. Let me remind us that the person we're hugging is the most important person we have in our life.

After the morning session Louise and I visited the Exhibition Hall. There, dozens of booths offered women's studies books and paraphernalia. Witchcraft and goddess worship supplies were in aisle one. Adjoining aisles sold handmade jewelry, leather crafts, ponchos, and other peasant apparel. One booth offered videos on do-it-yourself menstrual extractions and home abortions for those who want to avoid "patriarchal medicine." Available for viewing throughout the conference were such films as *Sex and the Sandinistas* and *We're Talking Vulva*.

The philosopher Paula Rothenberg spotted me and approached. She knows I am a skeptic. "I am very uncomfortable having you here. I saw you taking notes. We are in the middle of working through our problems. I feel as if you have come into the middle of my dysfunctional family, and you are seeing us at the worst possible moment."

But Rothenberg's "dysfunctional family" has had many such moments. Ouchings and mass therapy are more the norm than the exception in academic feminism. Last year, at a meeting of Women's Studies Program Directors, everyone joined hands to form a "healing circle." They also assumed the posture of trees experiencing rootedness and tranquility. Victim testimonials and New Age healing rituals routinely crowd out the reading of academic papers at NWSA conferences. Out of approximately one hundred workshops and presentations at the Austin meetings, I counted no more than sixteen that could generously be called scholarly.

Does it matter that a bunch of high-strung, anti-intellectual, chronically offended, "dysfunctional family members" get together for a conference and say and do a lot of odd things? It does, because on more and more campuses these consciousness-raisers are driving out the scholars. Within the past fifteen years the academy has witnessed the inception of more than five hundred Women's Studies Programs and more than thirty thousand courses, along with the formation of some fifty major feminist institutes. Most of the women who attended this conference are in the academy in one capacity or another: either teaching women's studies, directing programs, or in the administration. Others head women's centers.

These women run the largest growth area in the academy, and they have strong influence in some key areas, most notably in English departments (especially freshman writing courses), French departments, history departments, law schools, and divinity schools. They are disproportionately represented in the dean of students' office, in the dormitory administration, in the harassment office, and various counseling centers. They are quietly engaged in hundreds of well-funded projects to transform a curriculum that they regard as unacceptably "androcentric." Their moral authority comes from a widespread belief that they represent "women." In fact, their version of feminism falls short of being representative.

Most American women subscribe philosophically to an older "First Wave" kind of feminism whose main goal is equity. A First Wave or "equity feminist" wants for women what she wants for everyone: fair treatment, no discrimination. The equity feminist crusade that was initiated more than 150 years ago called for constitutional changes to guarantee equal opportunity, especially in politics and education. The equity agenda may not yet be fully achieved, but by any reasonable measure equity feminism is a great American success story.

Women's studies practitioners ride the First Wave for its popularity and its moral authority, but most adhere to a more radical "Second Wave" doctrine: that women, even modern American women, are in thrall to "a system of male dominance," variously referred to as "hetero-patriarchy," or the "sex/gender system." According to one feminist theorist, it is "a system of male-dominance made possible by men's control of women's productive and reproductive labor." Another describes it as "that complex process whereby bisexual infants are transformed into male and female gender personalities, the one destined to command, the other to obey."

Heady claims are made for the new way of looking at society and its impact on scholarship. According to the philosopher Elizabeth Minnich, "What we are doing is comparable to Copernicus shattering our geo-centricity, Darwin shattering our species-centricity. We are shattering andro-centricity, and the change is as fundamental, as dangerous, as exciting."

Some feminist scholarship is innovative, sound, and necessary. Literary scholars have discovered and rescued many gifted women writers from undeserved oblivion. Women historians and social scientists have found that much previous research did not apply to women. The best research on women does not use the gynocentric prism, but unfortunately a good deal of what is assigned in women's studies classes falls into the latter category. The amenable student learns to unmask the subtle, inimical workings of patriarchy. Committed instructors declare their classrooms "liberated zones" where "silenced women" will be free for the first time to speak out in a "safe" ambience.

What sort of approach to learning *would* satisfy the Second Wave feminist scholars? We get an idea by looking at a "model" introductory women's studies course developed by twelve Rutgers University professors. One of the stated goals of the course is to "challenge and change the social institutions and practices that create and perpetuate systems of oppression." Forty percent of the student's grade is to come from (1) performing some "outrageous" and "liberating" act outside of class and then sharing feelings and reactions with the class; (2) Keeping a journal of "narratives of personal experience, expressions of emotion, dream accounts, poetry doodles, etc."; and (3) Forming small in-class consciousness-raising groups.

The exhilaration of feeling themselves at the cutting edge of a new consciousness infuses some feminist pedagogues with a doctrinal fervor unique in the academy. "The feminist classroom," say four professors from the University of Massachusetts—Amherst,

> is the place to use what we know as women to appropriate and transform, totally, a domain which has been men's. . . . Let us welcome the intrusion/infusion of emotionality—love, rage, anxiety, eroticism—into intellect as a step toward healing the fragmentation capitalism and patriarchy have demanded from us.

The antirational character of feminist pedagogy has not impeded its burgeoning growth on today's campuses. Most faculty have been skeptical, but at the same time passive and permissive. Administrations have been cooperative. The one academic estate that resists are the students; but students have little political standing on the American campus.

An undergraduate may take Freshman Composition, Baroque Art, or Egyptology and discover on the first day of class that it will be taught from a "gynocentric" perspective. Students tend to like opinionated teachers who breathe commitment, but even so most are not buying the story of a gender war. Women's studies professors often describe their classrooms as being in "crisis" because of "rebellious students," a situation that has been aggravated because, on so many campuses, women's studies courses are now mandatory. Instructors tell of the inevitable "midsemester blowup" in which students protest angrily about the one-sidedness of courses. Feminist pedagogues call it the "blame the messenger" reaction, or the "denial" stage. Ordinarily instructors facing persistent student protests would be moved to reconsider their own methods and arguments. But in the feminist classroom, opposition, counterargument, or complaints about methods serve primarily to convince the instructor that she is encountering backlash. At the Austin conference the "White Male Student Hostility" workshop was packed.

To succeed as they have, feminist academics needed strong support from friendly administrators. They got this in two ways: first, by entering administrative positions in disproportionate numbers, and second, by doing all they could to get cooperative people into positions of power. Increasingly, aspiring presidents, deans, professors, and program directors in all academic fields have to pledge allegiance to feminist educational agendas. The American Association of Colleges disseminates a widely used questionnaire titled "It's All in What You Ask: Questions for Search Committees to Use." Among the questions: How have you demonstrated your commitment to women's issues in your current position? What is your relation to the women's center? How do you deal with backlash and denial?

THE PROPOSITION THAT "the knowledge base" must be radically "transformed" along feminist lines is now asserted by prestigious mainstream educational organizations such as the American Association of University Women and the American Council on Education (ACE). According to the ACE, the feminist challenges to "conventional ways of knowing and thinking" set a new agenda: "What has yet to happen on all of our campuses is the transformation of knowledge, and therefore of the curriculum."

At the root of all transformation projects is the thesis that not just people but also ideas and disciplines are gendered. But, as the academic promoters of the politics of sexual identity are beginning to learn, gender is not sacrosanct as a principle of social division. Why should identity politics be stabilized at two? A woman can be simultaneously a victim and, depending on her race and physical status, a white, able-bodied oppressor of Latinas, black males, and the disabled. The middle-class educated women who discovered the sex-gender system are now being forced to regard themselves as oppressors in a complex ecology of domination and subjugation.

One would normally expect that more objective academics would quickly demolish the claims being made for feminist theory. That they hold back is a tribute to the reputation feminists have for their ruthless ways of dealing with unfriendly comment. Adverse criticism is never examined with any seriousness. Instead, the critic is denounced as reactionary. Few disinterested scholars have been willing to take on the unrewarding job of critically examining feminist arguments. When the respected Shakespeare scholar Richard Levin took issue with some of the more fanciful feminist interpretations of Shakespeare's tragedies, he was denounced and ridiculed in the *Publication of the Modern Language Association.* One particularly nasty letter boasted twenty-four signatories: signing in groups is a standard feature of feminist critical response.

But the faculty's incapacity to impede the radical feminist colonization of the liberal academy cannot be ascribed to mere timidity. The deeper reason is that a confused academic community has persistently failed to distinguish between the "First Wave" equity feminism, which is responsible for the main achievements of feminism in this century, and the Second Wave gynocentric feminism, which since the early 1970s has taken center stage in the universities.

Gender feminists sometimes boast among themselves about the way they use naive liberal sentiment to gain their ends. Paula Goldsmid, a former dean at Oberlin College, muses: "You might wonder . . . how we managed to generate a Women's Studies program that has a catalog supplement listing more than twenty courses, that offers an Individual Major in Women's Studies, that has been able to involve several committees in really working to transform the academy in various ways." She then notes with cozy candor, "There is a great reluctance to say or do anything publicly that goes against the liberal and 'progressive' Oberlin stance. Oberlin's liberal values can be turned to *our* advantage."

But is it to the advantage of women students? Two years ago I wrote to the British novelist and philosopher Iris Murdoch, asking for her views on some recent trends in women's studies. In her response she said:

Men "created culture" because they were free to do so, and women were treated as inferior and made to believe they were. Now free women must join in the human world of work and creation on an equal footing and be everywhere in art, science, business, politics, etc. . . . However, to lay claim, in this battle, to *female* ethics, *female* criticism, *female* knowledge . . . is to set up a new female ghetto. (Chauvinist males should be delighted by the move. . . .) "Women's Studies" can mean that women are led to read mediocre or peripheral books by women rather than the great books of humanity in general. . . . It is a dead end, in danger of simply separating women from the mainstream thinking of the human race. Such cults can also *waste the time* of young people who may be reading all the latest books on feminism instead of studying the difficult and important things that belong to the culture of humanity.

The universal liberal ideal of a culture of humanity was not a theme of the Austin conference. On the contrary, the self-imposed segregation of women was everywhere in evidence.

This convention received a warm letter from Governor Ann Richards welcoming us to the Great State of Texas. The governor called the assembled feminists "the vanguard of the latest incarnation of the women's movement," praising their leadership as essential. The NWSA audience broke out into thunderous applause as the letter was read aloud. It is, however, unlikely that Richards was aware of the goddess worship booths, the menstrual extraction videos, the teddy bear puppets, the paranoid exposés of "phallocentric discourse"—let alone the bullying of students and the implacable hostility to all exact thinking as "male." Less innocently benighted are such government agencies or foundations as the Department of Education, the Ford Foundation, and the Mellon Foundation—which keep groups like the NWSA "empowered." Those who irresponsibly abet the spirit of Austin have much to answer for. Perhaps, in penance, they should be made to view the tapes of the conference and then asked to hug themselves till they "ouch."

A Darkness in Massachusetts

Dorothy Rabinowitz

ON LABOR DAY 1984, sixty-year-old Violet Amirault—proprietor of the thriving Fells Acres Day School in Malden, Massachusetts—received a call about a child abuse accusation against her son. Two days later the police arrested thirty-one-year-old Gerald (who worked at Fells Acres) on charges of raping a five-year-old boy, a new pupil.

In short order, the hideous crimes supposedly committed by Gerald began to multiply—as did the number of the accused. Soon, Violet Amirault herself and her newly married twenty-six-year-old daughter, Cheryl, were also charged with having perpetrated monstrous sexual crimes against children ages three to five. Police asked the Amiraults no questions. Instead, they summoned parents of Fells Acres children to a meeting at the station house—where they were instructed to look for symptoms of sex abuse.

Within three years, Gerald Amirault was convicted of assault and rape of nine children. In a second trial his mother and sister were convicted of roughly the same crimes against four children. Gerald, sentenced to thirty to forty years, has now been in prison since 1986. His mother, now seventy-one, and sister Cheryl, now thirty-seven, were given eight to twenty years. Both have been imprisoned, at the Massachusetts Correctional Institute at Framingham, for nearly eight years.

At the time of their sentencing, prosecutor Lawrence Hardoon complained that the punishment was too light for such crimes: and indeed, the prosecution had brought forth some remarkable accusations against the Amiraults.

A "Magic Room"

CHILDREN had supposedly been raped with knives—which miraculously failed to leave any signs of wounding or other injury—and sticks, and been assaulted by a clown (allegedly Gerald) in a "magic room." Some children told—after interrogations by investigators—of being forced to drink urine, of watching the Amiraults slaughter blue birds, of meeting robots with flashing lights. Violet Amirault was accused of shoving a stick into the rectum of a child while he was standing up, and of raping him with "a magic wand." Mrs. Amirault was convicted of these charges. The child also testified he was tied naked to a tree in the schoolyard, in front of all the teachers and children, while "Miss Cheryl" cut the leg off a squirrel.

Who would have credited such witnesses, such testimony? The Amirault family was charged in the midst of the great wave of high-profile child-abuse cases sweeping the country in the 1980s—all of them magnets for ambitious prosecutors. Among them was that of day-care worker Kelly Michaels, reported on these pages. But the prime child-abuse extravaganza—and the one the Amirault prosecutors clearly took for their model—was the now notorious McMartin Preschool case in California, involving alleged abusers Ray Buckey and his mother, sixtyish administrator Peggy McMartin Buckey.

True, there was a certain inimitable grandeur to the McMartin epic, involving as it did claims of abuse in underground tunnels, of molestation in hot air balloons, and similar marvels. As recently as three years ago die-hard believers among the plaintiff parents were still to be found at the school site, faithfully conducting their searches for the underground tunnels.

That the wave of spectacular child-abuse trials emerged in the 1980s was no accident. The passage in 1979 of the Mondale Act ensured a huge increase in funds for child protection agencies and abuse investigators. With the outpouring of government money came a huge increase in agencies and staffs, which in turn begat investigations and accusations of child sex abuse on a grand scale. An industry had been born.

Nowhere was the fervor of the search for abuse more evident than in the case constructed against the Amiraults. Her husband gone from the household, an impoverished Violet Amirault had built her highly successful day-care center—in operation for twenty years—alone, and from nothing. Over the years the school became her life, next to her children. It was clear, when the sensational prosecutions began, that of the thousands of children previously graduated from Fells Acres, none had any stories of abuse to tell.

So the world was left with the state's contention: that Mrs. Amirault, at the age of sixty, had suddenly taken to raping small children and terrorizing them into silence. When her daughter, Cheryl, was married in 1983, all the pupils and their parents were invited to the church—an event that occasioned a front-page picture of the "kindergarten teacher with a hundred children" in the *Boston Herald.* Among those children happily giving their teacher kisses were those who some months later would be served up to tell of terrors inflicted by Miss Cheryl, her mother, and brother.

As soon as the accusations surfaced, the school's teachers were grilled—but none could be found who saw anything wrong going on at the school. One or two of them disliked Violet, an exacting school head, but still they could come up with nothing, frightened though they were by unsubtle threats from the police, who repeatedly accused them of lying.

Still, the police investigators' effort to find abuse testimony pales beside the surreal interrogations conducted by such as pediatric nurse Susan Kelley, who developed most of the children's allegations of abuse. Over and over, the interviews show, the children say nothing happened, nobody took their clothes off, they know nothing about a magic room or a bad clown. But the interviewer persists. In the world of these examiners, children are to be believed only when they say abuse took place. Otherwise, they are described as "not ready to disclose."

The Fells Acres children were bribed with gifts, assured that their little friends had already told about the bad things and "helped so much." At one point the interviewer tells a child that her friend Sara had said "the clown had you girls take your clothes off in the magic room."

CHILD: No, she's lying.

NURSE: She's lying? Why would she lie about something like that . . . ?

CHILD: We didn't do that.

Next the interviewer tells the child, "I really believed her [Sara] because she told me all about it, and she even told me what the clown said."

CHILD: What was it?

No sane person reading the transcripts of these interrogations can doubt the wholesale fabrications of evidence on which this case was built. Nor could any reasonable person who looked at the trial transcript doubt that three innocent citizens were sent to prison on the basis of some of the most fantastic claims ever presented to an American jury.

Forced to come up with motives, the prosecutors hit on child pornography. With no evidence whatsoever that the Amiraults had engaged in such crimes, the Commonwealth brought forth a postal inspector Dunn to regale the jury with detailed descriptions of child pornography. When the Amirault women's appeal was refused, Justice Paul Liacos said, in an eloquent dissent, "The court today condones the admission in evidence of highly inflammatory and prejudicial evidence." Clearly, the justice charged, the Commonwealth wanted the jury to infer that because pornographers having no connection with the defendants took pictures of children, so had the defendants.

The accused in the McMartin case are now free. Kelly Michaels, too, now has her freedom—but for the Amiraults, a far grimmer story from the outset, prospects remain bleak. The thought of the whole family in prison, Cheryl says, "is too much for any one of us to endure. I can't look into my mother's eyes."

When the Amirault women were sentenced, Prosecutor Hardoon announced that it was "impudent of them" to continue maintaining their innocence. Nevertheless, after eight years in prison they continue to do so—as does Gerald, in Plymouth Correctional Facility. One parole board member told Cheryl that until she confessed she'd be going nowhere. None of the Amiraults are about to confess to what they have not done.

After the first time the women were refused parole, the judge who presided over their trial decided they had served enough time and issued an order to revise and revoke their sentence. Agitated prosecutors succeeded in getting the courts to overturn the revise-and-revoke order—a ruling unprecedented in Massachusetts history. As in some crude melodrama, the women, unaware and thankful to be going home again, were stopped just before they got to the exit. Back they went deeper into the system—to be refused parole again and again.

Silence Reigns

SCOTT HARSHBARGER, the district attorney whose office prosecuted the Amiraults—and who ran for reelection advertising that fact—is now attorney general of Massachusetts. Some months after the Amiraults were all convicted and in prison, Mr. Harshbarger presided over a celebratory convocation on the Fells Acres case, billed as "a model multidisciplinary response." Prosecutor Hardoon is now in private practice—in a firm specializing in civil awards for sex abuse.

In Massachusetts armies of journalists from the *Boston Herald,* the *Boston Globe,* and local TV followed this prosecution and its preposterous evidence. Today only silence reigns on the Amiraults and the great abuse trials that occasioned so much fevered reporting. Not long ago a *Boston Globe* editor dismissed a would-be contributor on the subject, saying, "I sent two reporters to cover the story at the time, and they said the Amiraults were weirdos."

Can such a miscarriage of justice—if one can use so bland a term for so horrific a tragedy—be sustained by the will of state prosecutors? As was true of the witch trials of an earlier Massachusetts, this prosecution will, in time, be the source of amazement and horror. In the meantime Violet Amirault lies locked in prison along with her son and her daughter, while the days and years of life slip past.

The Week of Smoking Dangerously

Joe Queenan

ONE RECENT AFTERNOON, I lit a Marlboro and slipped into a Times Square strip joint. I sidled into a peep-show booth, inserted a dollar bill, and, when the glass partition had risen to reveal the exotic dancer inside, exhaled.

"Whew!!!" hissed the girl inside the booth, disdainfully, waving the smoke away with her hands. When the stench had dissipated, she leaned down and said gruffly, "We work on tips: three dollars to strip, five dollars to touch."

"Do you mind if I smoke?" I inquired.

"Do what you want," she sneered. "It's your show."

I handed her a five, evaluated her "dancing" for thirty seconds, and left. I was immensely discomfited. Here was a woman with more tattoos than the Seventh Fleet working as a stripper in the sleaziest dive in Manhattan, yet even she looked down on me as a smoker. At that moment, I realized that the antismoking movement was a thundering juggernaut that had penetrated even the lowest substratum of American society, and that smokers, as a class, were doomed.

My epiphany in the strip joint was the culmination of a long, psychologically draining week spent smoking in various public and private places throughout the Greater New York area. I had given up smoking cigarettes ages ago, and in recent times my only nicotine-related activity was the occasional cigar puffed in the presence of people who had annoyed me. Now, years later, I decided to revisit the old habit as a way of gauging how much the mores of smoking had changed.

My week as a smoker got off to an odd start when I popped inside a Citibank at the corner of Sixty-fourth and Madison to get some cash. Although a No Smoking sign was clearly posted right next to one of the four ATMs, I lit up a Marlboro and took my place in line. There were three women using the machines, though the fourth was vacant. A stubby, Hispanic blue-collar type, who looked a lot like a smoker, was standing in line ahead of me, but he ignored the empty ATM. Nipping past him, I inserted my cash card, while puffing away furiously, flicking the ashes directly at the No Smoking sign.

The machine said it could not read my card. Scary. Did the machine know I was a smoker? Had Citibank, caving in to pressure from its antismoking clientele, equipped its ATMs with anticarcinogenic sensors that would prevent smokers from getting more cash to feed their habit? I didn't know.

What I did know was that the machine didn't work. But that was okay because one of the other machines was now vacant. I zipped into it, aware that I had now committed two antisocial acts: smoking and line-jumping. I stubbed out my smoke on the floor, lit another. When I'd finished, I made eye contact with the Hispanic man as he took my place. He had every right to be ticked off because I'd jumped ahead of him, but he wasn't mad at all. A conspiratorial glance passed between us. He had taken my cue. Now he was smoking.

It is the fear that a single renegade puffer may inspire others to ape him that makes antismokers so aggressive in their attitudes toward illicit smoking. I discovered this as I made my way up Madison Avenue, ambling into various fashionable boutiques with a cigarette dangling from my lips, knowing that I was going to be asked to put it out or leave. What fascinated me was not whether I would be asked to leave, but *how* I would be asked to leave. Would I *politely* be asked to get rid of my cigarette? Or would I be treated like a subhuman and told to get out and stay out?

My first encounter was surprisingly congenial. At the Metropolitan Opera Gift Shop on Madison Avenue, I strolled in, smoking a Marlboro, and began spewing poison all over the Ravel CDs. Within seconds, a fiftyish, well-dressed man came over and whispered, "I'm sorry, you can't smoke here."

He said this with a smile on his face and a twinkle in his eye, not wanting to scare off a reasonably well-dressed man who, however vile his personal habits, looked like he might be willing to overpay for a huge stack of CDs. Nor did the smile leave his face when I remarked, "Mario Lanza smoked!" an assertion that may or may not have been true.

There was certainly no twinkle in the eye of the tennis ladies at Canard & Company at Ninety-second and Madison when I strolled in with a Winston protruding from my lips. Wheezing carcinogens all over the Vine Ripe Belgium Tomatoes ($1.79 a pound), I was immediately singled out as *persona non grata*. No sooner had I opened the door with the sign reading

> *Our Pledge to Our Customers*
> *To Our Cows*
> *We do not use BST, BGH, or any bovine growth hormone*
> *of any kind. Never did. Never will.*
> *Ronnybrook Farm Dairies*

than a harridan with a politically correct tote bag hissed: "You can't smoke in here. *And you should know it.*"

I should have known it, I should. I had been tactless, insensitive, uncouth, uncaring. On the other hand, I had not behaved like John Wayne Gacy, Son of Sam, Charles Manson, or Pol Pot. I had not devised a homemade subnuclear device, or put an entire African nation to the sword. Yet she treated me like the scum of the earth.

This encounter set the tone for the rest of the week.

Two patterns emerged. One, it was the *patrons* in upscale establishments, not the personnel, who were most likely to tell me off. And two, women were far more likely to upbraid me than men. At Godiva Chocolatier, Dean & De Luca, and several upscale gourmet shops, the employees could have cared less if I smoked; they're all actors anyway, so they probably smoke themselves, and at five bucks an hour who's going to tangle with the weirdo with the cigarette? No, it was the customers, mostly females, who wafted their hands about and pointed to the No Smoking signs.

There are several explanations for this behavior. One, patrons of these shops are almost exclusively yuppies who believe that all human activity can be codified according to a rigid moral template. Yuppies either are lawyers or are married to lawyers, and have persuaded themselves that it is possible to establish hermetically sealed universes in which all human activity can be classified as licit or illicit. Boutiques thus become minicosmoses that yuppies can control through a Hammurabi's code of acceptable behavior.

Yuppies also arrange their daily lives so that they always occupy the moral high ground. A boutique presents them with a perfect social setting in which, in an atmosphere relatively devoid of personal danger, they can make another human being feel totally worthless. You'll notice that yuppies do not, as a rule, go out into the streets to tell grown men to stop using walls as urinals, to tell black teenagers to turn down their radios, or to tell thieves to stop pulling radios out of cars. Yuppies are all like Molly Ivins: they like to sermonize, but they only want to do it on the Mount. If they did it on the street, they'd get a punch in the nose.

One day I started walking north on Madison Avenue, stopping into every business establishment that had a French name. I had a revolting Gauloises Caporal hanging from my lips, Jean Gabin–style, but I figured people would cut me some slack if I pretended to be French, because French people smoke like chimneys: Hey, give me a break; it's a *cultural* thing. No such luck. At Au Chat Botte, they didn't want me hissing fumes all over the forty-dollar baby bonnets. Yves St. Laurent didn't want cigarette smoke up the cravats. At Godiva Chocolatier, a patron pointed to the NO SMOKING sign with a gesture that signified in any language that I was a hopeless jerk. At Pierre Deux, a fabric store, the cashier studied the unlit French coffin nail dangling from my lips with a look that said, "Just try it, mon vieux." Not until I hit a food emporium called the Madison Marché at Seventy-fifth and Madison did I find a place I could light up without being told off. Of course, the Madison Marché is run by Koreans.

Consider how different things were over at Forty-sixth and Eighth, where I spent fifteen minutes one day smoking my way through all the businesses on the west side of the Street. Did anybody care if I smoked at the Palace peep show? They did not. Did they care if I smoked at the Eighth Avenue Grocery? They did not. Did they care if I chain-smoked at Nilupul Video, the Full Moon Saloon, the Big Apple Gift Shop, Le Rendez-Vous Cafe, the Caravan Restaurant, Scruffy Duffy's, the Adult Video Store, the Friendship Hotel, the Subway, or the Acropolis Restaurant? They most certainly did not.

Smoking forces you to bond involuntarily with your social inferiors. Bums. The homeless. Drunks. Teenagers. Four of the twenty cigarettes from my first pack of Marlboros went to beggars: a bag person and three kids who surrounded me on Ninety-fourth Street demanding smokes. But most people, including most smokers, don't want to think of themselves as people whose personal idiosyncrasies will be tolerated only in a grubby, dangerous neighborhood. That's what's really discouraging. Go over and smoke in some whorehouse on Eighth Avenue—don't smoke here in this upscale boutique we named after a French cat.

The sad fact is that, while antismokers almost all think of themselves as allies in a moral and ecological crusade, smokers do not feel a similar rapport with other smokers. Smokers may engage in rehearsed solidarity—at bars, at tailgate parties, in men's rooms—but deep down inside they do not feel instinctive solidarity with one another. I realized this when I spotted a frowzy, fiftyish woman chain-smoking Winstons at a corner of Sixty-fifth and Madison, and sidled up to her with a Marlboro dangling from my lips, muttering, "There aren't many of us left, are there?"

She simply walked away.

One extremely interesting development in the world of nicotinophobia is the burgeoning antismoking bias one detects in places where you are actually allowed to smoke. Let me give you an example. One night I arrange to have drinks with a friend at Harry Cipriani, the cigar-box lounge in the Sherry Netherlands Hotel. *You are allowed to smoke in the bar.* But it doesn't matter. I can sense that the waiters want me out of there. I smoke a Gitane. I smoke a second. A third. A cloud of Gallic smoke is starting to waft across the room to the cheesecake. A waiter comes up and yanks away a chair from the table. "We need this," he says, not terribly politely. A few seconds later, a second chair is removed. The waiter is perhaps terrified that I am planning to network with a vast constellation of Gitane enthusiasts. Finally, the maître d' comes over and says, "We're setting up for dinner now." He doesn't ask me if I want to stay for dinner. He doesn't ask if I want another drink. He doesn't ask if everything was to my satisfaction. He just tells me in a polite, courteous way to take a hike.

The five most devastating words in the antismoker's vast lexicon of derision are these: "I didn't know you smoked." Whether the speaker is a waitress in my favorite diner, a friend at my outdoor swim/tennis club, or a colleague who knows that I am working on a story about smoking, the contempt inherent in those five words is almost nuclear. The phrase isn't a euphemism for "I feel sorry for anyone foolish enough to endanger his health by putting a cancer stick in his mouth." It's a euphemism for "I didn't know you dismembered tiny dogs."

Burdened by my sense of being a social menace, I spend the entire week deliberately eluding my normal, noncarcinogenic friends and spending all my free time with people who are going to die of cancer. One of them tells me that I hold the cigarette the wrong way. Another asks why I am smoking Russian Sobranies (because bag people are puzzled by black cigarettes with gold foil, and usually won't accept them). Inevitably, we spend all our time talking about how awful antismokers are. One friend tells me about a music lover who was smoking at an open-air Pavarotti concert in Central Park when a woman flew into a fit and demanded that a cop arrest him. (The cop told her to get lost.)

By the fourth day of my experiment, I am starting to get a bit combative. I visit a tobacco shop in midtown Manhattan and load up on some elegant Sobranies, another pack of Gauloises, a tin of Schimmellpennick slim cigars, and a couple of Monte Cruzes. Then I make an odd request.

"Could you please recommend the most repugnant cigar you carry?"

"It depends on what you're trying to accomplish," he says. "Are you trying to draw attention, or are you trying to clear the area?"

"I want to really offend a bunch of people who've been getting on my nerves lately."

"Then I highly recommend De Nobilis," he responds, passing me a tiny box containing five dwarflike, dangerous-looking cigars. "This is what I smoke when I'm out fishing. You light up one of these and it's just you and the fish."

"Do you catch a lot of fish?"

"I catch a lot of fish."

I study the box. Even the low-rent packaging (Made in Scranton, Pa.) suggests that the cigars are profoundly offensive. They look like Mesozoic tootsie rolls.

"Are these like Toscanis?" I inquire, recalling the diminutive tree stumps a French friend of mine uses to clear a large area of the Riviera for himself every July.

"Same principle, less money," he replies. "These will get the job done."

"There are also the Amaretto-soaked ones," a colleague volunteers. Intriguing: Amaretto-soaked logs. But the tobacconist waves him off. "Why spend seven dollars when you can get the same effect for a dollar-ninety?"

I load up my arsenal and walk up to the Central Park Reservoir, which is used almost exclusively as a jogging track. Lighting up one of my De Nobilis, I begin strolling around the track in a generally counterclockwise direction, blowing smoke directly in the faces of the mostly twenty-something and thirty-something joggers who pass me.

No sooner do I get that sucker lit than a short man in an Italian T-shirt sporting a stopwatch the size of Naples jogs past me, coughing theatrically. (Theatrical coughing will become a leitmotif in my stroll around the reservoir.) I keep a running tab of reactions to my offensive behavior. There are seventy-nine women and twenty-one men, of whom roughly eighty percent are under thirty. Of the one hundred only five, three men and two women, look threatening. Four people cough to express displeasure. One whispers "A—hole" as she passes, and I call after her, "Give me a break. It's a boy." A second says, "People are jogging here," and I mutter, "I'm sorry, I'm French." One woman, a true reservoir dog, actually says, "Can't you find any better place to smoke that thing?" I fired back, "Yes, but I missed the last plane to L.A." But the most impressive reaction of all comes from the three people who physically *leave the track* to run on the dirt off to the side.

As the week drags on, my sense of being a social leper increases. In a French bistro called Le Ferrier, several people at the next table make faces about my smoking, even though we are seated outdoors and there are ashtrays on the table. When I go to have a cocktail with a British friend in the private lounge of the Ritz-Carlton, everybody else clears out.

Even when I am not smoking, I feel like a pariah. One area that has not been sufficiently examined is the right to *exude a smoky odor* in a nonsmoking environment, even though you are not actually smoking at the time. When I visit my local YMCA and climb on an exercise bike, the man sitting on the bike to my left promptly snorts and leaves. As the antismoking juggernaut gains momentum. I am certain that No Smoking signs will be replaced by No Having Smoked signs.

I'll tell you another thing we can look forward to. Kids who grew up in the 1950s were taught that Davy Crockett and Daniel Boone and Buffalo Bill were genuine American heroes: brave, courageous, and free. Then, along came the Native American movement of the 1960s, and we all realized that these guys were a bunch of racist infanticides and fakes. Something like that is surely going to happen with Humphrey Bogart and Bette Davis and all the great chain-smoking movie stars of the past. As the antismoking movement gains momentum, those scenes where Bogart smokes cigarettes in *Casablanca* will be colorized out, and the smokes will be replaced by mints. By the time the millennium rolls around, schoolchildren will be taught that even though cigar aficionado Winston Churchill was the Lion of England, we might all have been better off submitting to the Nazi boot.

The entire week that I masquerade as a smoker, only a handful of strangers are nice to me: two foreigners asking for directions and a quartet of tourists who crowd around me in the lobby of the David

Letterman show, asking how to get standby tickets. (My gargantuan Dominican cigar must have beguiled them into thinking that I am a friend of Dave's.)

As my sense of cultural ostracism grows, I am driven to increasingly idiotic gestures of rebellion. During a phone interview with Don Imus, I light up a cigar and then sneeringly apologize to his millions of listeners for subjecting them to transtelephonic secondary smoke. I furtively smoke a cigarette in the lobby of Avery Fisher Hall and the Metropolitan Opera. I smoke in the backs of taxi cabs, which is illegal, and am twice told to put it out or get out. Once I descend indignantly after two blocks, and the driver becomes incensed when I demand a $1.75 receipt. But even in cabs where the driver lets me smoke, I can't enjoy it because the ashtrays have all been removed. I start to get a clear idea of how insurmountable the antismoking opposition is when I stride into an Eighth Avenue *pawn shop* with a cigarette in my mouth and am told to get the hell out.

Incidentally, how do the antismoking forces know that these acts are deliberate? Couldn't it be an accident? A couple of times I said that I'd simply forgotten the cigarette was in my mouth. Several times I said I had believed that people could still smoke in places that sold coffee. Twice I said that I was a French citizen having a nicotine fit. Each time I was greeted with the same look: You are scum. You revolt me. *You deserve to die.*

I got a vivid sense of how loathsome the vice of smoking is now considered when I walked up to a few women on upper Madison Avenue, in the museum district. All of the individuals I approached were fantastically dressed women of leisure who looked like they had husbands with good jobs—perhaps running tobacco companies. When I approached them with a cigarette between my fingers and asked for a light, they looked insulted. How could I possibly think that they smoked? *Do I look like white trash? Do I look like a hooker?*

The last day of my experiment, I have double epiphanies. First I get the cold (tattooed) shoulder from the stripper. Then later that day I meet a friend for lunch. We are seated in a pasta joint on Eighth Avenue, she having meatless lasagna, me the manicotti. There is no smoking in this eatery. We are chatting amiably when I detect a familiar, fetid smell wafting up through my nostrils. For once, it's not coming from me. It's coming from a young man who's sitting a few feet away, eating a tuna sandwich while puffing on a cigarette. I don't say anything for the longest time. I just nosh. But as my companion leaves, I double back (first having sized him up as a bit of a wimp), and say, "Excuse me, but there's no smoking in here."

He apologizes and starts to put the cigarette out. But I cannot resist a final parry.

" . . . *and you should know that.*"

Part 2

PLEASURES

The Wonders of Washington: A Memoir

John Podhoretz

I T HAS BECOME a matter of form for politicians and writers and talk-show callers to engage in ritualistic denunciations of Washington and all the permutations of life inside the Beltway. You can't go wrong with it; those of us who had the honor of writing speeches for Ronald Reagan knew that if you needed an applause line, nothing worked so well as an anti-Washington jibe. Of course, Reagan didn't need a speechwriter to denounce D.C.; he practically invented the mode, and the city is still struggling with the change he helped to effect in its reputation from the Home of the Wise it had seemed in the wake of the New Deal and the Second World War to the Cesspool of Elitist Vice it seems today.

As for me, though, I genuinely love Washington. And I do mean love, the way people talk about loving Paris, or Provence, or Hawaii—I love it as a place of excitement, romance, and mystery. Before you laugh at the very idea, you should know that this enthusiasm is shared secretly by most of those who live in and around Washington. It's a secret because it's unseemly—everybody in Washington knows he is to some degree a parasite whose host is the American body politic. And not just the government workers, either. From reporters who write about the place to think-tankers seeking to influence the policies of the place to shopkeepers inside the gigantic malls who take advantage of the acquisitive desires that come with the nation's highest per capita household income, Washingtonians are all parasites. And even parasites have a little discretion; they try to keep it down so that the landlord will not feel terribly ill and go in for a colonic.

So they stay quiet, even among themselves; they bitch about the atmosphere and quote Harry Truman's line about how the only friend you can really have in this town is a dog. They use the phrase "in this town" like a negative mantra, invoking "the way things work in this town" with weary resignation as though they are beyond disgusted by the practices they have seen. But they don't mean it, not at all.

If you want to know why term limits are so unpopular here, why the Georgians who came with Jimmy Carter and the Californians who came with Ronald Reagan and the Yankees who came with George Bush do not return home with their leaders—if you want to understand Washington you must understand that it is a wondrous place, a place that its adopted residents do not leave if they can help it.

I began thinking about all this when I decided to leave Washington and return to New York to take a new job. I came to Washington a hirsute kid of twenty-two with a wild head of curly hair and full thick beard and I left it exactly one decade later clean-shaven and a poster child for male-pattern baldness.

I arrived in Washington in the first place from a shared apartment virtually in the middle of Times Square, with no kitchen and flying cockroaches, on a block with thirty-three tourist-trap restaurants and two tenements that seemed to house the city's entire population of transvestite hookers. New York was the city I had been born and raised in, and I never really thought of living anywhere else after finishing college. After all, I was a writer and budding intellectual with ambitions to be a novelist and a journalist and a playwright and just about anything else involving writing, so where could a person live but New York?

It quickly became clear that neither the warm but scruffy New York in which I had grown up nor the mythical New York of a young writer's dreams existed any longer. During my four years of college, the city had gotten mean-spirited and its social pathologies no longer amusing. New York was in the middle of a spurt of economic growth that seemed only to be making things worse. Construction everywhere led to vicious traffic snarls. The fortunes that seemed to be coming so easy all over the place left those who weren't making fortunes in a state of ugly, perpetual want and envy. People talked of nothing but real estate, the way people during the Stalingrad siege probably talked about food—thirty years of scarcity due to rent control had done this to a once-sane populace.

Even if you wanted to live like a starving artist in a garret, you couldn't find one you could afford except somewhere in a middle-class neighborhood of Brooklyn, which defeated the purpose of the whole enterprise. The coffeehouses of Greenwich Village were no longer filled with Trotskyites, but instead with kids from New Jersey and Long Island in for an evening's entertainment. And the balance of power in the city's cultural life had shifted from the arts and publishing to banking and lawyering—for perhaps the first time in history, musicians had a harder time getting girls than Wall Streeters in braces and yellow ties.

Several things happened in the space of a single week that led to my exodus. First, I suffered a severe romantic disappointment that led me to write some hysterical poetry—*We cannot steer clear / Of water where the fathom-darkened depths cannot be sounded, / or from the rent despair of drowning men.* I was probably thinking about rent and drowning because as I wallowed in my sorrow one cold night in February the pipes burst in my apartment.

Most important, I was refused a promotion from researcher to writer at *Time* magazine, where I had gone to work after college. The reason I was given was this: I was too young. The reason I was not given was this: I was too ideological. But the latter was probably closer to the truth. When I was interviewed for the *Time* job, I was asked by the chief of research what I would do if I had to work on a story with which I disagreed. I said I would do my job, and then, heart pounding in my throat, asked whether this was a question she put to everybody who came to see her. She smiled and said, "Touché."

So I was sitting in my office, feeling bereft, and the phone rang. It was a man named Woody West, who introduced himself as the managing editor of the *Washington Times*. The *Times* was looking for someone to serve as a general culture critic; would I be interested in coming down to talk to him about it?

I had the same concerns everybody has about working for the *Times*. Was I joining a disreputable organization, owned by Sun Myung Moon's Unification Church, whose purpose was proselytization? Did anybody read the thing? Was I leaving the mainstream of journalism for a conservative ghetto? People in *Time*'s Washington bureau told me that the *Times* had in its first eighteen months achieved a certain standing in the city because it was read eagerly in the White House and didn't seem quite as bad as they expected. That was good news. And I was less concerned about the idea of being in a conservative ghetto because I was proud to be a conservative and fighting the good fight in the nation's capital—not to mention that the world of mainstream journalism wasn't exactly opening its doors and its heart to me.

Thus began my seven-year association with one of the most extraordinary organizations on earth—in every sense of the word "extraordinary." There is its extraordinary building, sitting at the northeast end of the city on a barren industrial corridor. A depressing place to work? Not at all, because the newsroom is new and airy, with a ceiling thirty feet high and one entire wall that is simply a gigantic picture window looking out onto the National Arboretum. The grandiosity of the paper's physical plant reflects the grandiosity of its animating force, the Reverend Sun Myung Moon, who thinks he is some combination of Jesus Christ and Mohammed and the Lord God Himself, and so when he does things, he builds them to last.

How could I work for such a man? Arnaud de Borchgrave, when he came to the *Times* as its editor in chief, put it best: "Every boss I've had thought he was God, including Kay Graham." Probably because Moon believes in his own omnipotence, and thus imagines he can reorder reality merely by wishing it, he agreed over the course of a decade to spend close to a billion dollars on the *Times* while sacrificing any and all control over the content of the paper.

Nobody outside the place ever quite believes that could possibly be the truth, and it's very hard to believe even when you're inside, but it is. Never before in the annals of publishing has anybody done anything quite so foolish, self-aggrandizing, or bizarrely noble. At a dinner in 1991, Moon made a nearly indecipherable speech crediting his sponsorship of the *Times* and its sister newsmagazine, *Insight,* for the collapse of the Soviet Union. Those of us civilians in the Shoreham Hotel ballroom listening to him struggle with the English language figured we ought to applaud politely because it was the least we could do for a guy who had dropped a billion dollars to let us play around with a newspaper and a magazine.

In many ways, life at the *Washington Times* was a perfect analogue to the life of any conservative in the 1980s. We were flush, awash in possibilities, and because the paper was in constant turmoil, the opportunities were unbelievable. I got to write two different columns, edit whole sections of the newspaper, and on two different occasions found myself in day-to-day charge of my own newsmagazine. And yet, and yet. We *Times*men felt disrespected and insulted by the wider culture we both yearned to be a part of and had nothing but contempt for. People felt free to say the most appallingly rude things at parties—"I work at the *Washington Times,*" I would say, and more than once the answer would come back, "Oh, that's disgusting"— just as conservatives were constantly hearing that we were (a) greedy, (b) racist, (c) unfeeling, and (d) generally a bunch of yahoos.

I don't want to give the impression that everybody working at the *Times* was a conservative. Far from it; in fact, the loudest complaints about the supposed "conservative bias" in the paper's news columns came from inside, from reporters and editors who came from the world of newspaper hackdom and were both unsympathetic to and fearful of the paper's editorial mission. And so like everyone associated with conservative causes, people at the *Times* always felt they had an out: they could go public and denounce the institution they worked for.

This Washington ritual, which could be called the Stockman syndrome, was a peculiar feature of life in the 1980s. Liberals and the mainstream media were not just interested in battling conservatives, but were actually consumed with the notion of delegitimizing us. And so there were sizable rewards for public statements of dissociation from conservative orthodoxy. For people in the political sphere, like David Stockman, there were book contracts and televised stories about growth in office; for the hapless dissatisfied *Times*people, there were a couple of stories in the *Washington Post* Style section and Jack Shafer's *Times*-baiting column in Washington's free town rag, the *City Paper.* A moment of stardom after the relative anonymity of a *Times* byline—that was the prize.

ON MOVING to Washington, I discovered the feeling that everyone who is happy there discovers—that the subjects and ideas that have obsessed you for years are no longer on the margins of your experience, but are central to it. If you are interested in large political ideas about the nature of the United States and its place in the world, you are so profoundly in the minority that you always feel sheepish. The United States is the only country in the world in which knowing the names of its political leaders is seen as a kind of dilettantism, a matter for trivia rather than the most important thing you can know. This is a wonderful thing, because it means that Americans have the profound luxury of ignoring politics instead of worrying obsessively about them.

But for those who do care, it can be a solitary life. When you start talking passionately about politics in a nonpolitical setting, people flee from you as though you were beginning to explain to them how you built your ham radio; they want to talk about sports. But politics is your sports—Phil Gramm's trade from the Democratic party to the GOP is far more transfixing to you than Darryl Strawberry's journey from New York to Los Angeles. Before the advent of C-SPAN and Rush Limbaugh, ideologically minded people in the heartland really were cast adrift in America, even in New York. Working at *Time* in the section devoted to world news, I found only one person who was actually interested in world news there. Everybody else talked about real estate and their kids and the sales at Saks Fifth Avenue at lunch hour.

New Washingtonians, on the other hand, find they have arrived in a city full of people who are even more obsessed with the sport of politics than they ever were. There is a breathless liberation to living in a place where you can have not one, not two, but ten conversations a day about the staff director of the House Banking Committee. Endless variations on the same subject, each conversation leading to a new tidbit, a new piece of gossip, a new and completely spurious and scurrilous rumor about Vince Foster.

In Washington, the material of most people's lives—their job, Little League, the mortgage—is subsumed by more abstract concerns: What's happening with the markup of the crime bill? Was there cloture on S-45? People are actually apologetic when the conversation turns from gossip about people they don't know—politicians—to gossip about people they do know—neighbors and coworkers.

So is this city, this wonderful daily gathering of the faithful and knowledgeable, going to be merely a temporary refuge, a place to do brief business and then go back home? This is home. Life is too boring back there, too—well—ordinary.

My first tour of duty at the *Washington Times* came to an end in 1987, when I left to work at *U.S. News & World Report.* The *U.S. News* experience was a disaster, because I moved from a workplace where I was valued and had authority to a place where, once again, I was suspect in some part because of my ideological predilections. My boss was the now-infamous David Gergen, whose vaunted reputation in Washington makes all of us who worked for him at *U.S. News* scratch our heads in wonder. He was a comically hapless manager, chronically late and dilatory, and prone to blaming his staff for the magazine's perpetually tardy closings on Friday nights when they were, in fact, his fault.

The experience at *U.S. News,* which I left after six months, was instructive in one regard: I learned that the temptation to "mainstream" myself was doomed to failure. The stigma of working as a conservative journalist is purely in the eye of the beholder, but there is terrific pressure to internalize the criticisms of the mainstream and try to defend yourself against them, rather than reveling in pleasures of being unconventional. One of the stranger facts of the 1980s was that the people who spent the 1980s defending the rights and views and ideas of the American bourgeoisie were far more unconventional, even oddly bohemian, than those on the Left who had for so long held the mantle.

It sounds strange to say that someone who found himself some months after leaving *U.S. News* writing speeches for the president of the United States could ever have felt himself a bohemian. But as William Kristol says, while the Right has been on the ascendancy politically for two decades, culturally the Right is farther out on the in/out scale than it has ever been. And most of us, even those of us with a passion for politics, experience life culturally, not politically. We listen to music, we go to the movies, we watch TV, and these give us more of a sense of our country than anything else. My contemporaries and I were desperate to find commonality with popular culture. I once threw a party at my house on Capitol Hill where forty right-wingers danced with crazed abandon to "Burning Down the House" by the proto-punk band the Talking Heads. A pretty blonde who worked for then Secretary of Transportation Elizabeth Dole shouted out, "It's our anthem! Burn down the House! Smash the State!" I can assure you this is not what David Byrne intended when he wrote the song.

Parties like that one are a hallmark of my years in Washington. Washington is the place of my bachelorhood, and my feelings for the city are wrapped up in the comic melodramas I created to keep myself enthralled with the enormity of my own problems.

I fell in love for the first time—on two separate occasions with two different women—in Washington, each time late at night on the grounds of the Jefferson Memorial. Each time we looked into the Tidal Basin and tried to ignore the hordes of tourist kids and the scaffolding from the endless repairs to the statue of the Sage of Monticello and the dozens of other couples doing exactly what we were doing at exactly the same time, at a distance of ten feet or so. Each time I later decided that I never loved A—— (or J——) anyway.

I spent a breathtaking amount of time engaged in insanely compelling and positively addictive philosophical conversations about love and pain and women and men in bars and restaurants throughout the city. At Café Lautrec in Adams Morgan, where E——, B ——, and I discussed the phenomenon of what Bismarck called "negative creative capability"—how the only way really to attract a woman was to be genuinely and truly indifferent to her charms—while a guy named Johnny who spelled it *Johné* got up and tap-danced on the bar. At Paper Moon in Georgetown, where B——, and T——, and I discussed whether sexual chemistry was real or delusional—I, as usual, arguing that it was delusional just for the sake of argument—and later getting so drunk that we forgot where my car was and I decided it would be a good idea to lie down on the corner of M and Thirty-first while B—— and T—— tried to remember. At the Hawk 'n' Dove on Capitol Hill, where we eyed the heart-stoppingly pretty college-age interns working in congressional offices and wondered whether it was taste and morals, or just plain cowardice, that kept us from approaching them.

But Washington is not really a party town, and as we all got older the parties got more and more staid, my friends paired off and got married, and our friendships are now conducted mostly by telephone. My friends moved onward, with children and second mortgages. They have become by turns apologetic and even a little smug about the whole thing. Apologetic because the kids and the mortgages were distractions from the really important things, like how much blood there was around Vince Foster's body. A little smug because that is the way all young marrieds seem to their bachelor friends.

Meanwhile, I found my life repeating itself—a return to the *Washington Times,* for two years after my tour in the White House, suffering déjà vu while picking up a woman for a date only to realize that I had been in the same building, the same apartment, before, picking up some other woman some other year.

It began to feel like it was time to go, because there was nothing left in Washington I wanted to do, and the hermetic quality of those ten conversations a day about the placement of the gun in Vince Foster's hand began to pall.

I remember that within two years of my exodus to Washington in 1984, almost everybody I knew in New York had made the journey down I-95 as well. So had the *American Spectator,* on another interstate, from Bloomington to Arlington, Virginia. My friend Tod

Lindberg wrote a wonderful article about this mass migration for *Commentary*, called "New York Down, Washington Up," that captured the feeling we all had—the feeling that Washington, a city modeled in part on the physical charms of Paris, was our Paris. It had become cosmopolitan enough to satisfy the gourmands with its array of restaurants, highbrow enough to make Philip Larkin's collected poems the city's number one fiction best-seller for a time, and safe enough that nobody I know worries about the crime even though the city is the nation's murder capital. Not where they live, it isn't.

I was not followed back to New York. The children of my friends are native-born Washingtonians, with parents who continued their discussions of the horror of political consultants and Hillary's hairstyles, while I was already doing emotional battle with the homeless conmen who stop in every subway car and make a big political speech about self-reliance and benefit cutbacks before sticking a coffee cup in your face.

Upon moving to New York, I told myself that after spending a decade in the cozy hermetic world inside the Beltway, I began to find the intensity of a life lived in proximity to politics and power more than a little exhausting. For a sports fan, it would be like watching ESPN fifteen hours a day for ten years; at some point you even begin to dread the words "Vince Foster." I was sure I would enjoy the conversations about real estate and sales at Saks now, instead of being disappointed by them as I had been when I first lived as an adult in New York.

I was mistaken. People in New York no longer talked obsessively about real estate. Rather, the conversations centered on the various bars and nightspots in the city where one might brush elbows with supermodels. "How about Match?" someone would say when asked where we might go to dinner. "Models go there."

And so, eight months after my prodigal return to my boyhood home, I called a number in Alexandria, Virginia, and engaged the same moving van that had brought my possessions to New York. The movers arrived at my apartment on West Seventy-third Street on a cold December day to pack me up and bring me back to Washington for good. Back, for better or worse, home.

The *L* Word: Love as Taboo

Kay S. Hymowitz

"I CAN SEE NO TRACE of the passions which make for deeper joy," wrote Stendhal about Americans in his 1822 essay "Love." "It is as if the sources of sensibility have dried up among these people. They are just, they are rational, and they are not happy at all." Imagine the Frenchman's horror if he could hear today's Americans speak of *l'amour* in what *Mademoiselle* magazine calls this "Post-Idealist, Neo-Pragmatic Era of Relationships." Here is Wanda Urbanska, author of *The Singular Generation,* describing her peers in their twenties: "We . . . do not have affairs, we have 'sexual friendships.' We do not fall in love, we build relationships. We do not date, we 'see' each other." A student quoted in a recent article in the *Vassar Quarterly* adopts the same cool attitude. She doesn't care for the term "boy-friend" or "lover"; she speaks instead of "my special friend with whom I spent lots of quality physical time."

Even rock and roll, once a soulful forum for aching, lonely hearts or ecstatic lovers, is now just as likely to rap or croon a message of tough, don't-need-anybody independence. In a recent top-ten hit, Des'ree tells women they have to be strong, hard, cool, bad, and tough. Her counsel finds visual embodiment in fashion ads, such as that for Calvin Klein One unisex perfume—perfume, of all things, the primal sexual lure!—in which a line of grungy young men and women demonstrate, with snarling mouths and pointed fingers, various permutations of seen-it-all exasperation.

The emotional coolness and self-sufficiency of the Neo-Pragmatic Era of Relationships often finds much more easygoing expression than this. Television comedian Jerry Seinfeld portrays the benign, loopy side of casual sexual friendships in his top-rated series. He, his eccentric buddies, and Elaine, an ex-lover who seems more like his twin sister, drift good-naturedly through a landscape of sexual friendships that inspire about the same level of feeling as the tuna sandwiches Jerry's friend George orders at the local coffee shop. In the 1992 movie *Singles*, the theme song, "Dyslexic Heart," evokes the sad confusion of the young and disconnected. "For some people, living alone is a nasty hang," shrugs Cliff, one of the movie's slacker heroes, to a girl unaccountably and unsuccessfully pursuing him. "Not me. I'm a self-contained unit."

Of course, it would be absurd to suggest that romantic love is dead in America. After all, for every *Seinfeld* there's a *Mad About You*, a comedy series about a devoted newlywed couple. And for every Des'ree there's a Beverly DeAngelis, a romance guru who writes self-help best-sellers with titles like *Are You the One for Me?*

Still, if love in America is not dead, it is ailing. It is suffering from the phenomenon historian Peter Stearns describes in his book *American Cool*. American cool disdains intense emotions like grief, jealousy, and love, which leave us vulnerable, in favor of an "emotional style" of smooth detachment. If pop culture gods present an elegant vision of American cool, for ordinary mortals the picture is less glamorous. But the unintended consequences of this banal ideal are the same across the economic spectrum: emotional frustration, alienation, and a sexual scene that recalls the drearier imaginings of Nietzsche or Freud.

American cool goes hand in hand with a profoundly rationalistic vision of human relations, which looks with suspicion on mystery, myth, and strong feeling. Powerful cultural trends have combined to produce this general coarsening and flattening of the sensibilities: feminism, which feared that love and equality were incompatible; the scientific rationalization of experts from the helping professions, who have helped advance what Lionel Trilling called our "commitment to mechanical attitudes toward life"; and, above all, America's fierce individualism, whose ideal is the free and adventurous loner.

The beginnings of the disenchantment of love and the rise of

American cool are well worth examining if only to gauge the trade-offs we have made during this era of liberation. We've purchased our freedom from inhibition and guilt with a loan from imagination and fantasy. And to gain the array of pleasure once denied the bourgeois soul, we've paid the price of deep feeling.

Feminists mounted the first significant challenge to love's hold on the American imagination. Romantic love is a myth, they argued, a myth inextricably tied up with women's inequality. It reinforces the idea of separate spheres for the sexes, providing a "consolation," as writer Juliet Mitchell put it, for women's "confinement in domesticity." Further, feminists contended, the ideal of love strengthened the myth of weak, dependent womanhood in need of strong male protection. Though this view got some airing as early as the mid-nineteenth century, it took on angry, raw urgency in the early 1970s in works like Shulamith Firestone's *The Dialectic of Sex* and Marilyn French's *The Women's Room,* which called love a "lie to keep women happy in the kitchen so they won't ask to do what men are always doing." Ti-Grace Atkinson went even further: "The psychopathological condition of love is a euphoric state of fantasy in which the victim transforms her oppressor into the redeemer. . . . Love has to be destroyed." Not just a myth and a dangerous illusion, love was a disease in need of a cure.

Some Victorian feminists offered a cure, or at least an antidote, in the form of what they called "rational love." They advocated an "educated" or "organized" union between men and women, a union based on mutual interests and friendly companionship, with knowledge replacing fantasy, and reason superseding untidy passions like jealousy and obsession. In a similar vein, feminists in the 1920s supported the introduction of college marriage courses aimed at dispelling romantic myths with objective, expert knowledge. Companionate marriage—cemented with shared interests, common background, and sexual pleasure rather than strong emotion—became the new rational ideal.

A health and family-life curriculum that the New Jersey Coalition for Battered Women is developing exemplifies a contemporary version of this ideal. The curriculum sets up a contrast between bad, illusory "romantic love" and good, clearheaded "nurturing love." The latter entails responsibility, sharing, friendship, pleasure, and "strong feelings." But examples of "What Love Isn't" include jealousy, possessiveness, obsession, dependency, and giving yourself up—that is, just about every extreme of feeling that romantic love may arouse.

The feminist view of the myth of love contained a curious, counterproductive misreading of history. For if love served to subjugate women, it did no less to men. In many countries where romantic love has not been institutionalized, men's philandering is winked at while respectable women are kept veiled and hidden. In its first institutional flowering in the guise of medieval courtly love, stylized passion turned the wandering, brutish young men of the day—who might literally rape an unprotected woman as easily as slay that night's dinner—into sensitive, pining poets. The important point altogether ignored by early progressive reformers and feminists was that it was precisely as a powerful way of sublimating the passions that romantic love was a civilizing force. A man in love was a man subdued.

But a man in rational or nurturing love? As Peter Stearns points out, the changing articles of *Esquire* magazine suggest just how compelling men would find "organized," "educated" sharing. In the thirties, *Esquire* endorsed the new companionate marriage recommended by feminists and sociologists, publishing many stories and advice columns exploring what one writer called "Brave New Love"and cautioning against the excesses of romantic passion. But by World War II, the magazine, presaging the arrival of *Playboy,* dispensed with all love talk and got down to the nitty-gritty: sex. *Esquire's* trajectory from love to brave new love to sex suggested that lifting the veil of the illusion of love might reveal not the sweet smile of equal, harmonious sexual relations but the predacious grin of raw impulse.

Doctors and health experts, starting at the turn of the century, espoused theories that echoed the feminist disdain for passion and fantasy. Inspired by advances in the understanding and treatment of venereal disease, the medical profession argued against Victorian sexual repressiveness and in favor of a demystification of sex. "Sex mystery prevents progress," announced a book by a social hygienist, as progressive reformers devoted to the eradication of venereal disease called themselves. By releasing "sex mystery" from the murky control of priests and superstition and bringing it under the bright light of science, humanity would enjoy health and progress.

For all their innovativeness, the social hygienists were hardly sexual freethinkers; by and large they believed in the Victorian virtues of chastity and self-restraint. But they began a process of the medicalization and rationalization of sex whose basic assumptions continue to control much current thinking on the subject. They believed that sexual desire could yield easily to the discipline of logic and information; hence they became the first to advocate sex education in the schools. They would probably not be surprised to find that today it is still usually taught in health classes. And they introduced what author Barbara Dafoe Whitehead has called the "Scopes trial terms" that continue to make the sex education debate so stubbornly hyperbolic: the scientifically minded, enlightened realists versus the superstitious, religious flat-earthers.

Yet the social hygienists would surely be dismayed by some of what is done in the name of health today. For the idea of rationalized and demystified sex has been stretched to its logical limits, as sex mystery—the dense subject of poets, philosophers, mystics, lyricists, and sacred codes—has given way to sex mechanics.

Nowhere is this robotization of sex more glaring than in the curricula of modern sex educators, the intellectual heirs of the social hygienists. In what may have been a swan song of sexual love in 1959, a sex education manual began: "The end and aim of sex education is developing one's fullest capacity for love." Today nothing could seem more quaint. Most modern sex education programs center on teaching not just health but technical skills—communication skills decision-making skills, refusal skills, and, of course, condom skills. Some years ago the Massachusetts Department of Public Health produced an AIDS-prevention video in which a hip young nurse distributes flash cards depicting the fourteen stages of condom use. The students get together, look at one another's cards, and decide the proper order—which looks like this: "Talk with Partner," "Decision by Both

Partners to Have Sex," "Buy the Condom," "Sexual Arousal," "Erection," "Roll Condom On," "Leave Space at the Tip (squeeze out air)," "Intercourse," "Orgasm/Ejaculation," "Hold onto Rim," "Withdraw the Penis," "Loss of Erection," "Relaxation," and, finally, an environmental skill, "Throw Condom Out." Note the goose-step courtship suggested to today's robo-lovers: "Talk with Partner, Decision by Both Partners to Have Sex."

Today's sex educator sees his demystifying task as ensuring not only that kids have the information necessary to avoid disease and pregnancy but also that they have "healthy" attitudes toward sex. A healthy student is one who is "relaxed" and "comfortable" in the presence of the erotic and can speak of sex in the same tones and with the same lack of emotion he might bring to a discussion of carburetors. Giggling kids who appear to suffer from embarrassment or reticence, sure signs of "antisex" attitudes or irrational hang-ups, must undergo a program of desensitization. One exercise I recently heard about at a private school in Brooklyn attempted such a reeducation, much to the dismay of a number of parents: in a fifth-grade class students were required to pronounce the words for the genitals at increasingly louder volume. Children calculating math problems in nearby classrooms were serenaded by their ten-year-old friends yelling, "Penis! Vagina!!"

The push to rationalize and deintensify sexual desire is so total that some educators even try to reprogram their students' fantasy lives. William A. Fisher, a professor of psychology at the University of Ontario, and Deborah M. Roffman, a sexuality education teacher at the Park School in Brooklandville, Maryland, suggest one way to steer fantasies into conformity with the rational ideal. Because teenagers' sexual fantasies usually don't involve condoms, Fisher and Roffman propose, why not show them "fantasy walk-throughs" in stories, videotapes, or plays, where kids like themselves "successfully perform . . . sex-related preventive behaviors." "Such imagery," they continue, "should enter teenagers' memories as fantasy-based scripts for personally practicing preventive behaviors when or if such behaviors are necessary."

Striking the same chilling, Strangelovian tone of scientific detachment, sex educators object to Hollywood's dream vision of sex not because coupling is ubiquitous or mechanical but because it is "irresponsible" or "unrealistic," with so few references to birth control, diseases, or abortion. More "pro-social messages," according to this line of thinking, would solve the problem of the hypersexed media.

The examples I've cited are extreme; few children are treated to classroom exercises precisely like these. Nevertheless, such examples expose the inadequacy of the terms of the recent culture wars over condom distribution, the Rainbow curriculum, or the promotion of masturbation as a form of safe sex. What's happening is not as simple as a contest between enlightened liberals seeking to liberate sexual life from Puritan repressiveness, and life-denying conservatives who wish to imprison it in a web of moral and religious restrictions. On closer inspection, the sexual liberals turn out to be advancing their own rigid moral strictures. Their Eros lays down an updated Puritan law: pleasure and self-fulfillment, yes; passion, no. The question, it begins to seem, isn't whether a society will codify sexual behavior but how it will do so. "From authority," Philip Rieff has written, "there is no escape"; that authority has simply been transferred from the church to the clinic.

This medicalization of sex has deposed the irrational chimera Love and installed reasonable Health as king. Kids must have "healthy" attitudes; they must make "healthy" decisions. A 1993 *Good Housekeeping*/CBS poll asked teenagers to give reasons not to have sex. While 85 percent mentioned fear of AIDS or pregnancy, only 4 percent said "not being in love." And although the increasing popularity of abstinence as a value to be taught in the schools may seem like an important shift in cultural climate, it only perpetuates the medical-scientific mode of sexual thinking. An article entitled "AIDS Disinformation" in *Seventeen* illustrates the problem: "Seventy-eight percent of women are sexually active by age 19," it announces. "This is not to say that abstinence isn't an important option. It is the only way to be 100 percent sure of not getting HIV through sexual transmission."

Conventional wisdom has it that the hypersexed media encourage kids to "fool around." But this half-truth begs the question of where in today's culture a teenager can find any alternative vision, any language for imagining sex as a potentially powerful union. Many parents today mumble something like, "Be careful." Meanwhile, their own behavior is corrosive to the idealistic longings of adolescence. In her book *Erotic Wars,* sociologist Lillian Rubin quotes a promiscuous seventeen-year-old who was twelve when her father left her mother for a younger woman. "I don't want to hear about any of that love stuff," the girl says. "It's garbage, just plain garbage. If a guy wants to make it with a girl, he'll say anything. I just spare them the trouble, that's all. Anyway, what's the big deal?"

Educators second this kind of cynicism when they advise kids only to "talk with partner" or "make healthy, good decisions." On what moral terms should a teen ground this good decision? Here the educators come up empty-handed. A National Guidelines Task Force of sex educators looked into this problem and could offer only platitudes like, "Every person has dignity and self-worth," and the priceless, "All sexual decisions have effects and consequences." Is it any wonder that kids today, stripped of all spiritualizing ideals and with nothing but dismal "health" to replace them, would shrug and ask, "What's the big deal?"

Love's most powerful enemy may well be America's obsession with individual autonomy. The free, self-contained individual—or "unit," as Cliff puts it in *Singles*—looks with suspicion on emotions that threaten dependence on others, and he celebrates those that glorify his splendid isolation. From this point of view, love might well signal childish weakness. "Clearly, romance can arrive with all its obsession whenever we're feeling incomplete," writes Gloria Steinem in her best-selling 1992 book, *Revolution from Within.* "The truth is that finding ourselves brings more excitement and well-being than anything romance has to offer." Steinem's prissy rejection of powerful feeling echoes that of some of her precursors, the nineteenth-century feminists. But it goes a step further. From her perspective, the problem is not merely that love's urgent desire for the other can shade into out-of-control obsession. It is that this obsession sweeps us away from life's central project: finding ourselves.

Finding ourselves is a complex task these days. It means not only developing interests and talents but also "exploring" what we have come to call "our sexuality." While sex is an activity or behavior involving another individual, sexuality is a territory of the self. Its logic insists that we are all "self-contained units." Others must not interfere.

Watch Oprah or Donahue, pick up any academic treatise on "gender," flip through any sex education curriculum, or read any self-help book, and the creed of healthy sexuality will stare you in the face. "Sexuality is much more than 'sex' or 'sexual intercourse,'" explains one sex manual for girls. "It is the entire self as girl or boy or man or woman. . . . Sexuality is a basic part of who we are as a person and affects how we feel about ourselves and all our relationships with others." Though it may affect how we feel about others, it does not necessarily tie us to them, for sexuality is first and foremost a vital arena of self-expression and creativity, a central act in the drama of personal identity. Leah P., married eighteen years and interviewed on a National Public Radio show about sex and marriage, admits she would hesitate to have an affair but insists on her autonomy from any rules or institutions or even relationships: "My sexuality belongs to me. I can take it where I choose to. . . . It doesn't belong to my husband; it doesn't belong to my marriage."

The creed of sexuality demands that the individual "explore" or "develop" her sexuality fully by experimenting with different partners, in different positions, at different times of the day, or in different rooms of the house or office. During the seventies, when the novels of Anaïs Nin and Erica Jong were popular, promiscuity became almost a matter of principle for many women newly liberated from old-fashioned notions of what good girls could and couldn't do. Sexual variety and abundance did not merely promise pleasure; they asserted women's freedom and independence. ("That was the meaning of freedom," thinks Nin's heroine Sabine about a one-night stand in *A Spy in the House of Love*.) And further: to expand one's sexuality was to expand one's very identity.

But if sex is imagined as a meeting of free, autonomous, and creative selves, each engaged in an act of self-exploration, we are left with a problem: the lover—or partner, the current term and one better evoking the situation—is in danger of becoming an object to be used and played with. The connection between partners can then only be imagined as contractual: two free agents voluntarily and conditionally involved in a mutually agreed upon activity. Some of our best and most disenchanted bureaucratic minds have gotten to work on this, as exemplified by the fourteen Stages of Condom Use and the now famous Antioch College sexual harassment code. "Obtaining consent is an ongoing process in any sexual interaction," the code reads. "Verbal consent should be obtained with each new level of physical or sexual conduct in any given interaction. . . . The request for consent must be specific to each act."

Although it ostensibly prizes freedom and pleasure, the creed of "sexuality" instead produces this sort of leaden, bureaucratic vision of sex. Here, unlike the lover willing to risk opening his heart in hopes of joyful union, the partner becomes a skilled negotiator demanding and accepting conditions for his or her personal pleasure. Hence, "sexuality" inevitably restrains the emotional, truly personal connection between lovers, stifling what Stendhal called the "passions which make for deeper joy." Central to an age of personal health and fulfillment, "sexuality" flattens as well as enriches the self-contained, autonomous individual. It giveth and it taketh away.

How entirely fitting, then, that the latest terrain of the culture wars, highlighted by the firing of Joycelyn Elders, is masturbation. The multiple ironies of teaching the joys of masturbation to teenagers were largely lost in the usual Scopes trial terms of the brouhaha—either you are antisex and believe masturbation makes your palms hairy, or you believe, as one Los Angeles school teacher claimed, it is a "way to sexually express yourself without actually having sex." Not least among those ironies is that masturbation does less to enrich sexual life than to advance the project of rational self-sufficiency. No messy emotions here.

Equally ludicrous, but unfortunately dead serious, is the way in which the primacy of the autonomous, self-contained ego freed from the call of passionate love reveals itself in popular culture. Mariah Carey's 1994 hit song, "Hero," preaches that the place to find love is within yourself. Accompanied by rich orchestral melodies, the video shows her with the quivering lips and outstretched hands usually associated with deep longing for another. Camille Paglia may have said more than she realized when she joked about her own gigantic ego: "There's Tristan and Iseult, Romeo and Juliet, me and me. It's the love affair of the century!"

At times, the sadness of American detachment seeps through the glossiest of advice columns. One example appears in last September's *YM,* a teen magazine, in an article entitled "The Six Love Wreckers (and How to Avoid Them)." Five of the six "love wreckers," those things girls do that chase boys away, involve loving too much. They include: "You're too demanding. . . . You're too jealous. . . . You push for a commitment." "Some guys get really uncomfortable when you try to box them in," warns one expert. "Plus, you risk coming off as desperate and needy." "Get a life! . . . Doing your own thing will make him appreciate you more," barks another author, under the headline YOU'RE TOO DEPENDENT. Adult women get similar advice: pronounces a recent *Cosmopolitan* headline CLINGY IS OUT!

Jealousy, possessiveness, and dependence are the stuff of our contemporary morality stories. The man in love is neither a hero nor henpecked as he once was; he is now a stalker or wife-abuser, our contemporary villain. Both the mainstream media and teen magazines frequently carry updated gothic tales like "My Ex Tried to Kill Me" or "When a Lover Turns Evil; He Follows You—Spies on You— Loves You to Death." The O. J. Simpson trial fascinates us, in large part because it reminds us of the extremes of these tabooed passions.

In this way, popular culture subverts as well as endorses our tidy scientific-therapeutic view of the human condition. Its current fascination with sadomasochism is a perfect example. A recent article in *New York* magazine cited many examples, including the fashion photos in *Details* magazine, Gianni Versace's 1992 fashion show with supermodel Cindy Crawford in bondage getup, and plotlines on soap operas, including *One Life to Live* and—one for the teen set—*Beverly Hills 90210.* Though presented as the next stage in a continuing liberation from outdated taboos, the fascination with S&M barely conceals the misery of the robo-lover. Enthusiasts are quick to affirm that S&M sex is "consensual," but with its chains and whips, handcuffs and muzzles, it offers the "partner" one last, desperate chance at surrendering his hardened, encapsulated ego to strong feeling. These sex toys suggest a perverse, high-tech twist on sexual liberation: the man or woman who wants to be dominated and controlled, to give himself up completely to another.

But this interest in S&M reminds us as well that, especially in a rationalized world where a lover's joy pales into pleasure and his tormented longing into codependence, irrational fantasy and intense desire will always bubble up. Kids raised in a world without an enriching myth to humanize the Dionysian demons growling and scratching below the surface of civility and to intensify their attachments to another are not a happy sight. For if some teens have reaped the superficial benefits of the new dispensation's relaxation of traditional taboos, all too many suffer from its shallowness.

For girls, the results are not just the widely reported epidemic of sexually transmitted diseases and unplanned pregnancies. Also evident to many working with these young women is a sense of vacant joylessness. Fifteen-year-olds with ten or even more "partners"—sociologist Lillian Rubin interviewed one sixteen-year-old who said she had "forty or fifty"—do not merely fail to find love; ironically, they also fail at the pursuit of pleasure, for they are almost never orgasmic. They promise to become a new generation of embittered women, resentful of men, cynical about love, and ripe for single motherhood.

How could they be otherwise, given the boys they have to contend with? Without any humanizing myth to help quiet the demons, boys have begun to play out the truth of Freud's observation that lust and aggression are deeply intertwined. Reports of young studs "playing rape" in a Yonkers schoolyard during recess, of nine-year-old sexual harassers and fifth-grade rapists and sodomists, have become too common to pass off as simply anomalous. To be sure, boys have always striven to test their manhood through sexual conquest. But the Spur Posse, a gang of teenage boys from Lakewood, California, are just as surely creatures of a crippled emotional culture. The boys held a contest in which they "hooked up"—a tellingly mechanical phrase—with girls as young as ten. (The winner "scored" sixty-six girls.)

Dispiriting as they are, these examples don't totally capture the emotional alienation of this Post-Idealist, Neo-Pragmatic Era of Relationships. In his 1979 book, *The Culture of Narcissism,* Christopher Lasch described the recent crop of patients seeking therapy, who, unlike the general run of patients in the past, "tend to cultivate a protective shallowness in emotional relations" and who are "chronically bored, restlessly in search of . . . emotional titillation without involvement and dependence." Therapists today continue to find such emptiness and emotional blankness the most common complaint. In the past, love has had the virtue not only of satisfying our longing for profound connection but of lifting us out of mundane life into enchantment. While it may not have straightened the crooked timber of humanity, it respected and nourished its tortuous imagination. Today more than ever, the sources of that nourishment seem indeed to have dried up.

Dorothy Parker, Uncompassionate Liberal

Florence King

THE DOROTHY PARKER REVIVAL is putting liberals in a bind. Not that she wasn't one of them. She marched for Sacco and Vanzetti, had a thousand-page file at the FBI, and named Martin Luther King in her will. Politically she was flawless. What disturbs the sensitivity crowd is her rule of tongue: If you can't say something nasty, don't say anything at all.

This clearly was on the minds of the participants in a recent television documentary. An assortment of feminists and women-in-film types, they gave off the perky tension of people trying not to mention rope in the hangman's house.

No one quoted any of Parker's blood-drawing ripostes. Instead they called her "piquant" and even "elfin." This strange eau de Roget saturated the atmosphere until they discussed her suicide attempts. Only then did they relax and revert to standard Liberalese. As the word count for "vulnerable" mounted, it was obvious they preferred victims to torturers.

Mrs. Parker and the Vicious Circle also tamps her down. Although the movie contains many of her best lines, she seems to be beset by an invisible nineties image counselor who keeps urging her to show her soft side. A piquant elf will no longer do; she must be a depressed sprite, a lovesick imp, a weary pixy with attitude. The only vigorous scenes involve sex and suicide; the rest seem to have been filmed on the sunporch of a Swiss sanitarium where the nurses don't let patients upset each other.

The flattening of Dorothy Parker was inevitable because liberals run the Deconstruction Company. She reminds them of what Bob Dole would be like if he ever really let loose. She reminds them of the sound they dread: the gasp that ripples over a campus audience when a speaker violates the canon of political correctness. Most of all, despite her leftist credentials she reminds them of the lost joys of social hierarchy.

Wit is not a democratic form. Its invariable modifier, rapier, was an aristocrat's weapon. The last witty civilizations were the last bastions of aristocracy, eighteenth-century France and England, in whose conversational salons Versailles courtiers and Whig peeresses traded bons mots and double entendres in a race to insensitivity.

Parker-era liberals identified with these merciless patricians, as we see in her own definition of wit: "the humor of the indifferent." To see how far she carried this, take the morning she woke up and found husband Alan Campbell dead in bed beside her. After the undertaker and police had left, a hovering neighbor aching to do good asked, "Is there anything I can do?"

"Yes, get me another husband."

"Dottie, that's a terrible thing to say!"

"All right, get me a ham and cheese on rye."

This is now called being "in denial," but that only begs the question of why there is nothing in *The Prince of Tides* to match it.

Our need to get rid of the tandem threat of wit and hierarchy drives American politics. Currently we are passing it around like a hot potato. Liberals define wit as mean-spiritedness and attribute it to conservatives who insure their populist bona fides by calling liberals elitists; liberals must then profess their egalitarianism by calling for more compassion, thereby inviting more charges of elitism from conservatives whom they will then call mean-spirited. This has brought us to a nadir of plebeianism in which nobody is witty, nobody is classy, and nobody lets Dorothy Parker be Dorothy Parker.

Least of all the people who created the I AM A HUMORLESS FEMINIST T-shirt. If, like the suffragettes of Parker's day, feminists had concentrated solely on women and ignored other dispossessed groups, they could have helped women develop the healthy selfishness that underlies the merry outlook. But in their zeal to stroke every minority under the sun they created such a chaos of caring that feminism merely became liberalism for women. As such it declared war on wit, as in this statement from a book by Emily Toth: "We would like to think that feminism will help women develop a different sense of humor, one that is warm, loving, egalitarian, compassionate."

That's like recommending calm orgasms but feminists don't see it that way. They can excuse the woman who set fire to her sleeping husband because it didn't offend anyone, but Parker makes them nervous. Her retort to an importunate male—"With the crown of thorns I wear, why should I worry about a little prick like you?"—is not only mean-spirited but rife with Christian imagery and body parts.

Parker also offends many liberals with her classical literary style. "Good writing is counter-revolutionary," decreed Ellen Willis, and she was right. Bad writing is now on the Left with all the other sloppiness, but it was the opposite in Parker's day; her liberals valued the epigram as ours value the focus group.

Big Blonde obeys the rules laid down by Aristotle and Horace about the value of leaving things to the imagination. The best example of Parker's masterly indirection comes when Hazel Morse, having passed out from an overdose, is being revived by her cleaning woman. As she is turned over on her back, her breasts sag sideways and lodge in her armpits. This one brushstroke description says more about sadness than all the tears on television.

A Philosophy of Pleasure

Roger Scruton

HUMAN PLEASURE may be sensual, like the pleasure of a hot bath, or intellectual, like the pleasure of mathematical proof. But the pleasures that matter most to us, and that shape our lives and personalities, are neither purely sensual nor purely intellectual, but both at once. They arise in contemplation, when the senses feast on some favored object, or during practical activities, when we rise above our purpose and begin to enjoy what we are doing for its own sake, without regard to the results. They include aesthetic pleasures, whether in art or in nature; the pleasures of sport, whether enjoyed as a spectacle or through participation; the pleasures of the chase and the pleasures of sexual union. In all of these the human being is emancipated from sensuous existence, so as to encounter a world beyond purpose, a world in which thought and feeling come together in a synthesis that no animal can ever know.

Hence we are judged by our pleasures, which are the sign of our worth. The joy of a human being is also an expression of his moral outlook: those who see things with evil or perverted eyes have evil or perverted pleasures. It is a pernicious modern fallacy to believe that pleasure is a physical condition, a primitive sense of well-being located in some region of the body, and no more susceptible to moral judgment than is the digestive system or the sensation of pain. This "demoralization" of pleasure owes much to nineteenth-century utilitarianism, and also to Nietzsche's glorification of the instincts and Freud's theory of the "pleasure principle." If there is anything wrong with pleasure, those writers suggest, it lies merely in the causes and effects of it.

This demoralization of pleasure makes us look more like the animals than we really are. If infant "sexuality" has been a favorite concern of the demoralizers, it is because the infant is a bridge between the animal and the person. He is the proof that, whatever our final state, we begin life as animals, and become persons only by a slow process that by no means eliminates, but at most "represses," our essential nature. Freudians try to persuade us, therefore, that all our sexual experiences have their paradigms in infancy, where they exist as bodily desires and satisfactions, focused on "erotogenic" zones. In a famous passage Freud wrote that "no one who has seen a baby sinking back satiated at the breast and falling asleep with flushed cheeks and a blissful smile can escape the reflection that this picture persists as a prototype of the expression of sexual satisfaction in later life." This ridiculous observation—which tells us only that the baby's expression is the prototype of a postprandial doze—is about the only proof that Freud ever offered for his view that our later sexual experiences are all presaged at the breast, and are as animal and amoral as the gluttony of the infant. By describing adult sexuality in these infantile terms, you make it infantile. The demoralized view of human pleasure is self-confirming, since the more people believe in it, the more true it becomes.

But however brutish modern people may be, art and literature testify to a higher and purely human form of erotic pleasure. The sexual pleasure of animals bears no real resemblance to that which lovers feel. It involves no understanding of the other; it provides no triumph or commitment, is hedged around by no shame or prohibition; is free from judgment, praise, or blame. The sexual pleasure of an animal neither depends on thought nor responds to thought. Hence it can never be mistaken. By contrast, the literature of love is full of mistakes: the mistaken pleasure of Lucretia, as she lies with the rapist whom she thinks to be her husband (an innocent mistake, but one that only death can cure); the transgression of Emma Bovary, whose sexual pleasure empties her of hope; the desperate pleasure that gnaws the heart of Swann, in the bottomless pit of his love for Odette. Do animals make mistakes like these? The very idea is absurd. The sexual pleasures of humans stem as much from thought as from sensual contact: they involve knowledge, imagination, and judgment, and express the whole personality of the person who experiences them. That is why they can be praised and blamed—not for their effects, but for their very existence. The sexual pleasure of the child-molester is wrong in itself, and not in its consequences only. And the same is true of the predatory sexuality which we are not supposed to judge, but which we must judge if we are to retain our true humanity.

Our greatest pleasures differ from those of the animals in another respect: they are also *evaluations,* in which we appreciate what we enjoy for its own sake, as an end in itself. This extraordinary fact, which Kant made the cornerstone of his aesthetics, is the proof that we belong to another and higher sphere—the sphere of judgment. For it is not only in the aesthetic experience that people learn to contemplate the world and perceive its intrinsic meaning. Even when pursuing a purpose, they garland their acts with purposelessness, and the purpose becomes the excuse for a higher meditation. This is what happens when we build, and building turns to style, ornament, and decoration. (The crime of modern architecture is that it makes the purpose sovereign over its embellishment, and so negates what is truly human in the art of building.) It is also what happens in the greatest pleasure that I know: the pleasure of hunting to hounds. This has a purpose, which is to catch and kill the prey. The pleasure of the hounds consists entirely in their absorption in this purpose, and in the animal compulsion that presses them onward to the kill. But for the follower, carried across country by a horse, whose animal pleasure courses through the human veins above him, hunting is an end in itself. The animal pleasure is transcended into something sublime: a contemplation of nature, in which life and death briefly flow together into a meaning. It is as hard to describe such a meaning as to paraphrase a Bruckner symphony. But its existence would be denied by no one who has encountered it. In hunting, as in music, we are confronted with an intrinsic good, and the pleasure we take in it needs no justification. It is such pleasures that make life worthwhile; and it is their absence from the life of sensuality that is the real punishment of those who are lost in it.

The Rise of Politics
and the Decline of Black Culture

Tom Bethell

WHEN I ARRIVED IN THE UNITED STATES from England, "black studies" were unheard of, and politics were far from my mind. The idea that I would one day be regarded as politically conservative would have struck me as very surprising. The year was 1962, and at that time I was a mechanical, rote liberal. If quizzed, I would have accepted all the pieties of the day: McCarthyism was a greater threat than Communism. Democrats were more idealistic than Republicans, who were probably just out for themselves. America's treatment of Negroes was a national disgrace.

What drew me to America was black culture, although I didn't quite think of it that way. I wanted to go to the American South—but not as a civil rights worker. Voter-registration drives were not for me. I did occasionally meet people who were involved with groups like the Student Nonviolent Coordinating Committee. I wished them well, but I was never interested enough to pay much attention to what they were saying. I had something else in mind—something, as I saw it, higher: music.

My great interest was American popular music, particularly jazz, particularly the old New Orleans style. My desire was to meet some of the pioneers, then still living in New Orleans, still playing in some cases. I wondered if they could shed any light on this new musical style that had so suddenly emerged—almost miraculously, as it seemed. In a recent essay on the blues singer Robert Johnson, Russell Banks observes that the blues "suddenly appeared in a specific region in a fully articulated and evolved form." The same was true of jazz. There's no evidence of an antecedent, "primitive" period. The earliest jazzmen could read music. It was the later ones who didn't bother to learn. The idea that jazz had emerged from African tribal rituals reenacted in Congo Square is utterly without foundation. Yet one thing is undoubtedly true: All the great early jazzmen that we know of were black.

Music was my love, but the European classical tradition had utterly collapsed. The nineteenth century had been one long, sickening slide, followed by the musically moribund twentieth. The avant-garde stuff struck me then, as today, as a kind of pretense of creativity sustained by music departments, critics, and academics. But something new had magically appeared in the United States, around the year 1900. The great change was that the new American music was . . . democratic. I hesitate to use the word because it sounds so political, which is not my intention. I mean that the music had somehow emerged directly from the lives of working people, not from concert halls, academies, or the furrowed brows of theory-laden composers.

Jazz, ragtime, and the blues all started up in different places at the same time—certainly all within a few years. How and why this happened so suddenly no one knows. A creative peak was reached at some point in the first half of the twentieth century. It's impossible to say exactly when that was—my guess is around World War II. But others say much earlier than that—perhaps in the first decade of the century. Unfortunately, no recordings were made at the time. We know as much about the origins of jazz and the blues as we do about the circumstances in which Shakespeare's plays were written; which is to say virtually nothing. The crucial early years, circa 1895–1915, are a blank. A few hazy photographs and hazier recollections are all that we have.

What had particularly attracted my attention were some recordings of traditional jazz made in World War II in New Orleans. They were made not in studios, but "on location," so to speak, in dance halls. It was the most wonderful music I had ever heard, and I still think so: a relaxed, nonchalant, three-part polyphony as complex as the Brandenburg Concertos, and similar to them in other respects. All the musicians on these recordings were black. The leader was a trumpeter called Bunk Johnson, a man in his sixties who had been discovered and resurrected by the pioneer jazz researchers of the 1930s. The other musicians were in their forties or fifties—probably not far off their prime. They were described at the time as "old," but jazzmen then were thought to resemble baseball players: their legs gave out at forty.

The man who had made those recordings was an eccentric Missourian named William Russell, who later became a friend of mine. He had studied under Arnold Schoenberg at UCLA and wrote some avant-garde stuff himself; all very complicated and abstruse, for percussion instruments. But in the 1940s he gave up pretending to be a composer, he told me, after hearing Warren "Baby" Dodds playing the drums and doing things he knew he would never have been able to think up. Russell made the New Orleans recordings with his own equipment, lugging it down to New Orleans by train. They didn't have recording tape then, so he also brought along wooden boxes of glass-based acetate discs. By a miracle, not one of these discs was ever broken.

Some of the recordings were issued on Russell's own tiny, non-commercial label, American Music, and by the late 1950s they were collector's items in England. As soon as I heard them I knew I wanted to go to America, hear more, and find out more about the music. By the time I arrived in New Orleans, however, the music had unmistakably declined. The clarinetist George Lewis and others who had recorded with Bunk were still playing, but the style itself had somehow "hardened" into a mechanical routine. The actual notes played were more or less the same, but the creative spark had departed. It was as though the Muse had moved on—to other places and other styles.

I interviewed a number of musicians, George Lewis in particular, and later wrote a book about him. As a rule the musicians couldn't tell you much. They knew who played with Kid René in 1930, but they didn't know much more than you did about how the music really began. As for the "art," you were wasting your time asking about it. When I would ask foolish questions about the contrapuntal style and the like, George Lewis was so diplomatic that I never could tell whether he didn't have anything to say on the subject, didn't understand a word of what I was saying, or (what I now think may be the case) just wasn't interested but was too polite to let it show. His articulate phrases and brilliant, dancing arpeggios would just have to speak for themselves.

I remember once driving him to a recording session in my beat-up Peugeot. As we drove toward the Mississippi River bridge I was asking him some solemn question—even as he spotted a young woman in huge Day-Glo orange stretch pants walking along beside the road. His head turning practically through 180 degrees, he gave me a one-word answer: "Sheees." I was surprised to find that he didn't even have copies of his own recordings at home. Once I asked him to name any musicians he particularly admired, and he told me about someone he had seen on the Johnny Carson show the night before.

When I asked him about segregation, how bad it must have been, he obviously wasn't interested in that either. But there was one form of discrimination that still rankled him, forty years later. A dark-skinned man, he had from time to time been treated contemptuously by light-skinned "creoles," and he hadn't forgotten it. But he did not think of himself as one of society's victims. Nor was he in fact. In the 1950s his band had toured Europe, and in Japan in the 1960s he had received almost a hero's welcome. As a person with musical talent, he knew that he had been fortunate in the place and time of his birth: New Orleans, 1900; a few days and a few blocks from Louis Armstrong's birthplace. The "clay" of the new style was still soft, and the early jazzmen could leave their fingerprints on it. Few musicians in history have been that lucky.

Yes, but condemned to live in a segregated society? Here a little perspective is in order. Compared to many Irishmen in nineteenth-century Ireland, for example, most blacks in New Orleans lived in comfort, even in the "Jim Crow" years. As for those with musical abilities, they enjoyed the rare gift of a new musical language—one that was vital enough to reverberate around the world. They had musical instruments, the leisure to learn how to play them, music teachers eager to give them lessons, social clubs they could join, and above all an economy productive enough to keep literally hundreds of them in work. Is a man oppressed if he can support himself and his family by going off to work every day, clarinet in hand, as George Lewis did in the 1920s and 1930s? Tell it to the ditchdigger.

When I arrived in America, and for a few years thereafter, you could still walk around the black neighborhoods of cities like New Orleans in the middle of the night if you wanted to. I distinctly remember the change—I think it was in 1967 or 1968. I made some recordings of the old-timers myself in those years, and I was looking for a particular musician. The old drummer Cié Frazier, then playing at Preservation Hall in the French Quarter, told me that my man lived in the Desire housing project. But he told me not to go out there because it was unsafe—"worse than a gang of rattlesnakes," as he put it. Three or four years earlier I had been there many times. At the time, of course, I did not associate the change with the rising tide of welfare or anything of that political nature.

One statement I am prepared to make is that black music, pre–civil rights, was artistically much superior to what came later. At the first hint of ulterior political motive, I'm afraid, the Muse just slinks away embarrassed and ashamed. It would be nice if Grace and Beauty felt at home with Indignation and Protest, but they don't. Mahalia Jackson's gospel recordings in the 1940s and 1950s are far superior to the sentimental melodies she sang after becoming a mascot of the civil rights movement. And there is simply no modern counterpart to Bessie Griffin's "Too Close to Heaven," recorded in a "Sanctified" church in Memphis in 1953. And there will not be again, I fear.

At the same time, the Muse is surprisingly at home in a businesslike setting, with "art" subordinate to social function. All the New Orleans musicians grew up playing for real events—dances, weddings, funerals, and parades—for which they were paid. MUSIC FURNISHED FOR ALL OCCASIONS was printed on their business cards. They thought of themselves more as artisans than as artists. Their brothers were bricklayers, plasterers, roofers. One of the old halls where Bill Russell made some particularly good recordings was called Artisans Hall (pronounced *Artesians* by the musicians).

The best music ever played in New Orleans was in dance halls when dancing was underway and few in the room were consciously listening at all. By the time I was in the city, it was still possible to hear some of the old-time music in dance halls, but this was rare and dying out. The musicians were usually on display at earnest concerts, and one was supposed to sit still and appreciate the tradition of it. A similar change had taken place in Europe. Concerts, in which the pure aesthetic experience was supposed to have been liberated from social distractions, more and more replaced real events, such as church services, in which the art was servant to the occasion. In the process, the music became more self-conscious and intellectualized, and declined. I suspect the Muse is basically a shy creature, more willing to put in an appearance when people are looking the other way or not paying too much attention.

The same attitude toward culture prevails throughout the United States and the West generally today. It is thought that we can subtract the all-important functional setting that gave life and purpose to the original creation, and retain only the distilled aesthetic drops in the concert halls and cultural centers: art furnished not for all occasions but for art's sake, with the help of educational programs, community input, "outreach," national endowments, committees, and dedicated funds.

THERE WAS STILL some pretty good black music in 1962, and for some time after that. John Lee Hooker was playing in Chicago at or near his peak. On the hit parade: Esther Phillips's "Release Me," which today evokes a golden age. Music in the black churches was often outstanding—and what a pity more recordings were not made *in* the churches, as opposed to dull studios. Mahalia Jackson was never recorded in a church, Bill Russell once told me. Later on, one heard it through the grapevine, there were some outstanding groups playing in the Motown style. I sometimes used to go and hear them on tour, at the Municipal Auditorium in New Orleans. But by the 1970s these were increasingly occasions for sartorial display, and within a few years black music was unmistakably in decline. It went on declining, and I doubt if it has touched bottom yet.

I've never actually gone to a rap concert, and I know I should. But

I have made determined attempts to listen to rap music. We're looking at a quantum change here, not just a continuation of the slide. Take the group Public Enemy. Recently I made an effort to listen to the album called *Muse Sick-N-Hour Mess Age.* Not a bad double entendre, by the way: Music and Our Message—The Muse is sick in our messy age. In her book *Hole in Our Soul,* the critic Martha Bayles describes "the loss of beauty and meaning in American popular music." She's right about the beauty, but listening to Chuck D and Public Enemy, I'm not so sure it is devoid of meaning. Those who may wonder what life is like in the inner cities in the 1990s could do worse than listen to Public Enemy.

The album notes, by the way, acknowledge "All praises Due to Allah (God)." I'm told that such dedications are now standard on the liner notes of black groups. A recent Boyz II Men album includes separate dedications from each singer: "All praises are due II my Lord God Almighty and my Saviour Jesus Christ," says one vocalist.

The performance barely qualifies as music. A characteristic of rap is the assumption that we find pleasure not in beauty, harmony, or melody, but in an attitude of accusation and mockery. "Lyrics" have degenerated into harangue, and the overall tone is one of scorn and defiance of bourgeois sensibility. There's a veneer of irony and political radicalism. But rap belongs nowhere near the category of "protest" heard in civil rights ballads—Pete Seeger and the like. In fact, the political veneer seems almost designed to mask an underlying nihilism and contempt for the law-abiding. Rap comes not to change the law but to mock it. We are faced with the open jeering of quasi-outlaws who understand perfectly well that their disdain will be matched, measure for measure, by our toleration. This is the one virtue that is still insistently demanded of us, and meekly supplied.

Rap has a pervasive air of triumphant badness and raucous aural jostling—they're shouting us down even before we know what the charge is—but there is something more unsettling than that. Public Enemy's performance manages both to parody, yet also to flirt with, what one can only call evil. I think that's what makes the whole experience so unnerving: Muse sick, indeed. Repetitive phrases turn over and haunt us as in a bad dream; dybbuks hop about on pogo sticks, and imps squeak and tease from a multitrack electronic inferno that just won't quit. It's Bedlam, or worse.

Confronted with the blatant decadence of rap, the Progressive Myth is given one more public airing. *Newsweek* dutifully referred to the new style as "the next evolutionary step." A *New York Times* editorial writer found something very familiar in these sounds: the history of music has been one of "innovative, even outrageous styles," but no matter how outrageous they seemed at the time, they eventually "became mainstream." And so it will be with rap (goes the argument). If you don't want to look foolishly reactionary in the light of history, better pay your respects now—or, if you disapprove, at least preserve a discreet silence. Remember: Art that "breaks the mold" is not appreciated in its day!

I wonder if those who believe that rap is the "next evolutionary step" also believe that we are "building a new society" in the inner cities? Such claims used to be made, but they now look absurd. Nothing has been built, nothing will be built, and a great deal has been destroyed. The raucous ugliness of rap mirrors the fantastic decline and destruction that we have seen in our urban centers in the past thirty years, and to that extent it is meaningful indeed. It's not surprising that this decline occurred just as the politicization of life was vastly increased. It's not just the destruction of family life by welfare and the message, openly communicated, that responsible paternity is not expected of those who have been historically victimized. Artistically, there's an even more deeply rooted problem. The nurturing of grievance in a whole class of people is bound to produce the exact opposite of a healthy climate for creative endeavor. Art is based on the appreciation, not the denigration, of one's milieu.

I MOVED TO WASHINGTON IN 1975, not long after the collapse of Vietnam (enthusiastically cheered by my liberal friends), and the pardon of President Nixon (equally reviled—retirement in disgrace wasn't punishment enough, apparently). It struck me that there was a great sickness in these attitudes, so I turned more and more to politics myself. You knew by then that you weren't going to be able to escape its long reach, so you might as well try to oppose its worst tendencies.

In 1991 I returned to New Orleans for a few days. The old San Jacinto Hall, where William Russell had made his 1944 recordings of Bunk Johnson, had survived until 1967 but was then torn down, along with the entire surrounding neighborhood, known as the Tremé. This act of urban vandalism was called urban renewal. It may seem that I am making this up, but at almost the exact spot where the old dance hall stood, a "cultural center" was built. Later on it was incorporated into something called Louis Armstrong Park. I planned to walk across Rampart Street one day and look around there, but I was warned that it wasn't safe even in daytime.

Bill Russell was then still living, only two blocks from Rampart Street on the edge of the French Quarter. I went to see him one night; as usual he was poring over his old documents and precious memorabilia. His collection of manuscript and biographical material on the pianist Jelly Roll Morton was finally ready for publication. He was by then eighty-five. He told me, when I said good-bye, that he was going downhill fast and that I probably wouldn't see him again. I didn't, either. He fell down in his apartment and died in the hospital sixteen months later. At night, the French Quarter today is not safe on its perimeter, and as it was about 2 A.M. when I left (Bill was always very much the night owl) he offered me, as a final gift, a small, palm-of-the-hand container of mace. In his final years, he carried it with him as he walked to and from his apartment. I am glad that he never had to use it, but I am sorry that it came to that.

Tumbleweed Dreams

Dave Shiflett

A SOUTHERN AMERICAN PRINCESS contemplating a move from the Southland to the great beyond (beyond Tennessee) wonders if those of us who have left the South still think about the same things we did back home. Having left Virginia some thirty months ago for Colorado, I can give her an honest answer: Yes'm. But we might think about them differently.

Take death, for instance. Among other things, most Southerners know that one's death should be a glorious affair, the crowning touch to a life lived full. Accordingly, while many of our countrymen pass their time thinking about sports cars, trust funds, and other of life's hollow accoutrements, the Southerner (we're talking true Southerner) is stretched out in front of the fire with his hound and his jug, dreaming of the best way to die. These contemplations are the fruits of a superior upbringing, and we revel in them, whether we happen to be in Richmond or Santa Fe.

We do not revel as a suicide would, of course, for the suicide often wishes to leave a scar upon the hearts of his survivors, which is why there should probably be a rule that suicides pass through the bowels of dogs on their way back to the dust (with some medical exemptions available, to be paid in advance). Bathsheba was fed to the dogs, and few people would argue that it wasn't fitting.

Instead, we revel in the contemplation of the death that is so magnificent and perhaps noble that its retelling would leave our survivors beaming through their mourning veils—and perhaps even cause complete strangers to tip their hat toward our humble mausoleum. History is full of people who died this way: war heroes, the

Christian apostles, or, at a much baser level, even JFK, though history has by now sandblasted much of the adulation from his highrise tombstone, etching in its place high tributes to his restless and unflagging gonads. By way of contrast, we are not talking about being dropped down the stairs by stretcher-bearers from an emergency medical team, or falling into a tree chipper, or choking on a piece of pig fat. No, we desire something that is dramatic, something along the lines of the dream death of James Dickey, who once told a television audience that if he could choose the best way to go, he would like to be eaten by a bear.

For the stay-put Southerner, Mr. Dickey's dream death is nearly perfect. Chief among its attributes is that the bear would be at a great advantage, and no Southerner worth his pickup wants to be knocked off by anything puny. Better to die in an avalanche than a collapsing toolshed; better to be smitten by Satan than influenza.

But for us transplants, this vision may have to be radically altered, which is something our Southern American Princess needs to understand before pulling up stakes and lashing the mules toward a foreign port. By the time you get to the Denver area, for instance (1700 miles west, 5,280 feet straight up), Mr. Dickey's bear will have to become a trout.

How come? The answer has two parts. One, most Southerners—even tumbleweed Southerners—wish to die on familiar ground. Two, in some parts of the country, the earth is so alien (no trees, lots of rocks, big lizards all over the place) that rivers and streams are the only places we feel truly at home. It's where we go to water our severed taproots. And since there's nothing else in the water to kill us but a slippery rock or a runaway kayak (neither of which would lend to a dignified death), we're stuck with a trout.

So that's how a bear becomes a trout. This may be more of a transition than our damsel would care to make; in addition, she may not believe there's any way you can look good being killed by a trout. But there she would be wrong. You can die a glorious death in the jaws of a trout. It would probably go something like this:

An hour or so before sundown, somewhere high on the South Platte River, you make a perfect cast with a number 20 Royal Coachman (called by some the Cadillac of dry flies) just upstream of a feeding trout. You are determined to land the arrogant bugger (you have stalked him before, and he has refused you), but suddenly something very odd happens. A great flash of silver breaks the surface just below the tip of your pole, and you catch the slightest glimpse of a three-pound cutthroat coming out of the water like a Polaris missile, its side slashed with the telltale red.

"My Lord," you think, "it's coming for me!" Indeed. The fish flies straight at your throat, spins like a feeding shark, and quietly slices your jugular with its lower jaw. "Take me!"—those are your last words as you slip quietly into the river, too shocked to grasp at your death wound, though miffed that no one was around to record your death utterance.

Does our dream end here? No, for it is incomplete—it offers no rest for your vagrant soul, for you now realize that you must somehow get home to the Southland if you are to rest in peace. There's a problem, of course, in that you are dead. But you are not still. You are eight thousand feet above sea level, floating down the mountain. Can you make it all the way home?

The dream continues:

A miracle of nature causes your body to immediately resurface (face to sky), and as you float downstream (feet first), fellow anglers drop commemorative flies (drys only, please) onto your chest. From time to time a bottle of Olympia Beer is pulled from a creel and held skyward in salute, and at a bend in the river an old geezer whips through the Twenty-third Psalm, then hooks a nice german brown just off your starboard.

Down through the canyons the trout man goes, over dams, through narrow rock passages, across those deep pools he had fished those countless summer evenings. Hundreds of feet above, mountain rams watch as the body heads toward the high plains. High above the rams, the evening star shines.

"Where is he going?" a child asks his father as they view the wondrous procession from the riverbank.

"He must be going home," the father responds.

The next morning, as the body bumps and splashes across the

high plains, it is met by the Fort Morgan (Colorado) city council, which marks the occasion with a ceremonial plaque and a half-day vacation for all public employees. By now a dozen or so seagulls (yes, there are seagulls in the middle of the continent) have formed a halo above the drifting corpse and shadow it, as it were, across the cloudless sky. They are joined at ground level by a band of wandering evangelicals, who march alongside singing songs of thanksgiving and occasionally firing their revolvers at encroaching coyotes.

Then into Nebraska, eastward beside the Oregon Trail, picking up speed before dumping into the Missouri (at Plattsmouth), and from there through Kansas City, St. Louis, and finally into the Mississippi. "He is a metaphor for us all," the newspaper pundits explain, and, indeed, great mobs stand along the Big Muddy, waving to the trout man, as if he were running for office. Outside of Cairo, Illinois, an ROTC unit fires a salute, and when the honored one passes beneath a bridge in Memphis, dozens of girls rain camisoles and roses upon him. "I think I went out with him once!" screams a particularly stunning redhead just before dissolving in sorrow.

From Memphis, he cruises to Baton Rouge, past the piney woods and small groups of drunk Cajuns who fire 12-gauge goose guns at the bird-flesh halo, without success. Then, as the body slowly drifts into New Orleans, a chorus of sweet-singing women serenade the traveler, accompanied by the string section of the Atlanta symphony. "He has reached the end of the line," the governor points out to a capacity crowd at the Superdome, and as he speaks, the trout man drifts into the big water of the Gulf, sinking out of sight as the gulls peel off one by one and drift into the Delta mist. It is over.

But our damsel should realize that people who leave the Southland (again, we're talking true Southerners) try to dream their way back by conventional means. She should know, however, that out here in the great beyond, the things she once imagined—men riding on the backs of bulls, funnel clouds dropping from the springtime sky—will suddenly appear before her, while the old home place, with mama in the parlor and the expatriate's footprints undusted on the pinewood floor, will face forever toward Xanadu. Sometimes the only way home is on the back of a trout.

The Use and Abuse of Violence

James Bowman

G. K. CHESTERTON once pointed out the intellectual legerdemain involved in the prohibitionist case against "alcohol." Nobody, Chesterton observed, drinks "alcohol," and nobody wants to. People drink beer and wine and whisky and brandy and frozen daiquiris and piña coladas. "Alcohol" is merely some chemist's fancy, an attempt to render uniform drinkers' diverse behavior by identifying a common ingredient in what they drink. This is not a trivial point. We may not understand why someone chooses to drink, but it is a step away from understanding to deny that he has made a choice at all and instead to buy the chemist's story about how a mythical monster called "alcohol" has enslaved him.

The same thing is true, mutatis mutandis, of "violence." The word is torn from its natural context and made to stand on its own as a new bugbear to haunt the liberal imagination. Who commits "violence"—still less its evil twin "senseless violence"? The expression merely reinforces the implicit assumption of "violence" alone: namely that, like "alcohol," it is a ravening monster with a life of its own whose motivations are inscrutable. I think this monster is even more a chimera than "alcohol." People rob and assault and rape and kill each other not for the sake of violence but for some other end. And sometimes, as in the case of self-defense, violent acts are justified. To categorize all such acts under the generic head of "violence" is simply to turn away from the attempt to understand why a particular violent act takes place.

And if, having thus turned away, one then proceeds to ratiocination about "violence" in the abstract, the result is guaranteed muddy thinking—on the order of the self-evidently false New Age platitude that "violence never solves anything." It solves lots of things, as anyone who descends from Olympus and gets close enough to it to see what it is for will tell you. What's your problem? Not enough money to buy drugs tonight? Mugging somebody will solve it. Or maybe you're the muggee rather than the mugger. Then your problem is to avoid being mugged. Superior force, successfully threatened or applied, will solve *your* problem—and give the mugger back his. Violence is a wonderful problem solver, perhaps the most efficacious of them all, which is one reason why it is both forbidden and fascinating.

Now it appears that people who like to indulge this fascination without doing violence to the taboos by watching dramatizations of it on television are going to be in trouble with the government. Senator Paul Simon, speaking to a conference organized in Beverly Hills on August 2 by the National Council for Families and Television, told some 650 representatives of the broadcasting business who were present that he was giving them sixty days to come up with a plan to regulate themselves with respect to the portrayal of violence—or else they would face some sort of government regulation. Already, after hearings he held on the subject back in May, Simon had induced the four major broadcast networks to agree to a warning label on programs he found to include too much, or too graphic, violence: "Due to some violent content, parental discretion advised." At least fifteen cable channels, including HBO, USA, MTV, and Nickelodeon, have subsequently agreed to adopt the warning.

By itself, the label would be no big deal. I was irresistibly reminded of the attempt a few years ago by Channel Four in Britain to identify sexually explicit programming with a little triangle—which people proceeded to take as the network's recommendation bestowed on the shows it reckoned were *really* hot. The real point of Simon's speech was public relations: to make it clear that he really *cared* about television's effects on America's children and that he was not going to be satisfied with the supine posture of the networks on the warning label. He has got to keep an eye out over his shoulder for other congressional carers seeking to go out in front on this one.

Politically, the attack upon "violence" is shooting fish in a barrel for both Left and Right. Not even willing to wait the sixty days, Representative John Bryant of Texas introduced, on the day after Simon's warning, a bill to entrust the regulation of violence on television to the FCC. Shortly thereafter, Representatives Edward Markey of Massachusetts and Jack Fields of Texas introduced another bill to require all televisions sold in the United States to include something called a V-chip, which Newton Minow is pushing. The idea is that it could be built into all new television sets and programmed to filter out any shows marked by their makers (or their censors) with a code identifying them as being too exciting for children. Senator Byron Dorgan has a bill pending to require the FCC to issue a "violence report card" every quarter. There is no constituency for violence except among the television producers who do nothing but bleat, as usual, about the First Amendment.

They should be less sheepish about violence and more sheepish about some of the other rubbish they purvey. As usual, when the political herd is galloping all in the same direction, they are sure to do some mindless damage to the fences. In his speech in Beverly Hills, for example, Senator Simon intimated that his response to TV "violence" was going to be to try not only to suppress images of it but also to dictate its presentation. Giving voice to the currently fashionable psycho-political orthodoxy about the causes of antisocial behavior in adolescents, Simon urged—in fact insisted—that the industry should go beyond censoring or labeling violent acts on TV to "deglamorize" such acts.

This is a much more frightening proposition. No one can be fool enough to suppose that if, for whatever reason, we are suddenly deprived of the opportunity to see a head exploding on television we will be an appreciably less free people. The reticences of decorum cost liberty little, and they should require little in the way of backing from the law so long as there are not madmen crying oppression at them. One might well object that one is not allowed to see one's neighbors in their underwear. But if the government is telling the makers of television programs that violence either is or is not glamorous, that is oppression indeed. It amounts to the imposition upon artistic judgment of a political imperative which has nothing to do with it. The artists' purposes are not those of the social engineer, and only tyranny would commandeer them to "educate the nation," as Senator Simon wants to do, into an official view of violence.

Moreover, this view is grievously mistaken. It is true that the most recent study of the subject, "Television and Violent Crime" by Brandon S. Centerwall in the Spring 1993 number of *The Public Interest,* seems to establish a direct correlation between the amounts of time spent watching television and levels of violent crime. It is also true that governments have a legitimate interest in preserving the social fabric even if doing so is at the expense of artistic freedom. But the only proper conclusion from Centerwall's study is that television ought to be banned altogether. I would have no objection to such a radical act, but too many of my more temperate countrymen would for it to be politically feasible. And lesser measures to do with the *presentation* of violence can have no foundation in social science at its present stage of advancement. Centerwall's instruments are not sensitive enough to register glamour.

My own impression from the so-called violence that I see on television is that it is neither plentiful nor glamorous. Look at the top-rated programs in any given week: Apart from movies, which are expurgated, nearly everything on the list actually produced by the poor beleaguered television industry itself is either news and documentary like *60 Minutes* and *Primetime Live* (even Senator Simon doesn't want to censor the news) or situation comedies like *Roseanne* and *Murphy Brown.* In fact, over a period of several days as I was writing this column, I couldn't find anything violent to watch. *Murder She Wrote* looked promising, but turned out to be an old-fashioned mystery of the wholly decorous, Agatha Christie sort. The latest cop show, called *Sirens,* had not a drop of blood in it. Instead, it was a sensitive portrayal of a poor salesman thrown out of work by the Reagan-Bush recession who is talked out of killing himself by an attractive young policewoman. She convinces him that he can win back the love of his daughter by hugging her and telling her that he loves her. And while she is doing her good deed she learns something about improving her own marriage.

Such moralism about "relationships" is far, far more common on television these days than violence is—and probably far more harmful to people from the viewpoint of the social engineer. Think of all the bewildered children whose emotional lives are being wrecked by overdemonstrative, TV-crazed parents hugging away at them. Children who listen to the moronic theme song of Barney the purple dinosaur are sure to grow up into the sorts of people who write their own wedding ceremonies and demonstrate against the wearing of fur. How one longs for the days of *Gunsmoke* or *Wyatt Earp* or, one of my personal favorites, the World War II series called *Combat!* They may not have been much as art, but without being cute or priggish they put violence into a moral context. Most of them you can't even see in reruns anymore. The best I can do with my cable company is *Bonanza*—which is really, I think, the one that started all this beastly hugging business in the first place. Little Joe, I could tell even then, was secretly a hugger, as he went on to show he was in *Little House on the Prairie.*

Back in the 1950s and 1960s, though, it really was possible to "glamorize" violence—just as the *Chanson de Roland* or *Le Morte d'Arthur* glamorizes violence. Nowadays, *pace* Senator Simon, television is much more likely to trivialize than to glamorize it by making it seem the exclusive province of such social exotics as Amy Fisher or David Koresh. Does anyone consider them glamorous? Both have been the subject of more than one TV movie. Is Gian Luigi Ferri, the madman who murdered eight people in a law office in San Francisco in July, a glamorous figure because among his many delusions he treasured the hope of appearing on *Oprah* to tell his story? This is not to say that Oprah herself (like Phil and Sally Jessy and all the rest of them) is not glamorous, but her glamour derives not from violence but precisely from her ability seemingly to snuff with compassionate attention the inward violence (one of the range of sicknesses she treats) of such pathetic losers as Ferri, who are then rendered even more marginal figures than they really are.

Violence and pathology, these days, go together like cannon and ball. And where is the glamour in being sick? Where (on television anyway) are the Davy Crocketts and the Matt Dillons, latter-day descendants of Roland and Lancelot, who made it seem to little boys a fine and noble thing to be proficient in killing one's enemies? Instead we have only nutcases and cops who are meant to be more "realistically" portrayed as being concerned rather with survival and personal happiness than any more honorable aim. The paradigm figures are Mel Gibson and Danny Glover in the *Lethal Weapon* series: the one a half-crazy daredevil in love with violence for its own sake, the other a nervous type just hoping to make it to retirement. The violence seems not glamorous but (as increasingly in the movies) self-consciously cinematic and unreal. It elicits the skills of the choreographer and cinematographer rather than the moralist.

Likewise, soldiers on television, as in *M*A*S*H* or *Major Dad,* are almost exclusively comic figures and are seen, when they are seen at all, not in action but goofing off behind the lines. So far from the youth of America being endangered by the glamorization of violence, they are endangered by its absence. The craft of arms, by which our liberties are ultimately preserved, is a joke. There is nothing in between the extreme nonviolence of Barney the dinosaur and the comic, cartoon violence of the Teenage Mutant Ninja Turtles—one of several examples of more traditional children's programming, by the way, including *Leave It to Beaver, The Jetsons,* and *Super Mario Brothers,* which, by a splendid irony, are now being applied by broadcasters to satisfy the requirements for "educational" material mandated under the Children's Television Act of 1990.

If it means that there will be less Barney and more Turtles, this is the one hopeful development in the sad tale of government regulation of broadcasting. Everything young children experience, every image they consume, is educational. But the images must be considered in their contexts. In the case of the Ninja Turtles, there is still visible some of the moral context of violence so firmly and, it has to be said, mostly boringly predictably established back in the days of *Leave It to Beaver* and *The Jetsons.* The heroes on the half shell are still recognizably heroes, their opponents still recognizably villains. But so lurid are the characters, so absurd the plots, so fantastical the images of anthropoid turtles skilled in Oriental fighting techniques, that such stuff must be judged more than halfway toward the *Super Mario Brothers* and the cartoonlike violence characteristic of video games.

There is, presumably, the perfect example of "deglamorized" violence for Senator Simon's edification: two morally indistinguishable electronic images bashing each other in a simulacrum of combat to no other end than the exercise of youthful skills in hand-eye coordination. And all television violence these days aspires to the condition of the video game. It is an abstract ballet of moving images stamped with visual whimsy in such a way as to preclude their identification with *anything* in the real world, let alone with good or evil—or glamour. If we are to turn social engineers we must recognize that the problem pointed to by Senator Simon and Professor Centerwall and so many others is not a result of so-called "violence" on television but of a tendency for violent acts to be detached from any context which could give them meaning.

Maybe the image of the lone lawman standing up to the bad guys was factitious and hackneyed and artistically clumsy, but it provided such a context—one which has dissipated as much in reality as on TV since the glamour of Matt Dillon was superseded by that of Bob Dylan. We need the glamour of discriminating violence in order to offset the collective moral lassitude induced by too much of the undiscriminating kind. Playing Simon Says with the government is certainly not going to bring it back—even if Simon were less simple than he is. Maybe nothing else is either. But if we all work to get as much violence on television as possible, maybe the effort to make sense of it all will result eventually in something like a plausible moral context.

Me and My Cars

Fred Barnes

Y FAMILY HAS FOUR CARS. I drive only one, but the other three don't sit idle. My wife, my daughter in college, and my daughter in high school each use a car every day. I know all this driving doesn't please environmentalists, but I never thought it gravely affected the tenets of political correctness. Until now. Maybe I'm paranoid, but I sense the beginnings of a moralistic new crusade to persuade or force people to curb their driving. For example, talk is picking up—including in these pages—about the embarrassingly low price of gasoline in America. (Sorry, I don't feel embarrassed.) There's also been a spate of newspaper stories reporting on, and bemoaning, the rise in three-or-more-car families and the decline in carpooling and mass transit ridership. Even Washington's safe, clean, and generally reliable Metro system has experienced a drop. The unspoken message of these stories is What's the matter with you people, acting so selfish and stupid? Officialdom is joining the crusade. In traffic-clogged New Jersey, officials canceled $1.2 billion in new highway projects, choosing to spend the money on mass transit. In Sacramento I chatted with a California state official who wants to use zoning restrictions to halt expansion of the suburbs and force increased population density in close-in areas. The aim is to make mass transit a more attractive option and to pressure people into giving up one or two of their cars.

It'll never work. There's not much chance I'll go back to two or even three cars, and one car is downright unthinkable. I don't believe anybody else is going to cut back either. There's a reason, and it's not just that Americans are car crazy (though they are). It's the freedom, convenience, and flexibility that comes from having a car at your disposal. The automobile is the most freeing instrument yet invented. It allows folks to take jobs far away from their homes. It enables them to live far from central cities and, if they're antisocial, far from other people. Two cars make the two-earner family possible. Sure, there's a downside: traffic congestion and pollution. Most people are willing to put up with those, within limits. I'm amazed at the incredible commutes—an hour or more each way—some people are willing to endure daily just to be able to drive to work when and with whom they wish. But it goes to show how strongly attached people are to their cars. And the attachment has grown as cars have become an extension of home and office, with telephones, message pads, coffee cups, books (on tape), etc. Government officials ought to recognize this. And if they want to be responsive, they won't emphasize mass transit. They'll build more highways.

The fight over the automobile is another skirmish in the longstanding political war described compellingly in Jeffrey Bell's *Populism and Elitism: Politics in the Age of Equality.* Populists, Bell writes, are optimistic "about people's ability to make decisions about their lives." Elitists are pessimistic about people, but optimistic "about one or more elites, acting on behalf of other people." Elitists, be they liberals or conservatives, think people don't know the most efficient way to get to work or wherever they want to go. If they did, they'd opt for mass transit instead of driving in jammed traffic. Populists figure that people know what's in their best interest, even if that means inching to work on congested highways. Being stuck in traffic is no fun, but people weigh that against the advantages of driving their own car. If they want to take off early, they can (but couldn't if they were carpooling). With a car, they're free to work late (but couldn't if the last subway train had gone). By the way, Bell's book is about politics, not cars. His highly original thesis: American politics is a struggle not between parties or ideologies but between populists (Jefferson, Wilson, Reagan) and elitists (Washington, Hoover, Mondale). Bell, I've learned, lives near a subway stop. He drives to work.

I rode mass transit—first the bus, then Metro—for nearly two decades. I gave it up when I got a parking space (partially subsidized) at my building. I didn't mind riding the bus or subway, but I like driving a lot better. I'm lucky to have the choice. Most people don't. The vast majority of jobs are not downtown anymore. The workplace has been decentralized. Instead, "edge cities" like Tyson's Corner in Northern Virginia have sprung up on the fringes of every metropolitan area. And the result is that mass transit simply doesn't make as much sense as it used to. It's great for getting people downtown, but fewer want to go there. New rapid rail systems, like the fantastically expensive subway in Los Angeles, are instant white elephants. For jobs scattered about the suburbs, you've got to have a car. Or two or three or four.

I'm glad the Bush administration has finally proposed the obvious answer to the auto pollution problem: buy up all the clunkers, the pre-1982 cars on the road. Bushies latched onto this idea to help the auto industry—people will have to buy new cars to replace their clunkers. But a more persuasive reason is that clunkers emit 40 to 70 percent of all auto pollution, depending on whose estimate you believe. I've got a clunker, a 1975 Oldsmobile Cutlass. It still drives like a dream, but it also pollutes more than its share. I'd happily turn over my Olds, worth maybe $100 as junk, for a bounty of $700 to $1,000, the range suggested by Bush officials. The argument against this is that poor people wouldn't sell because the bounty isn't enough to buy a new car, or they would sell but then would pocket the money. I doubt they'd go without wheels. To make sure they could afford a new car, the bounty could be means-tested. I'd get less for my Olds than a poor person would. Sounds fair, and I'd still come out ahead.

The Clever Life

Richard Brookhiser

I N THE centennial year of Cole Porter's birth, I wanted to hear him played, not by someone who was cashing in on the calendar, but by someone who has played him year in and year out because he enjoys him and knows how to play him well. So I went to hear Bobby Short at the Café Carlyle on Madison Avenue.

Short made his entrance to a long roll on the drums, twenty minutes late. He is a short, plain man, balding, with a snub nose and a sandpaper rasp to his voice. He majors in the golden age of American popular song, from the twenties to the fifties, as do most dinner singers. But his repertoire extends beyond the standards to tunes on flip sides, tunes buried in second acts of Broadway shows, tunes dropped from Broadway shows in Boston or Philadelphia. He knows when they were written and who first sang them, and imparts the information in his introductions as if he were a *Grove's Dictionary* of popular music.

Short's sets always include a cluster of songs by Cole Porter. Of the three he did tonight, two were bravura joshing. "I'm Throwing a Ball Tonight," introduced by Ethel Merman in *Panama Hattie* (1940), was like fast-forwarding through old Walter Winchell broadcasts.

> *I invited Wendell Wilkie,*
> *I invited FDR,*
> *And for photographs,*
> *I asked the staffs*
> Of *Life, Look, Peek, Pic, Snap, Click, and* Harper's Bazaar.

"How's Your Romance?" from *Gay Divorce* (1932) was not topical, but no less clever.

> *In* Italia *the* signori *are so very amatory*
> *That their passion,* a priori, *is* l'amor.
> *And from Napoli to Pisa, ev'ry man has on his knees a*
> *Little private Mona Lisa to adore.*

The stars of the show, Short explained when he finished, had been Fred Astaire and Claire Luce—("*not* Clare Boothe Luce"). "For the film," Short went on, "they did two or three interesting things, I thought. They found another blonde girl, Ginger Rogers. The Censorship Board thought the title made divorce too attractive to the American public, so it was changed to *The Gay Divorcee.* And, what was unforgivable, they threw out all of Cole Porter's songs, except this one." And then he slipped, as if through a hidden door, into "Night and Day," skipping the "beat beat beat of the tom-tom" of the verse, and stepping directly into the passion of the refrain. As he sang, the spotlight narrowed to his head and shoulders, and the rest of the room sank into hurricane-lamp-lit dusk; old couples, and not-so-old (none were young), held hands.

Two manners, two kinds of songs. It is easy to understand, from his life, how Cole Porter managed to catch the mood of the first world—affected, witty, fashionable. Understanding how he plugged into the second world, of seriousness and held hands, is not so easy.

Porter was born in Peru, Indiana, only two generations after the first white man's log cabin went up there. His father was a druggist, and a cipher; his mother had the will in the family. *Her* father had the money, invested in Appalachian timberland, which turned out to be laden with gas and coal.

Propelled by his grandfather's cash and his mother's ambitions (she had his first juvenile compositions printed privately), Porter determined to say good-bye to all that. Said it, at first, unsuccessfully. As a freshman at Yale, "in a checked suit and a salmon tie, with his hair parted in the middle and slicked down," he looked, one Yalie later recalled, "just like a Westerner all dressed up for the East."

Maybe he looked so to the last; the carnation he always wore in his buttonhole suggests the anxious dapperness of the ex-rube.

However anxious he felt, from the beginning of his musical career Porter was a hit with the elite: first at Yale (where they still sing two of his football fight songs), then among the expatriates of twenties Europe. The musical historian Robert Kimball thought Porter's years in Europe gave him the perspective of the lost generation. But it was the lost generation of Dick Diver, not of Gertrude Stein—of the idle rich, not the idle bohemians. Porter had augmented his own means by marrying an older divorcee whose ex had settled over a million dollars of stocks on her. ("He covered them with useful things, / Such as bonds, and stocks, and Paris frocks, / And Oriental pearls in strings."—"Two Little Babes in the Woods.") They lived up to their incomes: when Porter wrote a song about a Jewish factory girl for Fanny Brice, he first played it for her on a grand piano in the ballroom of the Venetian palazzo he was renting. As Lucius Beebe observed, it was "the simple things of life which give pleasure to Mr. Porter—half-million-dollar strings of pearls, Isotta motor cars, cases of double bottles of Grand Chambertin '87, suites at Claridge's, brief trips aboard the *Bremen,* a little grouse shooting."

Although the Porters were attached to each other, their relationship was not sexual, for Porter was gay. "You've never been laid till you've been laid by a man who knows the ropes," he once told Moss Hart. And laying and getting laid seems to have been what gayness amounted to for him. Porter cruised bars and waterfronts for sailors all his life, or called for prostitutes. Depression rates, according to his biographer Charles Schwartz, were ten dollars for a white man, five dollars for a black.

Charm was a lubricant of Porter's life even more important than money. The pattern was fixed as early as Yale, where, although he hated athletics, Porter managed to run with the jocks by being a cheerleader. His looks were one instrument of his charm, and he tended them carefully: every morning he dabbed his eyes with chilled witch hazel, to keep the skin taut. When charm failed, he deflated; he broke off conversations and left parties (including his own) the minute they bored him.

This life—busy, lively, bright as a globe and just as hollow—is obviously the soil from which he harvested the clever songs: the catalogues of famous names, and names now famous only because he catalogued them; the rhymes and rhythms that clack like pool balls; the in-jokes; the double entendres. Other songwriters spun lyrics as adroitly as Porter did; none packed them with such loads of public figures, foreign words, and guidebook destinations.

But then there are the Porter standards about love and longing, which are as direct in their utterance as Irving Berlin, or Handel: "In the roaring traffic's boom, / In the silence of my lonely room, / I think of you." How did the playboy write them?

He had, it is true, a craftsman's earnestness. Hart testified to Porter's "prodigious and unending industry. He worked around the clock." Porter liked to boast about the time he had spent studying composition and theory at the Schola Cantorum in Paris. He boasted a bit much, in fact, for he had to rely on the services of arrangers throughout his career. But he oversaw their work carefully. He also paid particular attention to the ranges and the limitations of the singers for whom he wrote; *Gay Divorcee* did not force Fred Astaire to skate on the thin ice of his high notes.

But if hard work is necessary to express passion, it is not sufficient. Passion itself must be present. It is certainly present, as an end product, in numbers of the songs. Sometimes it throbs in the black and white of the lyrics, even when the lyrics are unlikely. "You're the Top," a catalogue to end all catalogues, breaks into passion by sheer exuberance. After the tenth or twelfth metaphor—Mahatma Gandhi, Napoleon brandy, the Arrow collar, the Coolidge dollar—the glittering superlatives fade into the act of finding superlatives. The song of admiration which seemed like an excuse to be witty actually turns out to be admiring. Sometimes the music carries an emotional charge even when the words do not. "I Get a Kick Out of You" looks on the printed page like a product of the clever life; love is equated with kicks, and one of the things the singer gets no kick from, besides "champagne," is "cocaine"; for years, records altered this to "a bop-type refrain" or "the perfumes of Spain," and sheet music still does. But once the words are fused to the languorous melody, the wit becomes gallantry of an affecting, almost bashful, sort, and we notice the heart behind the lounge lizard's carnation.

What Porter's passions may have been are, with one exception, undiscoverable. Although it had a basis in convenience, and no basis in eros, Porter's marriage was not empty. He and his wife stayed together for thirty-four years, until her death at the age of seventy. For sixteen of those years, she helped him deal with the effects of a riding accident which permanently crippled his right leg. In health, she supplied him with encouragement and security, much as his mother had done during his days in Peru. It is of course an irony that the life of the cosmopolite should have revolved around something as all-American as motherhood. Perhaps Porter appreciated it.

The rest is silence. Maybe there was no "rest"—no other emotions that Porter drew on for his emotional numbers. Maybe, by the alchemy of the psyche and the creative process, mother love produced "Begin the Beguine" and "Every Time We Say Good-bye"— though those are not sentiments typically found on Mother's Day cards. Maybe the passion of the songs existed only in the songs, and only in the songwriter as he wrote them: an emotional exoskeleton, like the shell of a crab.

At least shells last. In a hundred years, the emotional lives of all of us at the Café Carlyle will be as lost as Cole Porter's. Some of us will have left benchmarks in records of marriages contracted, or children reared—unreliable benchmarks, since couples and families can lead lives as coldly empty as those of promiscuous narcissists. Porter left several dozen tunes—which our successors will use, as we used them, to mark occasions in their own emotional lives.

As we made our way out, I saw that the crowd collected at the door for the 11:30 show was a bit younger: a woman in a shoulderless black evening dress, which her companion was slipping further down her shoulders; another woman with a small diamond set in the skin of her right nostril. So, both sides of Short's talent—and Cole Porter's—would be appreciated.

Part 3

ATTACHMENTS

Tough Guys Don't Dance

Christopher Buckley

ONE NIGHT I had the words "Fuck Off" tattooed on the outside edge of my right hand. Some explanation is, obviously, in order.

I was eighteen and drunk, both on the six-pack of beer I'd been plied with to ease the pain of the far more elaborate (and tasteful) tattoo being applied to my biceps and with the thrill of being a young merchant marine on my first night of shore leave in Hong Kong.

But, you logically ask, why those particular two words? A joke on the ship's officers. The offensive phrase was burned through my epidermis on the part of the hand most visible to the recipient of a salute. Get it? I didn't either, on waking up to discover three regions of acute distress: my head, my biceps, and my hand. In a nice bit of karmic comeuppance, my assigned task that day was to swab clean the cargo winches: twelve hours of one-hundred-degree heat, with my newly embroidered hand immersed the whole time in kerosene. Every letter sizzled memorably.

The second question begged by this act of juvenile idiocy is Why do men do these things? I don't mean, Why do men have four-letter words tattooed on their hands? The only other instance that I know of is the Robert Mitchum character in the 1955 movie *The Night of the Hunter.* (How lovely to share this distinction with a famous psychopathic murderer. I must have a swastika tattooed on my forehead and achieve affinity with Charles Manson.) No, what I mean is, Why must some men play the tough guy?

One of the nice things about not being eighteen anymore is

looking back on all those times when you practiced smoking in front of the mirror, impressed your date by revving the engine at the stoplight, tried on twenty pairs of sunglasses until you found the kind Paul Newman wore, talked fuel injectors and .357 Magnums while holding a long-necked beer bottle, and wore blue jeans so tight that you ended up with sore balls and a rash. Yes, one of the nice things about being forty-one and happily married is that you understand how ridiculous all that really was—and how ridiculous it still is.

Sometime between eighteen and forty-one I learned something: that the ones who are really tough never act tough. Unless—as with the saying about never drawing a gun unless you plan to use it—they intend to be tough, in which case it's usually over very fast.

After the merchant marine, I went to Yale, where there was very little macho posturing going on. A lot of intellectual posturing, for sure, but no "Me Tarzan" stuff. This was the early 1970s—Nixon, antiwar demonstrations, women's lib, Alan Alda, *homo sensitivus*—and anyone who even tried to look tough would have been laughed at and told to go enroll in TM (transcendental meditation, for you Generation Xer's).

It wasn't until I started work in New York City as a magazine editor that I met my first genuinely fake tough guy. He was a writer. (Surprise!) He wore mirrored sunglasses—the kind that look exactly like mirrors, that is—and he would come to the office wearing a Porsche racing jacket crammed with stripes and patches. It was made of this silvery material—faux flame-retardant?—so shiny it looked as if it had been made with cast-off astronaut-suit material. At first I was mightily impressed. After four years of Shakespeare, Blake, and Joyce, here was a real-world writer. He smoked Camels; drank "Stoli, up"; made a show of annoying our boss, the editor; and told lurid stories of hanging out with extremely brutal South Bronx street gangs to research the big piece he was doing for us.

But after a time I started to wonder. (The best thing about a good education is it equips you with a good shit detector.) His teeth were unappetizingly brown from nicotine. He coughed a lot and wheezed after climbing a flight of stairs. The editor whom he cast as Walter Burns to his Hildy Johnson confided to me with wry amusement that he had been escorted every inch of the way by New York police during his research on the South Bronx gangs. As for the jacket, it became pellucidly clear that he had never set foot in a Porsche or any other racing car.

The mirrored shades were, I suspect, to cover up the aftereffects of too many Stolis, up, at Elaine's, or, more subtly, perhaps they were just the perfect sunglasses for the Me Decade because they let the beholder see himself in the reflection, invariably improving his opinion of their wearer.

He died ten years later, in his early fifties, of a heart attack, on the tennis court. Not a terribly macho end.

I T WAS PARTLY MY MEMORY of that jacket that led me years later to lock horns publicly with one of my heroes, Garry Trudeau. I'd been working at the White House, writing speeches for then vice president Bush. At the time, Trudeau was going after Bush mercilessly for what he perceived as Bush's slavish loyalty to Reagan, raking him over the coals in strip after strip for sacrificing his "manhood." When the next Banana Republic clothing catalog arrived, I saw in it an effusive endorsement by Trudeau for a leather navy pilot's jacket. Bush had gone off at age eighteen to fly torpedo bombers in the South Pacific against the Japanese; Trudeau had not. I pointed out this irony in a repercussive letter to the *Washington Post*.

Ever since, I've been averse to military fashions on civilians. Flight jackets ought to be earned. Imagine standing in an elevator wearing one with a 388th Fighter Wing insignia and the door opening and someone who'd actually *been* with the 388th getting on.

I'm averse, too, to civilians who talk military, saying things like "Lock and load" when they're merely going into a meeting, or shouting, "Incoming!" when the boss sends down a sharp memo. One of my closest friends served with the Special Forces in Vietnam, and I have never, ever, heard him say, "Lock and load" or "Incoming!" because something wasn't going well that day at the office.

The White House, as anyone who's worked there will confirm, is a veritable platform for macho posturing. I was there during the early

Reagan years, and while it's true that the place did not lack for cow-boy boots, the smell of testosterone roasting around the campfire was by no means peculiar to the Reagan era. Nixon's chief of staff wore a crew cut, and JFK's people liked to one-up one another with the question "Is your wife pregnant? Mine is." White House toys are too tempting for many men (and women): flashing lights, motorcades, *Air Force One,* phone consoles with lots and lots of important-looking buttons, Uzi-toting Secret Service agents, and, most coveted of all, a White House pass on the end of a chain around your neck. I saw peo-ple wear those chains around their necks at dinner parties, pretend-ing they'd forgotten they still had them on. *Whoops. So then I said to the president . . .*

The most conspicuous practitioners of macho on any White House staff are the advance men, the ones who arrange presidential movements and events. They wield a kind of plenipotentiary power. Who's going to tell them no? They work for the president of the United States. I've seen twentysomethings reduce governors of con-sequential states to fuming impotence—and relish every second of it. I watched one tell a government official of a significant foreign power, after viewing the spectacular nineteenth-century palace where the bilateral event would take place, "The facilities will be ade-quate." The documentary *The War Room,* about the Clinton cam-paign staff, shows the swagger that develops when young men get a taste of power. The advantage of the American system of government over, say, the Rwandan system is that in ours the tools of power con-sist of pagers and passes, theirs of guns and machetes. It is harder to laugh off the macho pretensions of a sixteen-year-old Hutu pointing an AK-47 at you.

Guns are certainly more attention-getting than even the coolest sunglasses or the flashiest Porsche jacket. Posturing with guns be-came literal in the 1980s with *Miami Vice,* when Crockett and Tubbs held their *biiig* pistols with both hands, in the combat stance. Up until then, TV cops had been content to hold their weapons in just one hand. (The cooler combat stance was the result of *Vice* producer Michael Mann's having previously directed and produced the film that is recognized by both security and military types as the only one to portray the world of killers with technical realism—*Thief,* starring James Caan.) Dirty Harry managed to empty his .44 Magnum—"the most powerful handgun in the world"—with only one steady hand, but by the 1980s guns were too serious to handle with just one.

I'VE NOTICED, TOO, that guns have become icons of masculinity. Street gangs today initiate members by having them kill whichever passing motorist signals to them that their headlights are off. The last issue of *Spy* magazine carried a piece in which well-known rap musicians talked with fondness about their guns. Clearly we've arrived at a weirdly evolved stage of gun macho. A few weeks ago I was on a jury that convicted a man of gun macho. He had drunk "about twenty-four" beers one day—this according to his own defense witness—and then, when no girls would dance with him at a party, stuck a loaded .22 revolver in the temple of a man who'd got on the elevator at the wrong moment. The police call this type of posturing "ADW (Gun)," assault with a dangerous weapon. It can get you about ten years, but I have little doubt that he'll be back among us soon, probably in need of an even more urgent expression of his compromised manhood.

He was just a small-time punk loser, seeking to impose his own loser status on the other guy. The tough-guy act I find most repellent is the one affected by some Wall Streeters. Michael Lewis got their number in his delightful book *Liar's Poker* when he wrote about show-off million-dollar bets and swaggering traders with their cigars, scatologies, and crude misogynies. Most of the really sick jokes— of the *Challenger* disaster or the Michael Jackson variety—I'm told, originate on Wall Street.

Tom Wolfe found the perfect name for this breed of puffed-up bantam cock in *The Bonfire of the Vanities:* Masters of the Universe. In the ridiculous movie version, poor Tom Hanks did what he could with Sherman McCoy, given the deplorable script, and managed a few nice moments of swagger, as when he shrugs over losing half a billion dollars of a client's money and grins and says to a fellow MOTU, "We're not going to get upset about $600 million, are we?"

Michael Douglas did a fine job of showing the effect of too much money on the prostate with his portrayal of Gordon Gekko in *Wall Street,* shouting "Lock and load!" to his assistant as he launches another hostile takeover.

Give me the posturing of the businessmen of yesteryear any day. At least this one: Sally Bedell Smith, in her biography of William Paley, founder of CBS, recounts a gem of an instance. Paley was visiting his Long Island neighbor John Hay Whitney, owner of the *Herald Tribune.* "To Paley," Smith wrote, "Jock Whitney embodied the ultimate in American masculine style. . . . A gentle rivalry flecked their friendship as a result. Once while watching television with Whitney at Greentree, Paley wanted to change the channel. 'Where's your clicker?' Paley asked, figuring Jock would have a remote-control switch at his fingertips. Jock calmly pressed a buzzer, and his butler walked up to the TV set to make the switch."

Whitney had grown up in the era of Teddy Roosevelt's "Speak softly and carry a big stick." (And clicker.) Lately, U.S. foreign policy seems to be all talk and no dick. Here was Clinton on the campaign trail: "The Serbian aggression against Bosnia-Herzegovina . . . must end. It is time for America, acting in concert with its allies, to exert strong leadership." This is not to suggest that America ought to send in the cavalry in an attempt to eradicate religious and ethnic hatreds that go back half a millennium: only that talking tough without follow-through looks as ridiculous on nations as it does on eighteen-year-olds, but with far worse potential for trouble. Bush's words after Saddam Hussein's invasion of Kuwait, "This will not stand," would now sound pretty hollow if Saddam were still receiving his mail in Kuwait City. General Colin Powell was not putting on the macho when he announced his war plan with a matter-of-factness startling to our government pronouncement—jaded ears, "First we are going to cut [the Iraqi army] off," he said. "Then we are going to kill it." Powell was the most plainspoken military man since Sherman.

PEOPLE MADE FUN OF REAGAN for playing the tough guy, just an old ham actor turned president, but in the end there was somehow something convincing about his toughness. Certainly, the Evil Empire was convinced; after the fall of the Soviet Union, it was learned that in the early 1980s the Kremlin thought Reagan was planning to go to war against them if they pursued their policy of foreign aggression. This said more for their paranoia than it did for Reagan's bellicosity, but they blinked first, and the Iron Curtain came down within a year of Reagan's leaving office, so the historians may decide it was more than just acting. He certainly demonstrated toughness of the personal kind when he took Hinckley's bullet in the chest. It's a test I fervently hope I never have to take, but in the event I do, I hope I'll have the scrappiness, as he did, to ask the doctors as I go under if they're all Republicans.

The tattoo? The one on my biceps is still there, a little faded but clear enough to alarm small children on the beach. The one on my hand is no longer there.

About ten years after that night in Hong Kong, I was in the Zarzuela palace interviewing the king of Spain—a *muy macho* fellow and very admirable—and about halfway through our hour I noticed his eyes being drawn to my hand, which I then assiduously tried to hide, not wanting to have to translate "fuck off" into Castilian for His Majesty Juan Carlos de Borbón y Borbón, king of Spain. When I got back to New York, I went to a dermatologist. It was prelaser back then, so it took an old-fashioned glistening steel scalpel to cut it out—thank God I hadn't asked for "Don't Tread on Me"—and fifteen stitches to close it. It hurt, and this time there was no six-pack to ease the pain. Now, I look at the scar and think, What was I thinking?

Dialogues with the Dead

Christopher Clausen

MY GREAT-GRANDMOTHER'S EIGHTH PREGNANCY was a difficult one. After all, she was nearly forty-eight years old when it began. Of her five living children (two others having died in infancy), the two oldest, my grandfather and his sister Marie, were already in their mid-teens. Contrary to what might have been expected, however, she carried the fetus to term and in the autumn of 1896 gave birth to a healthy boy who would live through most of the following century. Her own prognosis was not so fortunate. Never fully recovered from the birth of her final child, after twenty-one months she knew she was dying. Moreover, she knew only too well that her grief-stricken husband—"not a good provider," in the language of the day—would be hard-pressed to maintain an infant and three other small children, whatever help the oldest son, now at work but eager to enlist in the Spanish-American War, might provide. She was, like her husband, an immigrant. Her own family was far away.

Promise me, she said to her daughter Marie in German, *promise me that you will keep the family together and raise your brother Charlie.* What could a late-nineteenth-century girl say to such an appeal? Besides, she adored her mother. *Mama,* she answered inevitably, *I promise.* In that world, that was how they did things. What is more, they sometimes meant it. My great-aunt Marie kept the family together, raised her brother Charlie, and, for good measure, helped raise his children and grandchildren. She never married and lived to be ninety-eight. When Charlie died a few years before she did, she felt reasonably enough that life had become absurd and that it was high time to depart. Her final wish was to be buried in the grave of her mother, to whom she had so spectacularly kept a promise made eighty-one years earlier, and with whom she had so long carried on a dialogue that furnished the pattern for an entire life. Near the end of 1979, the customs of the late twentieth century grudgingly yielded to the sentiments of the nineteenth, and the ancient grave was reopened for its second occupant.

The communication of the dead, according to T. S. Eliot, is tongued with fire beyond the language of the living. Death has freed them to tell us things they had no words for in life. Being dead, they presumably do not mind what shapes we impose on them. All the same, they have their revenge: by admitting their influence through dialogue with them, we impose lasting shapes and obligations on ourselves as well. The dead can strengthen and steady us; they can also drive us crazy. People in superstitious ages imagined ghosts to explain their sense of being haunted, of involuntarily carrying on transactions with those who had died. In more modern language, our conversations with the dead are the ultimate form of projection, in which we define ourselves most revealingly and recognize, consciously or not, our actual status in the world. Whether or not we choose to be buried in the same grave, there is after all that perfect bond of death between the generations.

According to Dr. Milton Helpern, former chief medical examiner of New York City, death is "the irreversible cessation of life. Death may be due to a wide variety of diseases and disorders, but in every case the underlying physiological cause is a breakdown in the body's oxygen cycle." Law, if not medicine, distinguishes rigorously between death from natural causes, accident, homicide, or suicide. So do the survivors; our dialogue with someone who has been murdered is quite different in tone and substance from our colloquy with one who died of heart disease. Much depends also on the age at death. Like cause of death, the age at which one's oxygen cycle breaks down communicates a definite view of the universe to the living. In contemporary America we hold far fewer dialogues with dead children than took place in centuries when infant mortality was a frequent guest in every family, and the death of someone who failed to live out a normal life span is a correspondingly more powerful cause of grief and bitterness. We tend to feel that such a person has been the victim of an outrage. In many ritualistic or traditional cultures, on the other hand, "to be a dead member of one's society is the individual's ultimate social status," according to John Middleton—"ultimate" meaning not only "final" but "highest." Such societies find it easier, at least abstractly, to accept the inevitability of deaths at many ages and to maintain an equable dialogue with their vanished members, although that acceptance does not necessarily lessen either the grief or the extravagance of its expression.

"Must I remember?" the extravagantly grieving Hamlet asks himself reprovingly two months after the untimely death of his father. Memory of the dead is of course the beginning of dialogue with them, a dialogue usually commenced with the rituals of funeral and commitment to the earth. In Hamlet's case, as in many modern ones, the ritual has been foreshortened, with the predictable consequence that memory and dialogue acquire an unhealthy power over the survivors. This power is all the greater for being unanticipated. For we address the dead constantly if they were close to us; and if they had a powerful effect on us in life, they answer. Oh yes, they talk back, make demands, insist on undivided attention. Raise my family, share my grave—these are benign exigencies. Too often, the ghost demands revenge.

> Remember thee?
> Aye, thou poor ghost, whiles memory holds a seat
> In this distracted globe. Remember thee?
> Yea, from the table of my memory
> I'll wipe away all trivial fond records,
> All saws of books, all forms, all pressures past
> That youth and observation copied there,
> And thy commandment all alone shall live
> Within the book and volume of my brain,
> Unmixed with baser matter.

How to converse with a ghost who demands vengeance? To adopt its wishes as one's own is to become possessed, whether the ghost's name is Hamlet the elder, or Moses, or Mohammed; whether the essence of its demand is to kill the usurper or repossess the land he took. Share my grave. To deny the ghost, on the other hand, may involve such a renunciation of one's own identity as to be nearly impossible—and the ghost will still be there in any event, as dead as ever. Falling between two stools, as Hamlet did, may be the worst of all choices: as in the play, it may simply widen the power of the ghost to encompass other fates besides that of the individual possessed, leaving the family and the state in ruins and Horatio alone to tell the tale. But possession rarely involves much choice.

Hamlet, in the opinion of many critics, is a modern figure trapped in an archaic drama: a man not given to believing ghosts or committing bloody acts of revenge. That is his tragedy. The enlightened mind becomes genuinely unhinged when faced with such demands, or with such a demander. Ghosts, after all, are written into plays to entertain the groundlings, whose benighted state makes them more susceptible to haunting. Although groundlings still exist and ghosts are still created for them—television and Hollywood give ample recent instances—the dead, whether friendly or hateful, hold no dialogues with the truly modern mind. We have learned to outgrow all that. Life is for the living; the healthy mind looks to the future. We cremate the dead and scatter their ashes, dissolving not only the spirit but the material body itself into thin air. There is no grave to share. Nobody can haunt us.

"A ghost in search of vengeance," asks the ghostly narrator of Robertson Davies's novel *Murther & Walking Spirits*—"what is it to do in such a world as ours?"

The ghost, of course, was really Hamlet's unconscious speaking. Self-assertion and the desire for revenge, muddled up with Oedipal longings for his sexually accomplished mother, projected themselves quite naturally onto the image of the dead father, who then walked the stage as a ghost. Of course. The word "psychology" would not be invented for another two centuries. We know how to understand the character Hamlet and the play itself not just differently but better than any Elizabethan. In a sense, that is prefectly true. How important that sense may be is more debatable. In Shaw's *Saint Joan*, an indisputably modern play, the title character is informed that the voices of long-dead saints who talk to her are in fact the product of her imagination. "Of course," she answers unabashedly. "That is how the messages of God come to us." To take the ghost out of its shadowy existence in the world and enshrine it in the mind only increases its power, unless the implication is that understanding the true locus of the haunting somehow dispels it. Clearly it does no such thing. The dead whose final resting place is in our mind are no less potent than those who are assumed to keep an unquiet vigil in the world of space. Real ghosts could appear only at certain times and places, and they could be exorcised. Psychological ghosts, even of the friendly dead, have no such limitations. Once our dead are buried within us, they can stay there for as long as we live—longer insofar as the patterns they embody are passed on through us to others by way of upbringing or genetic inheritance. Ignoring them is no solution. The less we hold dialogue with them, the more unruly their effect on us becomes. We can never get away from a voice that lives inside us.

Sometimes the voices within are collective and historical rather than individual as are the ghosts of our private dead. My father-in-law was a career naval officer who served as a carrier pilot during World War II. Like a surprising number of American officers in that war, he was the grandson of a Confederate veteran and half-consciously saw his own war as a prolongation of his grandfather's, not in terms of the issues involved but rather as an opportunity to vindicate an honorable defeat by winning an even greater struggle eighty years later. Somehow the significance of the past could be changed by valor in the present, not exactly avenging a loss but perhaps removing the shame or sting of it. Although this particular way of looking at World War II was restricted to a small part of a single generation, the habit of seeing a current series of events in the light of the Civil War was not. Much of twentieth-century American history involves a dialogue with the ghosts of the Civil War, a conflict in which more Americans died than in all our other wars combined. If the civil rights movement had in some respects to defeat the ghosts of the Confederacy all over again, it also drew strength from the black heroes of Fort Wagner and many another battle a hundred years before.

The ghost of Abraham Lincoln, the commander in chief, remains the most potent figure in American history, now reinforced by that of Martin Luther King, Jr.

In the last year of his life, when his eyesight and many other things were failing, my father-in-law asked my wife to read him long stretches from Shelby Foote's narrative history of the Civil War as a preparation for death. It was not that he had any wish to refight the war, still less that he expected Stonewall Jackson to meet him on the threshold of Valhalla with an entrance examination. He was a modern man with, for the most part, modern beliefs. No, it was rather that having (again like many Southern men of his generation) lived in the shadow of these events all his life, he wished to be as clear as possible about them before he died. There were lessons to be learned about living and dying; this seemed the best available way for him to learn them. What the dead had to say now was very different from what they had communicated forty or sixty years ago. One last long conversation with the ghosts, perhaps, and then he would be ready to join them. The Crater was the battle he liked to hear about most, but there was nothing bloodthirsty or sentimental in his reactions. Rather he was closing a circle that had begun when he first heard about Southern victories and defeats in childhood, preparing for death in a way that was appropriate to the life he had lived, like a cheerful stoic.

"Then with the knowledge of death as walking one side of me," wrote Walt Whitman in 1865, commemorating Lincoln and the dead of the Civil War,

> And the thought of death close-walking the other side of me,
> And I in the middle as with companions, and as holding the hands
> of companions,
> I fled forth to the hiding receiving night that talks not.

Because he had so thoughtfully assimilated himself to the dead at the end of his life, and because, in the almost forgotten phrase, he was full of years, the ghost of my father-in-law is a quiet one, a familiar daily presence that inspires and does not disturb.

EARLY DEATH is something else again. To die with manifest unful-filled promise, to leave grieving parents behind, seems a violation of the natural order. These dead, if we were close to them, are the object not just of mourning but of shock and guilt, as though we should have been able to foresee and prevent. They speak of inconsolable loss, and a long time must pass before we can hear anything else they have to say.

The Boston cancer specialists thought they had cured my brother of lymphoma not once but twice. A political scientist of great talents, he had had a somewhat unlucky career, owing to the depressed academic job market of the seventies and, after he had gone into government, the change of administrations in 1981. But he had begun to work his way back, interrupted by chemotherapy and a marrow transplant, and had even managed to complete a book on nuclear proliferation in which many publishers expressed interest. A few days after he signed a contract for its publication, his doctor informed him that he had at most three months to live.

We drove up to visit him immediately. When we arrived he was in the hospital, and they discharged him after a few days. Perhaps there was hope—perhaps new therapies as yet untried—there are doctors and there are doctors. One of them was optimistic. My sister-in-law pretended to believe, but there was no hope, really, and my brother was full of bitterness. It was not *Why me?* It sounded more like *Why now?* Why not earlier or later? He was anxious for his family in a way that only someone with a deep capacity for happiness, a beloved eight-year-old son, and hardly any life insurance can be. That anxiety was the strongest note in everything he said.

It would be pointless to give details of the conversations we had with him then, or later by telephone. All of them were like conversations with someone who is already dead, who is looking back from the other side and seeing something quite different from the other people in the room. How does one discuss plans for the future of a widow and her son when her young husband is the most determined of the discussers? From a great distance he watched us sadly as we talked about mortgages, school fees, the raising of a child in which he would have no further living part to play. From whatever place he now inhabited, he pressed all the right questions, asked for and received all the right promises from everyone, unerringly noticed every feature of the situation that would soon face his survivors. Unwilling to die but perceiving no alternative, he expressed in his speech and actions an equal mixture of courage and anger. Eventually the anger faded, leaving only sorrow, courage, and deep concern for the two who needed him most.

"There must be wisdom with great Death," Tennyson wrote after the death of another young man: "The dead shall look me through and through." My brother unwillingly put his house in order, made such peace as he could, and died on an afternoon in early summer, the three months proving in the end to be thirty-eight days. At the funeral his father and two of his brothers were pallbearers, while his mother sat among the mourners, and I felt that whatever was in the casket was looking us through and through.

A depressing story, certainly, though far from a unique one in this or any other century. What kinds of dialogue will follow such a death? Of course it's too early to say. Like those of a true ghost, my brother's purposes must be fulfilled in the lives of others, in contrast to those of most people who live to what is thought to be a normal age. For the time being, he is an unquiet ghost who speaks only of loss and incompletion, who asks only about his wife and son and can be answered only with reassurances. Later on he will have other things to tell those who knew him, and they will speak to him less frantically. He was a much-loved person, not only by his family, and the value of his legacy—and consequently the richness of the dialogues in which he will participate while those who loved him are still alive—will be very great. The scope of those dialogues, like everything else in which the living take part, is unpredictable.

In a sense, any remembered dead person eventually says to us: *I lived in a different time, subject to different pressures, part of a story that has now, if not ended, at least reached a different stage, with different characters.* And later still, if anyone is around to hear: *Even if I had lived a normal life, I would be dead now.* Beyond that, is everything they tell us projection? Perhaps, in a way. If so, it is projection of a very special kind, in which by virtue of their being dead we find ourselves extended far beyond our everyday limits of understanding and learn things about ourselves and our world that no living person would tell us. In these strange dialogues, the dead do indeed look us through and through.

MANY SURVIVORS of the Final Solution feel that they carry the dead within them, an unbearable burden of guilt and remembrance. Here the conversation with the dead, who may include all the members of one's family, must surely reach the limits of possibility. Those who survived the atomic bombings of Hiroshima and Nagasaki tell a slightly different version: they sense that they carry death itself inside them. Perhaps such extreme calamities offer one reason that our time is so reluctant to be reminded of death as the common fate or of any claims that the dead might have on the living.

> They used to pour millet on graves or poppy seeds
> To feed the dead who would come disguised as birds.
> I put this book here for you, who once lived
> So that you should visit us no more,

Czeslaw Milosz wrote in the ruined Warsaw of 1945. If we pay them too much or too little attention, the dead can eat us up.

Even to us ordinary people, the dead speak all the time. Willingly or not, we conduct endless dialogues with them. People who live in periods with no widely accepted way of visualizing the status and influence of the dead will invent new ones or try to revive old ones; hence the widespread half beliefs in reincarnation and New Age varieties of spiritualism. On a more everyday level, the husband who has lost a wife, the wife who has lost a husband, says, *How could you do this to me?* The other answers, *I had no choice. I would much rather have gone to the beach with you as we planned.* And sometimes, *You should get out more.* And even, *You should remarry, for your own sake and the sake of the children.* Often enough, we do what the dead tell us.

Finally, it is the dead who tell us who we are, not just as individuals (though that too) but as a species of animals that needs reminding. They tell us constantly that life is a rough place and nobody gets out of it alive. Or as Montaigne put it, "Live as long as you please, you will strike nothing off the time you will have to spend dead." Our dialogue with the dead is a conversation between equals. As late-twentieth-century people, we tend to find this familiar news morbid and tasteless, like a Victorian funeral. After all, we make a fetish of youth and health, the unbounded liberation of the self from all forms of oppression, which must surely include the freedom not to die if we so choose. The impersonal objectivity of death is an affront to everything we want to believe.

That reaction only increases the power of the ghosts whom we try so hard, and with so little success, to confine in the safe, invisible place we call the dead past. But the ghosts tell us, either kindly or cruelly depending mostly on our willingness to hear, that they actually represent our future. Share my grave whether you will or not. That irrefutable announcement, which they are now free to speak, is the beginning of all the other things we can learn from them, and if we pretend not to hear it, the rest of what they have to say will be unintelligible.

You'd Cry Too If It Happened to You

Peggy Noonan

N HIS LIFETIME he had seen America rise and rise and rise, some sort of golden legend to her own people, some sort of impossible fantasy to others . . . rise and rise and rise—and then . . . the golden legend crumbled, overnight the fall began, the heart went out of it, a too complacent and uncaring people awoke to find themselves naked with the winds of the world howling around their ears. . . . A universal quilt enshrouded . . . all who participated in those times. . . . Now there was a time of uneasiness . . . when all thinking men fretted and worried desperately about "how to catch up" and "how to get ahead"; and also, in the small hours of the night's cold terror, about what it would be like if America couldn't catch up, if history should have decided once and for all that America should never again be permitted to get ahead.

Well, so much for Camelot.

When Allen Drury wrote those words—they set the scene for his classic political novel, *Advise and Consent*—he was trying to capture the mood of America in 1959, as the peaceful and composed Eisenhower era receded, John Kennedy geared up for the presidency and the go-go sixties waited to be born. We remember those days as innocent and hopeful; Drury recorded them as anxious and depressed. Which demonstrates a small but not insignificant point: It is writers—journalists, screenwriters, novelists, newswriters—we turn to more than anyone to tell us exactly how our country is doing, and they are precisely the last people who would accurately point out that in the long tape of history this is a pretty good few inches.

There are many reasons for this—catching and tagging whatever angst is floating around is their job—but the biggest is simple.

Writers always see their time as marked by pain because it always is. Children die. People lose their homes. Life is sad. To declare the relative happiness of your era is to sound stupid and uncaring, as if you don't know people are suffering, when people always are.

I am inclined toward the long view. The life of people on earth is obviously better now than it has ever been—certainly much better than it was five hundred years ago when people beat each other with cats. This may sound silly, but now and then when I read old fairy tales and see an illustration of a hunchbacked hag with no teeth and bumps on her nose who lives by herself in the forest, I think: People looked like that once. They lived like that. There were no doctors, no phones, and people lived in the dark in a hole in a tree. It was terrible. It's much better now.

But we are not happier. I believe we are just cleaner, more attractive sad people than we used to be.

THERE ARE SERIOUS reasons members of my generation in particular are feeling a high level of anxiety and unhappiness these days, but first a word about how we "know" this: the polls.

I used to like polls because I like vox pop, and polls seemed a good way to get a broad sampling. But now I think the vox has popped—the voice has cracked from too many command performances. Polls are contributing to a strange new volatility in public opinion.

A year ago, at the conclusion of the Gulf War, George Bush's approval ratings were at nearly 90 percent. As I write, they are 30 percent. This is a huge drop, and in a way a meaningless one. President Bush didn't deserve 90 percent support for having successfully executed a hundred-hour ground war; Abe Lincoln deserved a 90 percent for preserving the nation. Bush didn't deserve 30 percent support because the economy is in recession; John Adams deserved a 30 percent for the Alien and Sedition Acts. It is all so exaggerated.

The dramatic rises and drops are fueled in part by mass media and their famous steady drumbeat of what's not working, from an increase in reported child abuse to a fall in savings. When this tendency is not prompted by ideology it is legitimate: Good news isn't news. But the volatility is also driven by the polls themselves. People think they have to have an answer when they are questioned by pollsters, and they think it has to be "intelligent" and "not naive." This has the effect of hardening opinions that haven't even been formed yet. Poll questions do not invite subtlety of response. This dispels ambiguity, when a lot of thoughts and opinions are ambiguous.

And we are polled too often. We are constantly having our temperature taken, like a hypochondriac who is looking for the reassurance that no man can have, that is, that he will not die.

I once knew a man who was so neurotically fearful about his physical well-being that in the middle of conversations he would quietly put his hand to his wrist. He was taking his pulse. When I was seven or eight years old, I became anxious that I would stop breathing unless I remembered every few seconds to inhale. This mania was exhausting. At night, on the verge of sleep, I would come awake in a panic, gulping for air.

People who take their pulse too often are likely to make it race; people obsessed with breathing are likely to stop. Nations that use polls as daily temperature readings inevitably give inauthentic readings, and wind up not reassured but demoralized.

THERE ARE REASONS for our discontent. Each era has its distinguishing characteristics; each time a big barrel of malaise rolls down the hill there are specific and discrete facts rolling around inside. Here are some of ours:

Once in America if you lost your job—if you were laid off from the assembly line at Ford, for instance—you had reason to believe you'd be rehired. Business cycle, boom and bust—sooner or later they'd call you back. There was a certain security in the insecurity. Now it's different. Now if you're laid off from your job as the number two guy in public affairs at the main Jersey office of a phone company, you have reason to fear you'll never be hired back into that or any white-collar job, because employment now is connected less to boom and bust than to changing realities, often changing technologies, in the marketplace. The telephone company doesn't need you anymore.

You are a boomer, and obscurely oppressed. But there is nothing obscure about your predicament. So many people are relying on you! You and your wife waited to have children, and now they're eight and ten and you're forty-eight—too late to start over, to jeopardize the $75,000 a year you earn. And if you tried, you would lose your medical coverage.

Your mother and father are going to live longer than parents have ever lived and will depend on you to take care of them as they (as you, at night, imagine it) slide from mild senility to full dementia. Your children will have a longer adolescence and expect you to put them through college just as Mom and Dad are entering a home.

Your biggest personal asset is your house, which has lost value. You have a hefty mortgage, your pension fund is underfunded, you don't think your Social Security benefits are secure, and you do not trust the banks.

The last may be the most serious in terms of how people feel. In the years since the depression we have been able to trust that the institutions we put our savings into would be there tomorrow and pay us interest. We don't know that anymore; most of us are afraid that all of a sudden a major bank, strained from its own feckless investments to middle-aged mall builders who make political contributions, will fold, taking the other banks with it.

We wonder, "in the small hours of the night's cold terror," if there is another depression and the banks fail, how will I and my family live? How will we buy food and gas and pay for electricity? We don't know how to grow things! What will we eat if it all collapses?

I THINK THE ESSENTIAL daily predicament of modern, intelligent, early-middle-age Americans—the boomers, the basketball in the python—is this: There is no margin for error anymore. Everything has to continue as it is for us to continue with the comfort we have. And we do not believe that everything will continue as it is.

It is embarrassing to live in the most comfortable time in the history of man and not be happy. We all have so much!

Think of the set of *The Honeymooners*. What did Ralph and Alice have in 1955? A small rented apartment with a table, two chairs, a bureau, a picture on a faded wall. The set designer was spoofing the average.

Think of the set of *Family Ties*: the couches, the lamps, the VCRs, the color TVs. There is art on the walls. The children had expensive orthodontia.

You will say, one show was about the working class, the other the middle class. But that's the point: The average couple was working-class then and is middle-class now.

We have so much more than Mom and Dad that we can't help but feel defensive about feeling so bad, and paying off our charge cards so late, and being found in the den surfing from channel to channel at 3 A.M., staring back at Brian Lamb's eyes.

And there's this: We know that we suffer—and we get no credit for it! Sometimes we feel the bitterness of the generation that fought World War I, but we cannot write our memoirs and say "good-bye to all that," cannot tell stories of how our boots rotted in the mud, cannot deflect the neighborhood praise and be modest as we lean against the bar. They don't know we're brave. They don't know we fight in trenches too.

I find myself thinking of Auden's words about the average man in 1939, as darkness gathered over Europe—the "sensual man-in-the-street," barely aware of his emptiness, who promised that he will be "true to the wife," that someday he will be happy and good.

Auden called his era the "age of anxiety." I think what was at the heart of the dread in those days, just a few years into modern times, was that we could tell we were beginning to lose God—banishing him from the scene, from our consciousness, losing the assumption that he was part of the daily drama, or its maker. And it is a terrible thing when people lose God. Life is difficult and people are afraid, and to be without God is to lose man's great source of consolation and coherence. There is a phrase I once heard or made up that I think of when I think about what people with deep faith must get from God: the love that assuages all.

I don't think it is unconnected to the boomers' predicament that as a country we were losing God just as they were being born.

At the same time, a huge revolution in human expectation was beginning to shape our lives, the salient feature of which is the expectation of happiness.

It is 1956 in the suburbs, in the summer. A man comes home from work, parks the car, slouches up the driveway. His white shirt clings softly to his back. He bends for the paper, surveys the lawn, waves to a neighbor. From the house comes his son, freckled, ten. He jumps on his father; they twirl on the lawn. Another day done. Now water the lawn, eat fish cakes, watch some TV, go to bed, do it all again tomorrow.

Is he happy? No. Why should he be? We weren't put here to be happy. But the knowledge of his unhappiness does not gnaw. Everyone is unhappy, or rather everyone has a boring job, a marriage that's turned to disinterest, a life that's turned to sameness. And because he does not expect to be happy the knowledge of his unhappiness does not weigh on him. He looks perhaps to other, more eternal forms of comfort.

Somewhere in the seventies, or the sixties, we started expecting to be happy and changed our lives (left town, left families, switched jobs) if we were not. And society strained and cracked in the storm.

I think we have lost the old knowledge that happiness is overrated—that, in a way, life is overrated. We have lost, somehow, a sense of mystery—about us, our purpose, our meaning, our role. Our ancestors believed in two worlds and understood this to be the solitary, poor, nasty, brutish and short one. We are the first generations of man that actually expected to find happiness here on earth, and our search for it has caused such—unhappiness. The reason: if you do not believe in another, higher world, if you believe only in the flat material world around you, if you believe that this is your only chance at happiness—if that is what you believe, then you are not disappointed when the world does not give you a good measure of its riches, you are despairing.

In a Catholic childhood in America, you were once given, as the answer to the big questions: It is a mystery. As I grew older I was impatient with this answer. Now I am probably as old, intellectually, as

I am going to get, and more and more I think: It is a mystery. I am more comfortable with this now; it seems the only rational and scientific answer.

My generation, faced as it grew with a choice between religious belief or existential despair, chose . . . marijuana. Now we are in our cabernet stage. (Jung wrote in a letter that he saw a connection between spirits and The Spirit; sometimes when I go into a church and see how modern Catholics sometimes close their eyes and put their hands out, palms up, as if to get more of God on them, it reminds me of how kids in college used to cup their hands delicately around the smoke of the pipe, and help it waft toward them.) Is it possible that our next step is a deep turning to faith, and worship? Is it starting now with tentative New Age steps?

It is a commonplace to note that we have little faith in our institutions, no faith in Congress, in the White House, little faith in what used to be called the establishment—big business, big media, the Church. But there's a sort of schizoid quality in this. We have contempt for the media, but we have respect for newscasters and columnists. When we meet them we're impressed and admiring. We respect priests and rabbis and doctors. But we are cynical about what they're part of.

It's also famously true that we hate Congress and keep reelecting our congressmen. I don't know how to reconcile this. Sometimes I think there is a tinny, braying quality to our cynicism. We are like a city man in a Dreiser novel, quick with a wink that shows we know the real lowdown, the real dope. This kind of cynicism seems to me . . . a dodge. When you don't believe, you don't have to take part, invest, become part of. Skepticism is healthy, and an appropriate attitude toward those who wield power. But cynicism is corrosive and self-corrupting. Everyone at the top is a moral zero; I'll be a moral zero too.

B UT OUR CYNICISM is also earned. Our establishments have failed us. I imagine an unspoken dialogue with a congressman in Washington:

VOTER: Do what is right!

POLITICIAN: But you'll kill me!

VOTER: Maybe, but do it anyway! I hired you to go to Congress to make hard decisions to help our country. Take your term, do it, and go home. Kill yourself!

POLITICIAN: But I have seniority and expertise and I'm up to speed on the issues. Replace me and it'll be six years before he knows what I know.

VOTER: Well maybe we don't want him to know what you know. Maybe we want someone dumb enough not to know what's impossible and brave enough to want to do what's right.

POLITICIAN: But I love this job.

VOTER: But we never intended Congress to be a career. We meant it to be a pain in the neck, like jury duty. And maybe I won't kill you. Maybe I'll respect you. Take a chance!

The biggest scandal of the modern era, and the one that will prove to have most changed our politics, is the S&L scandal, in which certain members of both parties colluded to give their campaign contributors what they wanted at the expense of innocent taxpayers who will pay the bill, in billions, for generations.

Watergate pales, Teapot Dome pales. It is what was behind the rise of Perot. The voters think Washington is a whorehouse and every four years they get a chance to elect a new piano player. They would rather burn the whorehouse down. They figured Perot for an affable man with a torch. They looked at him and saw a hand grenade with a bad haircut.

Finally, another thing has changed in our lifetimes: People don't have faith in America's future anymore.

I don't know many people aged thirty-five to fifty who don't have a sense that they were born into a healthier country, and that they have seen the culture deteriorate before their eyes.

We tell pollsters we are concerned about "leadership" and "America's prospects in a changing world," but a lot of this is a reflection of a boomer secret: We all know the imperfect America we were born into was a better country than the one we live in now, that is, the one we are increasingly responsible for.

You don't have to look far for the fraying of the social fabric. Crime, the schools, the courts. Watch Channel 35 in New York and see your culture. See men and women, homo- and hetero-, dressed in black leather, masturbating each other and simulating sadomasochistic ritual. Realize this is pumped into everyone's living room, including your own, where your eight-year-old is flipping channels. Then talk to a pollster. You too will declare you are pessimistic about your country's future; you too will say we are on the wrong track.

Remember your boomer childhood in the towns and suburbs. You had physical security. You were safe. It is a cliché to say it, but it can't be said enough: We didn't lock the doors at night in the old America. We slept with the windows open! The cities were better. A man and woman falling in love could stroll the parks of a city at 2 A.M. Douglas Edwards, the venerable newscaster, once told me about what he called the best time. He sat back in the newsroom one afternoon in the late seventies, in the middle of the creation of the current world, and said, "New York in the Fifties—there was nothing like it, it was clean and it was peaceful. You could walk the streets!" He stopped, and laughed at celebrating with such emotion what should be commonplace.

You know what else I bet he thought, though he didn't say it. It was a more human world in that it was a sexier world, because sex was still a story. Each high-school senior class had exactly one girl who got pregnant and one guy who was the father, and it was the town's annual scandal. Either she went somewhere and had the baby and put it up for adoption, or she brought it home as a new baby sister, or the couple got married and the town topic changed. It was a stricter, tougher society, but its bruising sanctions came from ancient wisdom.

We have all had a moment when all of a sudden we looked around and thought: The world is changing, I am seeing it change. This is for me the moment when the new America began: I was at a graduation ceremony at a public high school in New Jersey. It was 1971 or 1972. One by one a stream of black-robed students walked across the stage and received their diplomas. And a pretty young girl with red hair, big under her graduation gown, walked up to receive hers. The auditorium stood and applauded. I looked at my sister. "She's going to have a baby."

The girl was eight months pregnant and had had the courage to go through with her pregnancy and take her finals and finish school despite society's disapproval.

BUT: SOCIETY WASN'T DISAPPROVING. It was applauding. Applause is a right and generous response for a young girl with grit and heart. And yet, in the sound of that applause I heard a wall falling, a thousand-year wall, a wall of sanctions that said: We as a society do not approve of teenaged unwed motherhood because it is not good for the child, not good for the mother, and not good for us.

The old America had a delicate sense of the difference between the general ("We disapprove") and the particular ("Let's go help her"). We had the moral self-confidence to sustain the paradox, to sustain the distance between "official" disapproval and "unofficial" succor. The old America would not have applauded the girl in the big graduation gown, but some of its individuals would have helped her not only materially but with some measure of emotional support. We don't so much anymore. For all our tolerance and talk we don't show much love to what used to be called girls in trouble. As we've gotten more open-minded we've gotten more closed-hearted.

Message to society: What you applaud, you encourage. And: Watch out what you celebrate.

(This section was written before Dan Quayle and Murphy Brown, about which one might say he said a right thing in the wrong way and was the wrong man to say it. Quayle is not a stupid man, but his expressions reveal a certain tropism toward the banal. This is a problem with some Republican men. There is a kind of heavyhanded dorkishness in their approach that leaves them unable to persuasively address questions requiring delicacy; they always sound judgmental when they mean to show concern.)

Two final thoughts.

1. We might all feel better if we took personally the constitutional injunction to "preserve and protect."

Every parent in America knows that we're not doing a very good job of communicating to our children what America is and has been. When we talk about immigration, pro or con, there is, I think, an unspoken anxiety: We are not inculcating in America's new immigrants—as someone inculcated in our grand- and great-grandparents—the facts of American history and why America deserves to be loved. And imperfect as it is, and as we are, we boomers love our country.

In our cities we teach not the principles that made our country—the words of the Founding Fathers, the moral force that led us to endure four years of horror to free slaves, a space program that expanded the frontiers of human knowledge, the free market of ideas and commerce and expression that yielded miracles like a car in every garage, and mass-produced housing. We are lucky in that the central fact of our country is both inspiring and true: America is the place formed of the institutionalization of miracles. Which made it something new in the history of man, something—better.

We do not teach this as a society, and we teach it insufficiently in our schools. We are more inclined to teach that Columbus's encounter with the Americas produced, most significantly, the spreading of venereal disease to their innocent indigenous peoples.

We teach the culture of resentment, of grievance, of victimization. Our children are told by our media and our leaders that we are a racist nation in which minorities are and will be actively discriminated against.

If we are demoralized we have, at least in this, demoralized ourselves. We are certainly demoralizing our children, and giving them a darker sense of their future than is warranted.

2. It's odd to accuse boomers of reticence, but I think we have been reticent, at least in this:

When we talk about the difficulties of our lives and how our country has changed we become embarrassed and feel . . . dotty. Like someone's old aunt rocking on the porch and talking about the good old days. And so most of us keep quiet, raise our children as best we can, go to the cocktail party, eat our cake, go to work, and take the vacation.

We have removed ourselves from leadership, we professional white-collar boomers. We have recused ourselves from a world we never made. We turn our attention to the arts, and entertainment, to watching and supporting them or contributing to them, because they are the only places we can imagine progress. And to money, hoping that it will keep us safe.

A Man, His Dog, and a Sad Story of Betrayal

Dave Shiflett

RECENT EVENTS, very sad events, have inspired deep reflections around our house concerning the relationship between man and dog. Similar reflections frequently accompany times of heavy grieving, and this is such a time.

At times like these, it becomes clear that a man and his dog share a special relationship, not as nations share special relationships, for nations will nuzzle at one moment and bite the next. No, the dog-man relationship is one of infinite trust and admiration, devotion and sympathy.

Indeed, in these days of creeping emasculation, a man's only true friends may be his hound (a male hound, of course) and his jug. When accompanied by both, he is able to face the modern era with the stoic resignation such a crisis demands.

Oh, that it would never end, this special relationship, in which hound and man walk quietly through life, brothers beneath the skin and fur, linked by a sort of trans-species empathy. When the hound drags, we drag. When he howls, our hearts ache. When he steps on a nail, our toes curl in response. Such is the price of love and devotion, and we would gladly pay the price, eternally, were that an option.

Yet it is not. Nothing gold can stay, as the poet says; all good things must come to an end. In our household, with our dog, an era has ended.

Has our dog died? No. But we did have him castrated last week. The master's empathetic teeth are still chattering.

DAVE SHIFLETT

This was not the master's idea, all should be assured, and if it would have done any good, the master would have taken his doomed companion to a secluded mountaintop and set him free. But little good that would have done. In the best of circumstances, someone might actually have picked him up, adopted him, and had him neutered anyway, which is hardly a gain. More likely, he would have starved.

So sadly we turned to the unpleasant task, initially hoping to keep the news from the unsuspecting victim, whose every lick of the hand became a searing indictment of heartless betrayal. Conscience-stricken, we decided to tell him. It was the least we could do for an old friend.

On the last preoperation walk around the neighborhood (taking pains to avoid the places where the females of the species flaunt their carefree immorality), we tried to explain that dogs—much like an ever-increasing segment of the human population—are hardly responsible enough to be left sexually intact. He responded with some ambivalence here; it was clear he did not think this justified his being made a eunuch.

We added that the veterinarian assured us that he would be much better off. His risk of cancer will be reduced, he will be more relaxed, and he will not lose one iota of his boundless energy. Still, he failed to endorse, by wagging tail, what was to come.

Nor was he impressed that the woman of the house, the master-mind of this atrocity, will no longer have to worry about his unto-ward advances on various sofa cushions and the smaller children in the neighborhood, whose looks of horror were truly heartrending.

We will all be better off, he was told.

Yet when the victim looked up with those sad eyes—for he knew something unpleasant was afoot—the master realized that treachery seldom reaches a higher level. We had been as one, laughing together at life, especially at those men who retreat to the woods to get in touch with their feelings, blaming their fathers for all their troubles, measuring their worth by the number of tears sent spilling down their highly eroded cheeks. We were different: We would live our lives without whining, and then we would die.

Now, these feelings have changed. For better or worse, one feels differently about a eunuch. He's no longer one of the boys. Perhaps this prejudice will be outgrown. It is hard to say.

In the meantime, the victim's silent objections ring loudly in his master's soul. "How could you let her do this to me?" he asked, in his inscrutable way. "When the thief comes calling at midnight, who advances with bared teeth and the willingness to battle to the death? Not her. Who sits through those long televised ball games, curled up warmly by your side and never—not once—glaring when yet another trip is made to the beer box? It is not her. Who is happy with horsemeat by-products, while the other demands steak? Who drags you into church when field and stream are beckoning?"

These truths smote like flaming arrows, and it would do no good to inform the old boy that his operation was, in fact, a birthday present to the missus. He has already suffered enough.

We are haunted by memories, and the sorrowful master will always remember leading the poor dog toward the operating room, through which he would pass into a different world. While the surgeon sharpened his pitiless knife and the receptionist prepared the bill, the dog looked up one last time, as if to say, "Empathy! Equality! Fraternity! Why don't you join me, so that we will always be the same?"

I hadn't the heart to respond: "Because we're not *that* close, pal."

Two Good Schools Are Not All We're Losing

Paul A. Gigot

WELL INTO THIRTYSOMETHING, I find myself more prone to nostalgia. I'm embarrassed to admit I got teary over *Field of Dreams,* an absurdly mawkish film about baseball, or something. Now my high school is closing down, and the sense of loss somehow seems greater than it ought to be. Perhaps more than a gilded memory really is being lost.

The local Catholic diocese has decided to shut down two high schools in Green Bay, Wisconsin, where I grew up. Abbot Pennings, the all-boys school my brothers and I attended, and St. Joseph Academy, an all-girls school my mother and sisters attended, have both declared this their final year. The baby bust has reduced the number of potential students, fewer priests and nuns are available to teach, and costs and tuition have gone up—the immediate reasons are unremarkable.

But the schools themselves are remarkable enough that their demise may speak to everyone. Only two months ago, St. Joe's was among 218 secondary schools from around the country cited by President George Bush for excellence. The selection process includes a two-day on-site visit and tracking the schools' graduates. St. Joe's sends 93 percent of its young women to college. Drugs are rarely a problem, and when they are teachers and parents descend to straighten it out. Not the sort of place to close amid an education crisis.

"Whatever the young women want to do, we really push them

and say, try it," explains Sister Helen Rottier, St. Joe's principal. "Our whole emphasis is on moral education." The school isn't afraid to put secular achievement in the context of what Sister Helen calls "the spiritual." With even Norman Lear now bemoaning the decline of spirituality in American life, maybe St. Joe's is ahead of the game.

Pennings in my day was atavistic without realizing it. The school had discipline; even in the efflorescence of the 1960s, kids wore coats and ties. (The bow to rebellious individuality was that most kids wore the same coat and tie all year.) It had committed teachers who enforced standards; Latin was taught as a long march of memorization. Conjugate or die—of humiliation. It had parents who paid attention, but not so much as to interfere when their rowdier sons had to be collared. Parents didn't sue.

What it has never had is money, or platoons of counselors, or high technology, or the other things our educators advise us schools must now have. The school building itself, a red-brick refugee from the warehouse era, might have been condemned at any time. The sweatbox of a gym ended with the baskets; to play run-and-gun basketball was suicide. This was no Dead Poets' Society for rich kids, either. Tuition in my day was $260 a year; now it's up to $1,800, but nearly 40 percent of the kids are on scholarship. Sons of machinists learn next to doctors' kids.

The school is run by the Norbertine order of priests, a teaching order not unlike, though not as renowned as, the Jesuits. They favored a curriculum that was James Madison basic. But far from offering dull conformity, the teachers took intellectual risks. A sophomore religion teacher introduced us to William James's *The Varieties of Religious Experience.* A history teacher forced us to debate topics of the day, once casting me to defend socialized medicine. (A fashionable McGovernite at the time, I kept tripping over my opponent's point about "incentives"; the seeds of common sense were planted.)

The same instructor, "Doc" Coyle, assigned "reports" from articles in the *New Republic* and *National Review.* One favorite was by sociologist Peter Berger on "The Paradoxes of American Conservatism."

DOC COYLE: First, please define "paradox" for the class.
STUDENT: Ummmm . . .

It is a paradox of modern life that the most intellectually tolerant are often those most grounded in orthodoxy.

The Norbertines, like most religious orders, have not multiplied with modernity. Many who once taught have since left the priesthood. One left teaching to become a marriage counselor and married a woman he counseled. The order now takes in only two or three new "vocations" a year. The Norbertines still run a couple of schools in the East, including one in Delaware that taught Senator Joseph Biden.

Modern culture has also changed the sisters of St. Joseph of Carondelet, who've run St. Joe's for ninety-four years. The Catholic Church's Second Vatican Council gave the sisters a broader choice of "ministry," says Sister Helen. Rather than teach middle-class kids, most of the nuns now prefer to work with the homeless, or in Peru or Chile.

Peter Berger—reading habits learned in school are hard to shake—and Richard John Neuhaus once wrote that modern America tends to shatter what Burke called the "little platoons" of community. Schools, voluntary groups, churches, even families are battered between our passion for individual rights and the giant companies and government that can seem so impersonal. Pennings and St. Joe's are two little platoons, smaller communities, on which bigger ones build. Tuition tax credits might have saved one or both, but the American public seems to have decided this is not a policy it can support.

So it does not pay to be nostalgic about what cannot be changed. Green Bay's public schools are better than most. A Catholic high school will remain open on the other side of the city for kids willing to make the commute. But come next September there will be two fewer little communities of allegiance, two fewer good schools, and something will have been lost.

Quantity Time

Fred Barnes

FATHERHOOD ISN'T BRAIN SURGERY. I say this in defiance of the new conventional wisdom that being a father is breathtakingly difficult, that it creates tough dilemmas and causes enormous stress and that fathers need a strategy, a plan, a vision, for carrying out their duties. I don't think so. Most men I know have an instinct for fatherhood that was triggered the day their first child was born. They instantly recognized the number one requirement of fatherhood: be there. Woody Allen may be a lousy father, but his rule for life applies to being a father. Yep, 90 percent of fatherhood is just showing up. Of course, millions of fathers don't show up at all because of divorce, out-of-wedlock births, and so on. And the absence of fathers has awful consequences. But that's a social problem, quite different from the personal crisis fathers supposedly face in their day-to-day interaction with their children.

Forget quality time. You can't plan magic moments or bonding or epiphanies in dealing with kids. What matters is quantity time. Judging from my own experience—four kids—children crave prolonged attention, preferably undivided. They want whole days and nights of it. Knowing this, I opted for an adventure in quantity time with my son, Freddy, in mid-June. He's eight. I took him with me for a weekend at The Balsams, an elegant old resort hotel in Dixville Notch, New Hampshire. All I had to do was give a speech Saturday morning (I was a last-minute substitute for David Gergen) to a group of Maine and Vermont bankers and their spouses. The rest of my time was Freddy's. The only dilemma I faced was figuring out what to do with him while I spoke. He's about as eager to listen to me hold forth on politics as President Clinton is to hear another question from Brit Hume. Since Freddy refused to participate in the hotel's program for kids, there was only one solution. I paid him off. I gave him $10 in quarters, hoping that would keep him busy for ninety minutes playing video games. It worked only too well. When I came to get him later he'd spent the money and was playing pool with an older kid named Zack. "Dad," he said, "what'd you come so soon for?"

I had no strategy for how we'd spend our time or what we'd talk about. We would play it by ear, by instinct. The hotel is situated beside a lake stocked with trout, so fishing seemed logical. "We're men, aren't we?" Freddy said. We got life jackets, a rowboat, oars, and two fly rods and headed for the middle of the lake. I rowed, and Freddy accused me of splashing him as I rowed. Sad to say, my knowledge of fly fishing consisted of having seen the movie *A River Runs Through It,* and that turned out to be insufficient. Fly fishing, like golf, is hard. By the time we'd casted a few times, the boat had floated back to the shore, and I had to stop fishing and row again. This process repeated itself a few times. After a half-hour, Freddy said, "Dad, we'll never catch a fish." I told him he was wrong, that if we stuck to it for a while more, we'd catch something. He was right. The fishing episode produced no moments of deep father-son rapport, only a shared sense of relief that the two young women who were fly fishing at the same time didn't catch anything either.

Basketball was better. Freddy showed me everything he'd learned earlier that week at basketball camp. We pretended to be the Bulls and the Suns. Hiking was better still. When we returned, it was time for dinner. Freddy and I were signed up to attend the bankers' formal banquet. I was worried that he would be bored and bad. Instead, I experienced two of the blessings of fatherhood (these apply also to motherhood). One is that people are unusually nice when you're with your children. When Freddy balked at prime rib, the waitress brought him a burger and fries. The other joy is when your kid unexpectedly displays his best behavior in public. Freddy acted like Little Lord Fauntleroy. He sat still, responded to everyone who talked to him, didn't once call anyone a "butthead," his favorite epithet. He got restless after roughly an hour. So I gave him $3 to play video games.

During the weekend, I managed to resolve what *Time,* in its June 28 cover story ("Fatherhood: The guilt, the joy, the fear, the fun . . ."), suggests are the two great dilemmas of modern fatherhood. You know, choosing between work and family and deciding whether to be a New Father or an Old Father. This was no big deal. In fact, it's a false choice, one most fathers don't really have to make. The weekend itself combined work and family. Nothing extraordinary there. Fathers balance work and family all the time. You go to work, but if your child is doing something eventful, or needs your immediate help, then you take off. (Those, that is, who have the luxury of skipping out of work when they choose.) You never get credit for being there with your kid. But you get blame—and suffer remorse—if you aren't. Only once have I ever been forced to make a conscious choice between work and family. It occurred when my daughter Grace had a weekday soccer game and her mother was away. I thought: I have so much to do I can't leave work at 4:00 P.M. But I did. Grace scored four goals, her best game ever.

As for new fatherhood—more nurturing and soft-edged, less rigid and aloof—you don't have to embrace it or reject it. You adopt the parts you're comfortable with and forget the rest. I never believed I'd find it thrilling to be in the delivery room to see my child being born. I was wrong. *Time* says that "it is still the mother who carries her child's life around in her head." Like many fathers, I try to keep track of what my kids are doing every day. But I can't be a second mother to them. Men, my friends anyway, aren't good at that. Robert Griswold, in *Fatherhood in America,* complains that American culture "lacks any coherent and unified vision of what fathers and fatherhood should be." He's right, but so what? That's a problem of our culture and its need to put a theory behind things that work in practice. Fathers get along fine without such a vision.

As the banquet was ending, Freddy returned from the game room, ready for attention. We went outside to reconnoiter the eighteen-hole putting green, where we intended to play the next morning. The sky was amazingly clear, the stars glistening like they never do through the haze over Washington. A couple from Camden, Maine, spent thirty minutes talking to Freddy and me. The wife took Freddy aside and pointed out the Big Dipper to him. He was ecstatic. "I couldn't see it before," he said. The husband talked about other wonders in the sky. Freddy was enthralled. As we walked back to our room, he said, "That man really knew a lot." It was 10:00 P.M., time for bed. Freddy jumped under the covers and insisted we sleep in the same bed. "Dad, Dad, there's so much I want to tell you," he said. Before he could remember exactly what, he was fast asleep.

The Legacy of Russell Kirk

David Frum

RUSSELL KIRK, WHO DIED THIS SPRING at his home in Mecosta, Michigan, at the age of seventy-five, has left behind an intellectual and literary achievement as huge as it is difficult to categorize. He was not exactly a political theorist, nor really a philosopher, certainly not a historian; and yet his work speaks profound truths about politics, philosophy, and history. An ardent enemy of Communism, he was barely more enthusiastic about the commercial civilization of America. An unrelenting critic of "King Numbers," he championed a Goldwaterite conservatism that owed far more to the populism of Jefferson, Jackson, and Tom Paine than to the prescriptive politics of Edmund Burke and John Adams. A scourge of ideology and abstraction in politics, he determinedly refused to pay any attention to the circumstances and context in which the thinkers he studied had lived. He loved old cathedral towns and country fields, ancient mansions and Gothic universities; he hated cars, television, and shopping malls. For all his patriotism, one has to wonder how comfortable he ever really felt in late-twentieth-century America. "Against the lust for change," Kirk wrote of his admired John Randolph, "[he] had fought with all his talents. And though he lost, he fell with a brilliancy that was almost consolation for disaster." Of course, it wasn't just Randolph he had in mind.

Russell Kirk came of one of the many small-town families hit hard by the depression. His great-grandfather had founded the little town of Mecosta, and his mother's father had owned a bank, but Kirk attended Michigan State on a scholarship and worked at Ford's Rouge River plant after completing his M.A. at Duke in 1941. Kirk was then drafted and stationed in Utah; according to George Nash,

author of *The Conservative Intellectual Tradition in America Since 1945,*
Kirk cast his first presidential ballot for Norman Thomas in 1944, to
reward the veteran socialist for his steadfast opposition to the Second
World War. Released from the army, Kirk resumed his studies and
began to publish. In 1951 came *John Randolph of Roanoke,* an enlarge-
ment of his M.A. thesis, and in 1953, *The Conservative Mind.* The
fame that second book won Kirk enabled him to return to Mecosta
and settle in his family's house.

A charming 1992 essay by Edwin Feulner, president of the Heritage Foundation, quotes Kirk's description of the place: "over everything brooded an air of faded splendours, vanished lands, and baffled
expectations." The house soon sheltered armies of young conservative
scholars, and other, more miscellaneous, guests: "unwed mothers,
half-reformed burglars, . . . Vietnamese . . . families, waves of Ethiopi-
ans, Poles fled from martial law, freedom-seeking Croats, students
disgusted with their colleges, and a diversity of waifs and strays from
Progress." (The sarcastic uppercase "P" on "Progress" is a characteristic Kirkean flourish.)

From Mecosta, for four decades, Kirk fired his observations upon
the world: two more major scholarly works, *Eliot and His Age* and *The
Roots of American Order,* books, essays, ghost stories, lectures, columns
for magazines and newspapers. From Mecosta, too, he cast a sharp
and often disapproving eye upon the conservative movement that
had sprung up in the years since the publication of *The Conservative
Mind.* He disliked libertarians, and apologists for big business, and
neoconservatives. He did not mind making enemies: he separated
himself from his old friends at *National Review* after 1980, and in a
1988 critique of neoconservatism he let loose the startling observation that "not seldom has it seemed as if some eminent Neoconservatives"—that capital letter again!—"mistook Tel Aviv for the capital
of the United States." By the end of his life, he had circled back to his
Taftite origins and joined the opposition to the war in the Persian
Gulf.

KIRK'S VOICE ECHOED LESS POWERFULLY in those later years than in
the 1950s and 1960s. In part, of course, he was the victim of his

own success: with conservatives in a position to exercise national political power after 1978, a political thinker who declined to preoccupy himself with the details of public policy—which he left to the "enlightened expediency" of statesmen—inevitably lost audiences to technical experts. Clad in out-of-fashion vested suits, immersed in his old books, smoking (as Feulner says) dark, thick Burmese cigars that looked and tasted like torpedoes, he looked oddly out of place among the sleek Republicans of Reagan-era Washington.

And these stylistic oddities hinted at an even bigger and deeper gulf between Kirk and his Reaganite audience. From the beginning, Kirk had denied key tenets of the American faith. He had openly defended class hierarchies; he doubted the value of technological progress; and, while disliking the growth of the central government, he cared very little for the danger to prosperity and economic growth posed by bigger government. In fact, Kirk regarded "growth," in most cases, as a misnomer for "decay."

> During the late 'fifties and the early 'sixties, I watched in Long Island the devastation of what had been a charming countryside, as dismaying as what was being done to our cities. To make room for a spreading population was necessary: but to do it hideously and stupidly was not ineluctable. Much of the mischief was accomplished by the highways of Robert Moses, generally supposed to be one of the abler of American planners. Speed was everything, speed by automobile from Manhattan to Montauk.

Many thinkers have damned suburbia, but Kirk uniquely dared to reveal the antiegalitarian implications of the aesthetic critique of American life. "This is my case: there ought to be inequality of condition in the world. For without inequality, there is no class; without class, no manners and no beauty; and then a people sink into public and private ugliness." Ugliness was for him no light accusation. "With Santayana," he said, "I believe that beauty is the index to civilization." By this index, contemporary America scored low. We now live, he bitterly complained in *The Conservative Mind,* in "a world smudged by industrialism, standardized by the masses, consolidated by government."

Nor was Kirk bashful about itemizing the differences between his conservatism and the enthusiastic Jacksonianism found on the right wing of the contemporary Republican party. He openly disdained populism, denouncing "those who, in the belief that there exists a malign 'elite,' cry, with Carl Sandburg, 'The people, yes!'" As for the Reagan-era project of identifying conservatism's cause as the defense of "democratic capitalism," an optimistic philosophy that commingled high-tech prosperity and ever-widening popular sovereignty . . . well, here's what Kirk had to say about that:

> Previously, even in America, the structure of society had consisted of a hierarchy of personal and local allegiances—man to master, apprentice to preceptor, householder to parish or town, constituent to representative, son to father, communicant to church. . . . This network of personal relationships and local decencies was brushed aside by steam, coal, the spinning jenny, the cotton gin, speedy transportation, and the other items in that catalogue of progress which school children memorize. The Industrial Revolution . . . turned the world inside out. Personal loyalties gave way to financial relationships. . . . Industrialism was a harder knock to conservatism than the books of the French equalitarians. . . .
>
> That the sudden triumph of democracy should coincide with the rise of industrialism was in part the product of intertwined causes; but, however inescapable, it was a conjunction generally catastrophic. Jeffersonian democracy, designed for a simple agrarian people, was thrust upon an acquisitive, impatient, and often urbanized mass of men.

Instead, Kirk throughout his life insisted upon the six "canons" of conservative thought he first identified in *The Conservative Mind:*

1. Belief that a divine intent rules society as well as conscience. . . .
2. Affection for the proliferating variety and mystery of traditional life. . . .
3. Conviction that civilized society requires orders and classes. . . .
4. Persuasion that property and freedom are inseparably connected. . . .

5. Faith in prescription. . . . Tradition and sound prejudice provide checks upon man's anarchic impulse. . . .
6. Recognition that change and reform are not identical, and that innovation is a devouring conflagration more often than it is a torch of progress. . . .

Kirk expressed his major ideas in highly general terms, and so it is hard to know exactly what these six canons imply, especially the final two. When pressed for specifics, Kirk's political advice tended to take the form of negative injunctions.

> Conservative people in politics need to steer clear of the Scylla of abstraction and the Charybdis of opportunism. So it is that folk of conservative inclination ought to decline the embraces of such categories of American political zealots or charlatans as I list below:
>
> Those who demand that the National Parks be sold to private developers. Those who declare that "the test of the market" is the whole of political economy and of morals. Those who fancy that foreign policy can be conducted with religious zeal on a basis of absolute rights and absolute wrongs. . . .

Etcetera. Even Kirk's journalism bears only indirectly on the controversies of his day.

Then again, uncertainty about the implications of his ideas in practice may not matter very much: for Kirk was, at bottom, much more concerned with morals and education than with politics as politics is usually understood. He reserved his energies for other themes, themes sometimes absurdly small, but at other times profound and urgent, as in his remarkable essay "The Rarity of the God-Fearing Man."

"We have to begin," Kirk describes himself telling a group of clergymen, "with the dogma that the fear of God is the beginning of wisdom." "Oh no," they replied, "not the *fear* of God. You mean the *love* of God, don't you?"

> Looking upon their mild and diffident faces, I wondered how much trust I might put in such love as they knew. Their meekness was not

that of Moses. Meek before Jehovah, Moses had no fear of Pharaoh; but these doctors of the schools, much at ease in Zion, were timid in the presence of a traffic policeman. Although convinced that God is too indulgent to punish much of anything, they were given to trembling before Caesar. . . . Gauleiters and commissars? Why, their fellowship and charity was not proof against a dean or a divisional head. . . .

Every age portrays God in the image of its poetry and its politics. In one century, God is an absolute monarch, exacting his due; in another century, still an absolute sovereign, but a benevolent despot; again, perhaps a grand gentleman among aristocrats; at a different time, a democratic president, with an eye to the ballot box. It has been said that to many of our generation, God is a Republican and works in a bank; but this image is giving way, I think, to God as Chum—at worst, God as a playground supervisor. . . .

In a Michigan college town stands an immense quasi-Gothic church building, and the sign upon the porch informs the world that this is "The People's Church, Nondenominational and Nonsectarian." Sometimes, passing by, a friend of mine murmurs, "The People's Church—formerly God's" . . . From the People's Church, the fear of God, with its allied wisdom, has been swept away. So have I.

KIRK'S LITERARY PRODUCTIVITY commands awe. He took particular pride in his ghost stories: His spare curriculum vitae modestly omits mention of nearly all his innumerable awards and honorary degrees, except for three that especially pleased him—one of them being the Ann Radcliffe Award of the Count Dracula Society. ("A child's fearful joy in stories of goblins, witches, and ghosts is a natural yearning after the challenge of the dreadful: raw head and bloody bones, in one form or another, the imagination demands.") In all the millions of words he set in print, however, he never amended or retracted any of the thoughts and formulations of the masterpiece he published at age thirty-two, *The Conservative Mind.*

"Professor J. W. Williams kindly read the manuscript of this book; and in his library at the Roundel, looking upon the wreck of St. Andrews cathedral, we talked of the inundation which only here and there has spared an island of humane learning like St. Andrews town." Those words, the opening sentence of the acknowledgments to *The Conservative Mind,* and the first of Russell Kirk's that most of his readers will encounter, demonstrate what a fine literary artist he could be. You might close the book right there, and Kirk would already have stabbed you with a pang of loss and regret. An old cliché has it that a great actor can wring tears out of an audience by reading a laundry list. Kirk could summon up nostalgia with a list of place-names. "These chapters have been written in a variety of places: in a but-and-ben snuggled under the cliffs of Eigg; in one of the ancient towers of Kellie Castle, looking out to the Forth; in my great-grandfather's house in the stump-country of Michigan; among the bogs of Sligo in the west of Ireland; upon the steps of Ara Coeli, in Rome; at Balcarres House, where what Burke calls 'the unbought grace of life' still abides."

Kirk was writing in the aftermath of the forty most catastrophic years in the history of Western civilization, and at the beginning of another forty of the most tense and terrifying. It must have seemed to him that everything he treasured had either been pulverized by war or would soon be bulldozed by one form of socialism or another. He strained all his powers to summon up a vision of the Anglo-American past that would stir the imagination and entice us to preserve as much of the vanished aristocratic age he loved as we possibly could. In form, *The Conservative Mind* appears to be intellectual history. Each of its chapters closely studies the writing of a conservative thinker or group of thinkers: Edmund Burke; John Adams, Alexander Hamilton, and Fisher Ames; Walter Scott and Samuel Taylor Coleridge; Benjamin Disraeli and Cardinal Newman; Irving Babbitt and George Santayana; and many others. In fact, history is the one thing *The Conservative Mind* is not. Kirk repeatedly declares his lack of interest in the tangle of facts and events from which his subjects' ideas emerged. He takes his ideas as he finds them, the way an anthropologist might examine an artifact or a New Critic, a poem. Was John C. Calhoun's dramatic midlife switch from nationalism to sectionalism motivated by his commitment to slavery? Kirk does not inquire.

DAVID FRUM

The whole grim slavery-problem, to which no satisfactory answer was possible, warped and discolored the American political mind, on either side of the debate, for the earlier two-thirds of the nineteenth century. So far as it is possible, we shall try to keep clear here of that partisan controversy over slavery and to penetrate, instead, beneath the froth of abolitionist harangues and Southern fire-eating to those conservative ideas which Randolph and Calhoun enunciated.

Are we really to take Benjamin Disraeli's flights of political fancy seriously as expressing a distinctive Tory philosophy? It doesn't matter whether we do.

In truth, Disraeli's positive legislation sometimes was inconsistent with his theory, and in any case inferior to it. His really important achievement, as a political leader, was implanting in the public imagination an ideal of Toryism which has been immeasurably valuable in keeping Britain faithful to her constitutional and spiritual traditions.

No, *The Conservative Mind* isn't history; it is a work of literature meant to achieve political ends.

This isn't to deny that Kirk could produce acute analysis of earlier times when it suited his purposes. Kirk's erasure of Alexander Hamilton—the hero of an earlier generation of conservative Republicans—from the conservative canon shows his historical intelligence at its best.

It hardly seems to have occurred to Hamilton's mind that a consolidated nation might also be a levelling and innovating nation, though he had the example of Jacobin France right before him; and he does not appear to have reflected on the possibility that force in government may be applied to other purposes than the maintenance of a conservative order. . . . All his revolutionary ardour notwithstanding, Hamilton loved English society as an English colonial adores it. His vision of the coming America was of another, stronger, richer, eighteenth-century England. . . .

[T]hat industrialization of America which Hamilton success-fully promoted was burdened with consequences the haughty and forceful new aristocrat did not perceive. Commerce and manufac-tures, he believed, would produce a body of wealthy men whose in-terests would coincide with those of the national commonwealth. Probably he conceived of these pillars of society as being very like great English merchants—purchasing country estates, forming presently a stable class possessed of leisure, talent, and means, pro-viding moral and political and intellectual leadership for the nation. The actual American businessman, generally speaking, has turned out to be a different sort of person: it is difficult to reproduce social classes from a model three thousand miles over the water. Modern captains of industry might surprise Hamilton, modern cities shock him, and the power of industrial labor frighten him: for Hamilton never quite understood the transmuting power of social change, which in its operation is more miraculous than scientific. Like Dr. Faustus' manservant, Hamilton could evoke elementals; but once materialized, that new industrialism swept away from the control of eighteenth-century virtuosos like the masterful Secretary of the Trea-sury. . . .

Hamilton was a straggler behind his age, rather than the prophet of a new day. By a very curious coincidence, this old-fangled grand gentleman died from the bullet of Aaron Burr, friend and dis-ciple of Bentham.

Thinkers whom Kirk sought to include, rather than exclude, from his canon sometimes met, however, more procrustean fates. It's fasci-nating to compare, for instance, the exegesis of a single sentence of Edmund Burke's both by Kirk and by Conor Cruise O'Brien in his recent study, *The Great Melody*. First, Kirk:

"I heaved the lead every inch of the way I made," Burke observed of his career, in the *Letter to a Noble Lord*. Heaving the lead is not a prac-tice for which Irish orators are renowned; Burke's flights of eloquent fancy everyone knows; and surely Burke did not seem at Hasting's trial, to frightened Tory spectators, a man sworn to cautious plumbing of the depths. Yet Burke spoke accurately of his general policy as a statesman, for he based his every important decision upon a close examination of particulars. He detested "abstraction"—by which he meant not *principle,* but rather vainglorious generalization without respect for human frailty and the particular circumstances of an age and nation. Thus it was that while he believed in the rights of Englishmen and in certain human rights of universal application, he despised the "Rights of Man" which Paine and the French doctrinaires were soon to proclaim inviolable.

Now O'Brien.

The occasion for the composition of *Letter to a Noble Lord* was an attack by two Whig peers, the Duke of Bedford and the Earl of Lauderdale, in the Lords on 13 November 1795 on the pension which had been granted to Burke in the previous year, on his retirement from Parliament. . . . It enabled Edmund to pay his debts and to be assured, during his last illness, that his widow would not have to face a life of poverty. . . .

Inevitably, Burke's many enemies, among the Whigs and the radicals, triumphed. . . . It was the thirty pieces of silver. . . . Burke had received an enormous amount of abuse and innuendo—more than any other politician—in his long political career. In *Letter to a Noble Lord* he called it "the hunt of obloquy, which ever has pursued me with full cry through life." Most of those attacks came from anonymous writers in the corrupt press of the time, faceless and unaccountable tormenters. Burke did not answer those ever. The Duke of Bedford, on the other hand, was a marvelous target. . . .

He was also vulnerable. The Bedford family, since the days of Henry VIII, had been beneficiaries of Crown patronage on a colossal scale. Thus, by attacking Burke's modest pension, the Duke had unwittingly laid himself open to the most devastating *argumentum ad hominem* in the history of English controversy. . . . It contains [in the "heaving the lead" passage], with much else, Burke's grave and succinct rebuttal to the charge of venality that dogged him throughout his life, and has clung to his reputation ever since.

In some respects, obviously, Kirk's reading of the sentence is better. Kirk never even acknowledged, much less succumbed to, the contemporary urge to psychologize and personalize every human utterance. His Burke is a public man, and a public man's public statements are given public meanings by Kirk. Too, Kirk relies only on what he can see in the documentary record; O'Brien's conviction that he possesses some special intuition into Burke's Irish soul that justifies leaps beyond the available facts would have irritated Kirk no end. Even so, and for all that, O'Brien's Burke is a *man*—maybe a badly misunderstood man, but a man all the same. Kirk's Burke is a repository of political wisdom, the author of a series of preternatural insights on which, two hundred years later, a political movement can be grounded.

RUSSELL KIRK HAS ALWAYS reminded me of those nineteenth-century Central European historians who promoted national consciousness by writing passionate histories of "nations" that had not existed until those same historians invented them. And just as the nationalist historians manufactured "Croatia" or "Czechoslovakia" out of half-forgotten medieval and baroque fragments, Russell Kirk inspired the postwar conservative movement by pulling together a series of only partially related ideas and events into a coherent narrative—even, although Kirk objected to the word, into an ideology. Kirk did not record the past; he created it. He gathered the words of his political exemplars to answer his burning question:

> What is the essence of British and American conservatism? What system of ideas, common to England and the United States, has sustained men of conservative instincts in their resistance against radical theories and social transformation since the beginning of the French revolution?

As a question, of course, Kirk's query takes far too much for granted. Can one in fact fuse the English and American political traditions together in this way? Was the dilemma of the English Tories—how to maintain aristocratic deference in a democratizing society?—truly identical to that of American conservatives in the North—how to maintain the virtues of the founders' way of life in the face of colossal, unexpected wealth and exploding, non–Anglo-Saxon, populations?—and South—how to preserve white supremacy in the face of Northern criticism and an agricultural way of life in an industrial age? But Kirk's question is not a question. It is a prelude to a romantic reading of the past for the purposes of the present. No wonder, then, that *The Conservative Mind* found little favor with professional historians. Writers of the Left may be able to get away with devising "usable pasts": Certainly Michel Foucault and the writers of women's history distort the past for their own polemical purposes on a scale and with a brazen falsity that would have made Kirk gasp. But in the hostile purlieus of the academy, writers of the Right must be more careful.

Yet if Kirk's great work cannot be counted as history, exactly, it ought to be esteemed as something in some ways more important: a profound critique of contemporary, mass society, and a vivid and poetic image—not a program, an image—of how that society might better itself. It is, in important respects, the twentieth century's own version of the *Reflections on the Revolution in France*. If Kirk was not a historian, he was an artist, a visionary, almost a prophet. As long as he lived, by word and example he cautioned conservatives against overindulging their fascination with economics. He taught that conservativism was above all a *moral* cause: one devoted to the preservation of the priceless heritage of Western civilization.

Remembering Allan Bloom

Clifford Orwin

ALLAN BLOOM WAS BORN in Indianapolis in 1930. He studied at Chicago and at Paris and Heidelberg and taught at many places, notably in Chicago's Basic Program in the 1950s, at Cornell in the 1960s, at Toronto in the 1970s, and at Chicago again from 1979 until his death this past October 7. I knew him as an undergraduate at Cornell from 1964 to 1968, as his colleague at Toronto from 1973 to 1979, again as his colleague at Chicago in the last year of his life, and as a frequent visitor in the years in between.

It was as a teacher that my friends and I first encountered "Mr. Bloom." The classroom was at the center of his life, and with him in it, it quickly moved to the center of ours.

As a teacher Allan hit the ground running, enjoying his greatest successes at the outset. In just one semester at Cornell in 1962, he inspired two brilliant students to transfer to Yale, where he was to spend the following year. When he returned to Ithaca, so did they. In the one year at Yale, teaching in Directed Studies where the best undergraduates were to be found, he inspired two of these students to transfer to Cornell immediately, and another four to resolve to attend graduate school there. These decisions to transfer were made within weeks of the students' first meetings with Allan.

Long before the public knew of Allan, he dominated the lives of those who did. I often thought of him as America's greatest unknown celebrity. On arriving at Cornell in 1964, I found my residence hall, a designated hatchery for intellectuals, wholly polarized around the subject of Allan Bloom. He had lived there the year before, and everyone either loved or hated him. The two parties therefore fell to warring for the souls of us freshmen. The Bloom question raged unabated inside the residence and on the campus generally for my entire four years at Cornell. It also raged within many of us, who were both attracted and repelled, amazed and disturbed, entranced and horrified by Allan and his mind-shaking arguments. One night my closest friend and I, fearing for our spiritual independence, resolved to flee Ithaca; then we decided that we owed it to ourselves to stay to fight it out; then we just laughed.

For us Allan Bloom was the foremost issue of the sixties, with which all the others were hopelessly entangled. Later, at Harvard graduate school, a leader of the New Left warned me that, come the revolution, students of Allan would be shot first. He was not alone; a great many people were obsessed with Allan. He remained throughout his life the consuming topic of discussion whenever his acquaintances gathered.

Allan's presence as a teacher was astonishing. Throughout his career he attracted large crowds. Even so he was never quite at ease in the lecture hall. His gestures were ungainly and he stuttered; if nervous energy was radioactive, his casualties would have dwarfed Chernobyl. Still, to watch him lecture was something. His dark eyes flashed over his aquiline nose as his face clearly registered his shifting moods. A frown of intensity was his basic expression, ceding to delight or concern at some sally by a student, then to pleasure as he savored a new formulation or to annoynace if he felt that the right words had eluded him. Often he would seem lost in his own musings. His powerful voice would fade to little more than a whisper, as all in the room strained to hear. Then the voice would boom again, and he would proceed with renewed confidence. All the while he filled the air with smoke rings. (Indifference to No Smoking signs was his characteristic form of lawlessness.) Juggling two cigarettes (the last and the next) while meditating on the profundities of life, Allan occasionally lifted the lighted end of one toward his unsuspecting lips. (He usually drew back in time.)

I have never known another teacher capable of so transporting an audience. In Allan's classroom, time stopped, and one felt oneself wafted to a higher plane of life and thought; to return to the outside world was always slightly depressing. He had the gift of making us feel that study was something exalted, one of the rarest human privileges, for the opportunity of which we should never cease to be thankful. (And for which therefore we should never cease blessing liberal democracy.) Other teachers could say as much, and have, but Allan made us *feel* it, in a matter in which only feeling is believing. Through knowing him it suddenly became credible that a life devoted to studying a couple of dozen mostly old books was one of surpassing nobility and joyfulness; in him we actually saw this life before us, and, however fleetingly, joined in it.

Allan's method was very simple. He proceeded slowly through books like *The Prince,* the *Republic, Gulliver's Travels, Madame Bovary,* and *Democracy in America,* spending an entire course year on just four or five of these. He went through them from beginning to end, reading each in its entirety. He wanted us not just to learn the author's official position on this or that issue, but to grasp each work as a rich and integrated whole that addressed the entire human situation.

Allan aspired to demonstrate that these old books still spoke to us, indeed that they spoke with greater power than the clamoring voices of our own day. He would therefore mix detailed textual analysis with discussion of current issues. As he saw it, to explicate a text was to make it speak, which he could do only by establishing that it had anticipated the questions that mattered most to us today—which upon examination always proved variants of age-old human problems. The drama of his classes was that of confronting oneself in a book that had at first seemed impossibly old and "academic." He imparted that most vivid and profound of all lessons in our common humanity, the recognition that Plato really was speaking *to us,* that he had thought more deeply about the problems that most gripped us than we had ever been going to think about them ourselves. Allan did not just make old texts speak; he made them sing. As his friend Werner Dannhauser put it at his funeral, he was a pied piper of philosophy.

Nor did Allan slight the great alternatives to philosophy, even if these, too, had largely receded from modern view. He movingly recreated the life of piety, that of the great statesman or soldier, that of simple patriotism, that of the gentleman, that of devotion to the family. In his great scheme of things, each of these finally ceded to philosophy, but not before he had restored it to such dignity that you appreciated it as never before. He saw that philosophy as a way of life could only emerge in contradistinction to the full panoply of other human possibilities and that, estranged as we were from the primary phenomena, it fell to him to begin by painting the background. In this he made excellent use of the Bible, Shakespeare, and the novel and always felt that his teaching suffered from students' progressive unfamiliarity with these.

Allan was a live wire, throwing off spark after spark. He thrived on objections, which was fortunate, as he provoked so many of them. Often these were hostile or inarticulate; he didn't mind. He treated every objection as a question and made a genuine effort to satisfy it. Occasionally, he turned the objection to laughter but would then proceed to try to deal with it. He distrusted students who agreed with him too readily, admired those who put up a fight.

With everyone's opinions always on the line, the tension in the classroom would have been unbearable were it not for Allan's wit. This was spontaneous and amazingly quick; most of its flashes were at his own expense. Allan evoked not chuckles or titters but waves of tumultuous laughter, again and again, lecture after lecture. Students who knew nothing else about him would enroll in his course simply because of the hilarity that flooded from it. It was hard to hate someone who made you laugh as he did.

Allan loved teaching, and no hardship could deter him from it. Once in Toronto he arrived in class with his face all distorted; up all night with a toothache, he had just been to the dentist for removal of the abscessed tooth, rejecting any anesthetic lest numbness cramp his style as a speaker. The show went on, as it always did, and he reserved some of his most powerful performances for situations of adversity. In 1974 the Toronto campus was convulsed because some New Leftists had physically prevented a distinguished visitor from speaking. This time Allan was both sleepless and furious, intending to devote part of his lecture on Plato to an angry statement. Our colleague Walter Berns and I deterred him, lest he go off half-cocked.

Allan refrained from mentioning the incident. Instead, in fielding a question about the dramatic character of the *Republic,* he spoke more movingly than ever about the rarity of the kind of discussion reported therein. He talked of how in times of darkness and crisis for Athens, a few people had gathered to consider the timeless issues of politics, of how the trial of Socrates cast its long shadow over the conversation, and of how we must cherish and defend the opportunities for such discussions that the university afforded us today. Having made his point, he proceeded as usual.

Allan later came to be called a conservative, a term that *The New York Times* obituary repeated like the mantra that it had become. Conservative, however, does not begin to capture his quality or his appeal. Since the climate of opinion on the better American campuses was leftish throughout his career, and since he questioned conventional wisdom relentlessly, "liberals" and leftists fumed about his influence with students. In fact conservative students rarely found him attractive; there was too much Voltaire in him. He was every bit as hard on "conservatism" as on "liberalism." All of his best students began on the Left, even if few remained there. Allan flushed out students from every thicket of current opinion: his target was lazy thinking and especially ideological thinking.

The least fair of all the accusations later leveled against Allan was that he was an ideologue. Like all of us, he harbored inclinations in that direction, inclinations all the more powerful in a man of such incandescent passion. He could be irascible and hasty, and he could oversimplify complex issues. Unlike most of us, however, he was wholly conscious of these inclinations and battled them constantly. He regarded the use of teaching to advance a partisan viewpoint as disgraceful, especially if one was teaching the works of great poets and philosophers.

Today we are admonished that to teach great books (books that the teacher asserts to be greater than most others, including almost all recent ones) is itself an ideological exercise. Allan turned to these books precisely to escape from ideology. He never offered a dogmatic teaching; he presented philosophy as that way of life for which the problems were always more evident than the solutions. He wanted to help students achieve a broader perspective on their own problems than was available in their own society, to survey themselves and it from the heights afforded by the works of the greatest thinkers. He stressed that these thinkers were neither Democrats nor Republicans; he noted for instance that Plato and Aristotle, while neither "socialists" nor "capitalists," were closer to the former than the latter. His aim was never to bring the cavalry of political philosophy to the rescue of any partisan position; it was to disclose the difficulties of those positions, thereby freeing the students from them.

Allan insisted that the books that he taught could speak to everyone, male and female, white and black, of Western background and of non-Western. Besides insisting on this, he proved it. In his last years, as North American universities became more polyglot, he drew many devoted students from non-Western backgrounds. His graduate students always included women, and he attracted some outstanding blacks. Allan was an "elitist" in believing that some books were much more worth reading than others, but he also believed that every student should read them. He opposed racial self-segregation because it discouraged blacks from reading them. He regarded some books as worth more than others precisely because they spoke to absolutely anybody who would take the trouble to listen to them.

As a graduate teacher, Allan ran an imposing seminar. He did most of the talking but evoked a lively response just the same. His sessions were famous for starting punctually and never ending that way. The scheduled two hours easily ran to four. In 1965 the great East Coast Power Blackout struck Ithaca and Allan's seminar, plunging the classroom into blackness. Perhaps Allan thought it his civic duty to deny us the opportunity of looting; in any case, he talked on and on. (I can no longer recall whether the blackout outlasted the seminar or vice versa.) In the seminar Allan could be peremptory, but often he would airily dismiss a question and return the following week to answer it at respectful length, having obviously mulled it over in the meantime.

Allan's advice to his graduate students was to find one great writer and stick with him. He himself focused on just four in the course of his life: Plato, Shakespeare, Rousseau, and Nietzsche. He believed that the key to learning was to live for a lifetime with the few great texts that most engaged you, to return to them again and again, and to grow as a thinker and human being along with your comprehension of them. If his students have anything in common, it is that they have honored this advice and immersed themselves in texts as diverse as their characters, ranging from the Bible to Heidegger.

Allan was equally a teacher outside the classroom. A visit to his apartment was a cherished if daunting experience. For his closest students he created an entire milieu. His favorite device was the reading group, an informal class held at his home. He also spent hours with these students individually, discussing the world, their work, their friendships and loves. Like most teachers, he overestimated his students; but unlike most, not by much. He was a superhero not least in possessing X-ray vision. He could be tactful and he could be frank. He understood in each case what could not be said to someone's face and what could only be said to his face. Still, after a session listening to Allan dissect my friends, I could hardly escape the conclusion that he also dissected me before them. At least that spared me the necessity of trying to conceal much from them. Allan's gossip of this sort was rarely malicious. He believed that all learning was personal, that you learned only by coming to grips with your own character and those of your friends, the cases of human nature that mattered to you.

Especially in his informal relations with students, Allan appointed himself a kind of ambassador of the past. He loved, in the first place, the America of his youth, that vanished world of FDR and Truman, of a Democratic party that had Americanized the immigrants, confronted the Great Depression, spearheaded the defeat of Hitler, and kept the Soviets at bay. This he regarded as the heroic age of modern American politics, and his sentimental identification with the Democrats persisted, even as he found it ever harder to vote for Democratic candidates. (In his last years he delighted in following the ins and outs of Chicago politics.) At Cornell he befriended the octogenarian Frances E. Perkins, delegate to the Bull Moose convention of 1912, pioneer social reformer, and FDR's secretary of labor. He accorded Madam Perkins (as she was always called) the rare honor of confining himself to playing her straight man, eliciting arch social commentary and anecdote after anecdote about Al Smith, Jim Farley, John Nance Garner, Harold Ickes, and the rest. These he repeated for the rest of his life.

Equally privileged were such last masters of the great tradition of Western thought as happened to come to town. Allan loved being host to a Gershom Scholem or a Hans-Georg Gadamer, treating him with filial reverence and doing his best to communicate the grounds of that reverence to his students.

Conversations with Allan were as full of laughter as his lectures. He was a wonderful raconteur because he had so many stories to tell on himself. He was someone to whom things just happened. A famous gloss on two Yiddish terms for haplessness identifies one as the man who spills his soup and the other as the man whom it gets spilled on. Allan was a thirty-second-degree adept of both categories; he spilled oceans of soup on himself.

One of his favorite stories involved a lecturing trip to New York during his Toronto years. His friend Walter Berns had entrusted him with a credit-card payment to mail inside the States. Allan was staying at the Plaza, and he realized only after he was in bed that he had forgotten to mail the letter. A dim sense of the urgency of this missive afflicted him, and so, after hours of insomnia, he got up and went to look for a mailbox. So groggy was he, however, that when he got outside his room, he discovered that he had forgotten the letter. He also noticed that he was less than half-dressed, that he had closed his door behind him, and that he didn't have his key. (As my wife has often said of me, things hated him.) After other misadventures, he finally regained his room, his clothing, and the letter, and stumbled down to the lobby to mail it. No sooner had he accomplished this demanding task, however, than a new doubt seized him. Had the letter been stamped with American postage? He wasn't absolutely sure. If not, the post office would not deliver it, and Walter Berns might be seriously embarrassed. Allan now resolved to retrieve the letter. Since the desk clerk was vague about when the box would be emptied, the sleepless Allan camped out beside it for the remaining early morning hours. When the postman finally arrived, an actual tussle ensued.

"Get your hands out of there! That's property of the U.S. govern-ment!" Allan finally got the letter back. It was correctly stamped. As he later learned from Berns, the payment was for $1.17.

This couldn't have happened to many people, but it was easy to believe that it had happened to Allan. He loved to tell of his early ex-periences in France, such as when a prostitute solicited him and, in-formed that he was only a *pauvre étudiant,* replied, *"Mais j'adore la théorie!"* (words that Allan later delighted in applying to himself). Then there was the time he was in a café with a group including a worldly older woman. Her cigarette went out, and Allan sprang to be helpful. *"Madame, permettez-moi de rallumer votre feu!"* She (with a withering glance): *"J'en doute, monsieur, j'en doute."*

Another favorite French story involved of all things *la Sainte Toile,* France's most sacred relic, the reputed wedding veil of the Virgin. At dusk one winter day in the early fifties, Allan found himself almost alone in the Cathedral of Chartres. A priest approached to ask his help with an urgent task. It proved to be that of transporting the reliquary of the veil from one place in the church to another. As they lugged it reverently, the priest inquired, *"Est-ce que vous êtes catholique, mon fils?"* *"Non, mon père,"* replied Allan politely. An awkward pause ensued. *"Alors est-ce que vous êtes protestant?"* *"Non, mon père."* There-after they proceeded in silence.

Paris was the next thing to heaven for Allan. He cherished the freedom that reigned there, the remarkable individuals, the range of human types, the intellectual intensity, the café society. He never felt pressure there, as he sometimes did in America, to conform to pre-vailing opinions. He hobnobbed with Rothschilds, with Commu-nists who declared that someone should blow up the Louvre, with the philosopher Alexandre Kojève, with the eminent liberal Ray-mond Aron, with publishers, writers, artists, politicians, academics, and *flâneurs.* He influenced younger scholars emerging from Marx-ism, some few of whom almost comprise a French contingent of his students. Over the years he made several close friends, and ten days in Paris comprised the happiest interlude of his final months. If there are to be Allan sightings, a likely venue is the Café de Flore.

Allan's French sojourns pervaded his teaching and were the chief means by which he sought to open his students' eyes to the existence of a world beyond America. For him France and America were the two poles not only of his own life but of Western modernity. This emerged especially in his teaching of Tocqueville. He loved to contrast the callow but touching innocence of our society with the worldliness and cynicism of theirs, the American suburban bungalow with its sign The Joneses Welcome You with the posh apartment building in Paris where not a single tenant has displayed his name by his doorbell.

Allan appreciated life's pleasures. A music lover, he acquired the best equipment that he could afford, and an infinity of records and, later, CDs. You could never get away from his apartment without listening to his latest discovery. He also came to love fine clothes, fine furniture, fine foods, gadgets, rugs, objets d'art. It was part of his superabundant vitality to care a lot even about rather trivial things; it was a side of himself that he often laughed at. His acquiring began in his Toronto years, before he had money. A colleague joked that at Christmastime the local Georg Jensen's displayed a banner reading "Thank you to our customer." By the time the wealth was there, the habits that presupposed it were well established.

Allan of course had vices, which, because his personality was so forceful, were obtrusive. His nervousness and intensity put people off. He could be abrasive and overbearing, and he sometimes argued unfairly. He loved attention, and he insisted on it. He dominated social situations so thoroughly as to drive hostesses to despair (he was grateful to those who put up with him). Parents never much liked him; he seemed too interested in their children's approval and not enough in their own. From his point of view, the case was simple. However nice the parents might be, it was too late to persuade them to devote their lives to studying Plato; there was hope only for the children.

Away from the limelight Allan suffered from bouts of gloom and agitation. He agonized deeply, for example, over the intertwined destinies of America and Israel, over the state of American Jewry, over the worsening crisis of race relations. In his last years, he was preoccupied with the future of the university and of the learning that it was charged with transmitting. He tended to fear that his prophecies of decay would come true by the following morning; in fact their ful-fillment usually took a little longer. Because of his moodiness, he could be difficult even or especially with his intimates. He often had a bee in his bonnet. His closest friends were those who knew how to argue with him; this for him established not only respect but inti-macy.

By 1969 Allan seemed set at Cornell. Just then, however, the uni-versity blew up and caved in, bowing to demands made at gunpoint. Allan, like most of his faculty friends, felt that he had no choice but to resign. He was fortunate to land at Toronto with the closest of these friends, Walter Berns.

Allan's years in Toronto were probably his most tranquil; on a later visit there he described them as his happiest. He much admired the unique combination of traditionalism and tolerance that charac-terized Canadian life. He regarded Canada as the archetype of a well-ordered liberal society. He felt that no people were more decent than the Canadians, no colleagues more gentlemanly. He was particularly impressed by the late George Grant, the best-known Canadian thinker to remain little known in the United States. Grant was a great man, the other professor whom I have met who was larger than life, and Allan, sensing a kindred spirit, loved and admired him, as he did Grant's remarkable wife Sheila. A devout Christian and a Canadian loyal to his Loyalist forebears, Grant had meditated deeply on the writings of Simone Weil, Martin Heidegger, and Leo Strauss. The result was a profound critique of technological modernity and of the United States as its vanguard. It bemused Allan that George was forever signing petitions demanding Canadian withdrawal from NORAD and NATO. Here, however, was a man who was a genuine thinker and a brilliant conversationalist, whose passions were as in-tense as Allan's, and who, despite his critique of Americanism, re-spected Americans who were as loyal to their country as he was to his. It would take a subtler pen than mine to do justice to their rela-tionship.

Allan enjoyed many other friends and admirers in Toronto. Per-haps nowhere else did he meet so many adults who, without quite understanding what he was about or without being able to enter into it, recognized his remarkable qualities and supported him loyally. He attracted many fine students in those years, and made great strides in understanding (especially in his work on Rousseau's *Emile*). After every class he would call me and excitedly share his new discoveries. In general he seemed in those years to be leading the life that best suited him.

For me, it was one thing to have studied with Allan as an undergraduate, quite another to study with him (for that was still what I was doing) as a colleague. The delicacy, the solicitude, the generosity that Allan showed me then remain among my most cherished memories of him. Recognizing the difficulty of my establishing my independence from him, he did everything to bolster it. When he heard that a certain undergraduate, reproached with being a Bloomian, had indignantly insisted that he was an Orwinian, he laughed delightedly. When I fumbled the ball, he recovered it, and, as he did not wish to wound my shaky self-confidence, months or years might pass before he would gently disclose to me how badly I had bungled.

Allan close up was very different from Allan at a distance. My wife and I soon learned that our education in human nature had scarcely begun. I learned many things, but above all I learned that my understanding was much too "idealistic." Allan saw that I would rather think the best of people (including myself and himself) than the truth about them. Allan had the strength to face harsh truths without wavering in his zest for life or his love toward friends. He taught us to accept the world as it was; he even persuaded us that it was more beautiful that way.

Allan finally became restless in Toronto, as he would have done after ten years almost anywhere. Besides, it was Chicago and the Committee on Social Thought that beckoned. Chicago shared with Paris the distinction of being home for Allan. There he had spent the decisive years of his life, studying with his great teacher Leo Strauss. There remained such intellectual titans of his youth as David Grene and Edward Shils, as well as good friends his own age and Nathan Tarcov, one of his best students. The great surprise of this second Chicago stint was his friendship with Saul Bellow. Each recognized in the other a genuine original. They regularly taught together, exploring their very different insights into a wide range of texts. Allan marveled at Saul's creative intelligence, so different from his own critical one; Saul saw in Allan the makings of a genuine writer. Allan had always taken great risks as a teacher; Saul encouraged him to take them as a writer. The result was *The Closing of the American Mind,* which began a new (and final) epoch in Allan's life.

Allan had always viewed himself as a teacher rather than a writer. Modest about his intellectual achievements, he had always deferred to the writings of Strauss. His previous publications had all grown out of his teaching, and most had been intended for use in it. They consisted primarily of commentaries on and translations of his favorite books, and they were meant for students. *The Closing* also grew out of his teaching, but it had the character of a report from the battlefront. It, too, was in a sense a modest book, which purported to recount nothing more than Allan's experiences as a teacher at three of North America's better universities. In it he accused such institutions of claiming to foster "openness" but of seeking, in the name of this very end, to stifle discussion of fundamental issues, thereby impoverishing education under the pretext of broadening it.

Allan elaborated this contention in detail, offering a provocative account of the whole history of Western thought culminating in this outcome. He also set out to explain why today's students and professors had become what they had become. He thus undertook to discuss the most controversial issues in American society: the decline of parental authority and the influence of feminism and of widespread divorce, the prevalence of drugs and rock music, the issue of race on campus, the effect of the New Left on the curriculum, the substitution of empty jargon ("psychobabble") for receptivity to genuine philosophic texts. Discussing these matters with a boldness and directness absent from other academic treatments, he opened many eyes and raised many eyebrows.

The phenomenal popular success of *The Closing of the American Mind* took Allan entirely by surprise. Overnight he found himself confronting wealth, fame, and notoriety. The wealth and fame he enjoyed with childlike glee, and he was amused to observe himself so doing. He loved to dial the 800 number that advised the caller of the coming week's *New York Times* best-seller list, and to hold out the receiver so his visitor could hear that Allan still commanded first place. He was thrilled when the business pages listed his book and Eddie Murphy as the two biggest moneymakers for the Gulf and Western Corporation that year. On a more serious note, he was heartened that the book seemed to have done some good by emboldening others to speak out as he had done.

The notoriety was another matter. Allan had always been sensitive to what others thought of him (too sensitive, as he thought; this too was a topic of his jokes), and it stung him to be insulted by critics, many of whom either had not read the book or had willfully distorted his argument. Attacks on him became de rigueur for establishing the writer's political correctness (a term that may not yet have existed), and he was routinely denounced as racist, sexist, and elitist. Whole conferences were convened to denounce him, one of which a *Times* correspondent likened to the "minute of hatred" in Orwell's *Nineteen Eighty-Four,* a staged frenzy of ritual execration. Allan did what a man of courage had to do: he fought back.

In the fall of 1990 Allan contracted Guillain-Barre syndrome, a rare neurological disease that causes paralysis and atrophy. The initial onset was almost fatal. Allan's body, always robust in spite of his habitual neglect of it, was ravaged; his limbs had lost almost all of their flesh. Bedridden for months, he had to relearn how to walk and never regained full use of his hands. Even so, the pace and extent of his recovery were remarkable. Unfortunately he was only to enjoy it for a few months. December 1991 brought a sudden and again nearly fatal onset of acute diabetes; from this too he managed to rebound. Finally he suffered from a perforated peptic ulcer and from liver failure; yet again he rallied, but this time unsuccessfully.

Through this all, Allan soldiered on, and addressed himself to unfinished business. He resumed teaching and holding reading groups: that much went without saying. He continued to follow politics and the state of the universities. As he had always done, he welcomed countless visitors and spent hours on the telephone with friends, many of them his former students. Above all he labored to finish the second book for which he had contracted with Simon and Schuster. A large advance was involved, as was a determination to see in print this work by which he most wanted to be remembered. Entitled *Love and Friendship,* it dealt with his lifelong favorite themes as treated by his favorite writers: Rousseau, the great nineteenth-century novelists (Jane Austen, Stendhal, Flaubert, Tolstoy), Shakespeare, and Plato. Spending hours each day dictating to an amanuensis, he not only produced a draft but completed his final revisions of it.

My wife and I happened to be present in Chicago for most of that final year. I'd like not to rhapsodize on the way that Allan handled it. The last thing he would have wanted was for me to depict him as J. L. David painted Socrates, all noble gesture and moral uplift. He feared death as much as (and loved life more than) the next man, but he faced it squarely. He wanted his friends around him, and he wanted to prepare them for the worst, but he also wanted to make this as easy for them as possible. For a man who had so many books in his head and who had taught them so eloquently, a signal achievement of his last months was that he never struck an edifying note.

Allan's death was an irreparable loss to all the members of his circle. That circle persists, however. His students are scattered throughout North America; he regarded as his greatest achievement the bonds of friendship that continue to unite them. They in their turn have succeeded in attracting students of their own. It has to be one of the more successful pyramid schemes around. And it's entirely legal; most of us even heed No Smoking signs. But, as none of us can be another Allan, so we can hardly hope to meet one. As Allan's favorite poet might have ended this (or some other) piece, we who are young will never see so much, nor live so long.

Part 4

ASPIRATIONS

Time to Shake Our Hypochondria

Robert L. Bartley

A S THE NEW DECADE DAWNS, a resolution for American society: Let us shake off our national hypochondria. The decade just closed has a special place in our history. In no other have we accomplished more and enjoyed it less.

We are now witnessing the worldwide triumph of American values and the collapse of the empire that threatened us for two generations. A decade ago we faced the prospect of worldwide inflation and economic collapse. Over the decade this threat has been confounded and almost forgotten. Last year our per capita gross national product was 17 percent above 1980 in real terms, 38 percent above 1970, and 68 percent above 1945. The economy expanded for nearly the whole decade; we have now reached a peacetime record eighth year of economic expansion. Peace and prosperity.

Yet the reaction has been one of unrelieved pessimism. We are by now accustomed to best-selling books like *The Rise and Fall of the Great Powers,* or *The Great Depression of 1990.* Even the Statler Brothers—or was it the Oak Ridge Boys?—have been proclaiming the good days are over for good. The hypochondria has been notable in the news media celebrations of the end of the decade.

Part of this is of course ideological sour grapes. The conventional media/academic wisdom has been repeatedly confounded through the decade and now wants to find reasons why it was right and Ronald Reagan wrong. But the hypochondria must have deeper roots. Many of my ideological allies and personal friends have joined the chorus. Wall Street figures such as Peter Peterson have harped to the point of boredom on borrowing from the future. Richard Darman, who could talk about the success of his own policies, gives speeches denouncing American society as a spoiled child crying for Maypo, Noooow.

The public is somehow frightened when Japanese investors buy into Rockefeller Center; the fear alternatively seems to be that they will pick it up and move it to the Ginza or that they will sell it back for less than they paid. A decade ago, we worried that the Japanese would sell us too many high-quality goods at too low a price; it was the Arab sheiks who would buy us up. In fact, foreign investment is a vote of confidence in the United States. As for being bought up, between 1981 and 1988, net foreign investment amounted to a cumulative $670 billion. Over the same years, the private net worth of Americans increased by $5.2 trillion. Quite a treadmill.

THE PUZZLE FOR THE NEW DECADE is to explain this pessimism. How can peace and prosperity give birth not to cheer, but to the new Malthusianism?

There may be some clues looking back to the actual age of Thomas Malthus, trying to discern what gave birth to the ideas that made him history's champion economic pessimist. Malthus's first essay on population was published in 1798. This was twenty-nine years after the first patent was issued to James Watt in connection with the steam engine. In other words, Malthus's gloomy theorizing took place in the midst of the Industrial Revolution. He was explaining why economic progress was impossible just as mankind was taking the greatest economic leap in history.

Joseph A. Schumpeter, our century's greatest economic historian and one of its greatest economists, devoted a chapter to it in his massive *History of Economic Analysis*. He related how ancient societies were worried about overpopulation, but that after about 1600 this changed completely. The prevailing attitude was "increasing population was the most important symptom of wealth; it was the chief cause of wealth; it was wealth itself."

"It is quite a problem to explain why the opposite attitude," Schumpeter wrote, "should have asserted itself among economists from the middle of the eighteenth century on. Why was it that economists took fright at a scarecrow!"

The pessimism associated with Malthus did not develop despite the progress of the Industrial Revolution, Schumpeter concluded. It developed because of the progress. Rapid progress means rapid change, and rapid change is unsettling. Long-run progress causes short-run problems. Schumpeter wrote, "In the Industrial Revolution of the last decades of the eighteenth century, these short-run vicissitudes grew more serious than they had been before, precisely because the pace of economic development quickened."

To be fair, this is not to say the short-run problems were imaginary. In the short run, technological advance destroyed agricultural jobs faster than it created manufacturing jobs, especially since guilds and the like created bottlenecks. A type of mass unemployment arose unknown in the Middle Ages, and with it urban slums, gin mills, and great social debates over the poor laws. Malthus's pessimism was echoed a few decades later by Charles Dickens. But we now know that through it all mankind was rapidly building wealth.

TODAY'S HYPOCHONDRIA SHOWS SIMILAR ROOTS; we are living through another such age today. We are, mankind is, currently making exceptional technological and economic progress. This is, if you will, the new Industrial Revolution. The world is changing so rapidly that old certainties are breaking down and no one seems in control. Naturally, pessimism is appealing and chic.

In technological terms, it's not at all hard to believe we live in a second Industrial Revolution. In what other lifetimes could you find technical advances such as the splitting of the atom, the development of the computer, and the decoding of the gene? Not even James Watt's time showed such a profusion of scientific breakthroughs. If Watt's steam engine was the popular epitome of the original Industrial Revolution, the epitome of the new one is William Shockley's transistor. Electronics—the transistor, computers, microchips, integrated circuits—is redrawing the face of society today.

As the first Industrial Revolution changed an agricultural economy into an industrial economy, today's industrial revolution is changing an industrial economy into a service economy. Or perhaps more specifically, into an information economy, in which the predominant activity is collecting, processing, and communicating information. We are headed toward a world in which everyone on the globe is in instant communication with everyone else, and this evolution is changing world society in a myriad of ways.

Most conspicuously, we are seeing a decline in the power of governments, and also other institutions that mediate between people. This is the meaning of Tiananmen Square and Wenceslas Square. In a sense, William Shockley produced Mikhail Gorbachev. A censor can tell what books are being brought through customs, but he'll never be able to keep track of all the computer disks. And we're finding that totalitarian states cannot survive the information revolution. Back in the 1950s, wags talked of conquering Russia by bombarding it with Sears & Roebuck catalogs; the policy, unwittingly followed, has been an astounding success.

The information revolution does not affect only totalitarian governments. Democratic governments are now subject to much closer scrutiny. Today's presidents and congressmen can't get away with practices that were more or less routine for their predecessors. The basic policies of a state and indeed a nation can be turned around by an uprising led by a Howard Jarvis. The leaders of Japan Inc. are finding that if they pass taxes after voters keep telling them not to, geishas suddenly become a scandal.

Similarly, too, big corporations are not as powerful as they once were. We can now all watch the poor chairman of Exxon writhing with an oil spill in Alaska. With international competition, the power of labor unions dwindles. But the individual entrepreneur with a good idea can find easier access to capital and markets.

A second important aspect of the global information age is increasing economic interdependence. Probably the world economy has throughout this century been more interdependent than anyone realized; probably the true explanation of the Great Depression lies in attempts to fight this interdependence, in particular the Smoot-Hawley tariff.

Today, with twenty-four-hour financial markets spanning the globe, interdependence is hard to miss. This also limits governments, which simply cannot afford economic policies that are too far out of step with those of other nations. The best example was François Mitterrand's first year as president of France. Here was a dedicated socialist experiment, starting with nationalization of banks. But the external costs were too great; within a year the experiment had to be abandoned for market-oriented policies like those of other nations.

Similarly, even the United States found that it could not maintain benign neglect of the dollar. But when the United States cut top marginal tax rates, other big governments found they were more or less forced to copy the policies. The global information network renders almost instant verdicts on changes in government policy. In the end the world is ruled not by politicians but by markets. National governments will evolve toward something like state governments today: Each will have its own industrial development program to show why it has the best business and investment climate.

By and large this is a happy development, but not all of its aspects are agreeable. Governing nations and running big corporations will be more difficult, and these are after all necessary tasks. Relentless exposure can probably destroy almost anyone, whether Richard Nixon, Jim Wright, or Michael Milken. Instant communications may put more emphasis on emotions and less on logic; public policy preoccupations may become faddish. We the citizens will have to educate ourselves on how to assess and manage these trends.

Beyond that, the evolution of an information economy will inevitably cause painful displacements. In particular, it's hard to envision a place in this kind of economy for the uneducated. There will be, there is, a new urgency about schooling that works. There will be endless debate over what to do with those left behind in the new workforce. Our crack problems today echo the gin problems of Malthus's England.

We will need to learn, too, a lot about managing an instantly connected, interdependent world. At the international level, nations have to learn about coordinating policies. In particular, it's hard to see how we can manage an interdependent world economy if real economic variables can be swamped by seemingly arbitrary changes in exchange rates.

On the national level, there will be attempts to fight the new trends. There will always be the temptation to believe that if only we could wall ourselves off from the intrusions of foreigners, we could stop this ceaseless change and restore the old certainties. This is a snare and a delusion. If protectionism and economic nationalism prevail, they will stop progress and growth, if not cause a new depression.

The task before us is not to stop the new information age, but to take advantage of its vast opportunities. We will have to learn to live in a world economy. We shouldn't try to fight the marketplace, but listen to what it is telling us. Clearly it is telling us to become more modern, more globally minded, more innovative, more entrepreneurial.

An appropriate policy for the new interdependent world, indeed, would be unilateral free trade. In the long run, trade and investment barriers hurt the nation that maintains them. We should be dismantling ours, and leave it to Japanese citizens to dismantle theirs. In recent elections, it seems to me they have already started to do this; voters and consumers in Japan are demanding a bigger share of their country's economic gains.

The main point as the 1990s open is that national competition is something we should stop talking about. We're all citizens of the world, all in this together. If Mexicans don't prosper, Americans will be poorer. If China stagnates, it drains the rest of the world. The real economic competition will not be between nations but between companies. Sony and IBM will sell in the same markets, build the same international workforces, draw on the same world capital pool, and respond to the same incentives. What will it mean to say one is Japanese and the other American?

Still, the world likely in the 1990s and beyond should be kind to the United States. Our polyglot and multiracial society has its problems, but it also uniquely equips us for an interdependent world. More than other nations, we have developed the strong suit of adaptability; we can handle rapid change better than probably any other society. We certainly have the world's best entrepreneurial tradition. Barriers to starting a business are still lower here than in other nations. Risk taking is even fashionable.

Finally, we have an ace in the hole, if only we recognize it. The integrated world economy will feature mobility of goods and capital. But its true key will be brainpower, that is, labor. The assets of a business will walk out the door every night. And the United States will lead the world in extending a welcome to such movable assets.

We have an immigrant tradition, and despite some recent silliness, we are still going to have the most open immigration of any major nation. Some of our leading entrepreneurs are immigrants, and in our schools and universities the science leaders are the sons and daughters of immigrants. The bright and ambitious of the 1990s and beyond will be attracted by our freedom and vitality, if only it isn't soured by continued hypochondria.

So welcome to the 1990s. From now on, let's feel free to enjoy our good fortune.

America's Best Infrastructure Program

George Gilder

WHEN THE DETHRONED KING of high-yield bonds, Michael Milken, left for Pleasanton prison some two years ago, the claims of his critics inspired Hollywood, ruled best-seller lists, and sealed the ledgers on a so-called "decade of greed."

So what is happening now, just two years later? Who is this balding young man emerging this week with a smile from his years in the slammer? Despite his recent diagnosis of treatable prostate cancer, Mr. Milken is coming out of prison ready again to take on the world and launch a revolution in educational video.

Since his incarceration, the entire case against him has collapsed. Never in history has a white-collar criminal been so luminously and elaborately vindicated during his years in jail.

Punctured Claims

THE CLAIMS that Mr. Milken's alleged crimes cost their immediate victims scores of millions have already been punctured on this page. (Federal District Judge Kimba Wood's own assigned experts appraised the damage at $318,082.) Still, the heart of the case against Mr. Milken came not in specific legalities but in the larger charge that his entire enterprise was basically fraudulent. But in 1993 the evidence presents its own clear verdict. Far from a Ponzi schemer, Mr. Milken was demonstrably one of the supreme investors in the history of finance. At a time when the air is full of talk of new investment in infrastructure, we can learn much from Mr. Milken's successful financing of the infrastructure for a new service economy.

Mr. Milken's largest commitment—some $21 billion—was to the information industry. The most important of these firms were MCI, Tele-Communications Inc. (TCI), McCaw Cellular, Turner Broadcasting, Warner Communications (now Time Warner), Twentieth Century Fox (now part of NewsCorp), and Metromedia Broadcasting. Virtually devoid of conventional collateral, none of these companies could have raised comparable sums from another source. Together they stand or fall as unanswerable evidence of the quality of Mr. Milken's unique vision and contribution.

Mr. Milken's $3 billion endowment of MCI's bold drive to lay a national network of leading-edge fiber-optic lines began at a time when MCI's revenues were $234 million and came in the face of AT&T's plans to delay completing its own system until sometime in the early twenty-first century. Not only was MCI's venture a success, but it also spurred the creation of several other fiber networks over the next five years and saved Corning's seventeen-year investment in the technology. MCI is now worth some $11 billion, Corning $7 billion, and these webs of glass and light are today an essential resource of America's information economy. Because of Mr. Milken's head start, the United States has laid about nine times as much fiber as Japan, which in the early 1980s was threatening to take over fiber production and installation.

Just as important to America's information infrastructure as fiber optics is cable TV. As a technology, cable is often underestimated. But some 80 percent of the cost of a telecommunications system comes in the local loop: the web of neighborhood connections to homes and offices. The cable industry offers to about 90 percent of America's homes the chance to link to a network with some seventy thousand times the bandwidth of telephone wires. With television rapidly becoming a branch of the digital computer industry, these cable connections, potentially capable of sustaining billion-bit-per-second two-way data, have become a crucial complement to the fiber long-distance network.

Without the vision and $12 billion commitment of Michael Milken to an array of cable companies, this huge resource of broadband communications could not have been laid. Lacking such financing and TV entrepreneurs, Europe and Asia command no comparable cable infrastructure. When Mr. Milken began funding TCI with a stream of investments totaling $814 million, it was worth a few hundred million. Now it commands a market value of some $10 billion. With recent announcements of major digital TV fiber projects in Queens, New York, and Orlando, Florida, Time Warner is challenging TCI for the technological lead in cable. Saved by junk bonds at the time of its Atari fiasco, Warner, too, has become an important asset of American competitiveness.

Mr. Milken's cable investments, however, would not have thrived without investment in complementary programming. When he funded Ted Turner's CNN and laid the financial foundation for TNT, the Turner enterprises were worth a few hundred million dollars. While turning down Mr. Turner's appeal for funding for purchase of CBS—on the correct belief that the networks were in decline—Mr. Milken financed Mr. Turner's acquisition of MGM's film library. At the same time, he helped finance the Fox Network, Viacom, and Lorimar. The cable and programming companies supported by Mr. Milken now are worth more than $100 billion.

Perhaps the most visionary Milken investment was McCaw Cellular. When McCaw Cellular came to Mr. Milken in 1986, it was a localized cable and cellular company with small profits and a large, apparently foolhardy goal: competing with the giant regional Bell operating companies by creating a national network of wireless phones. Mr. Milken raised more than $1.25 billion for the company. As we enter an era when most telephones will be wireless, McCaw, together with Lin Broadcasting, was valued in the recent AT&T equity purchase at some $11 billion, and Craig McCaw speculates in Forbes about the possibility of taking over AT&T.

Mr. Milken also funded an array of important companies in other fields. Among the famous failures, such as Kindercare and Integrated Resources, were a series of phenomenal successes. Among them are Medco, valued at $35 million when Mr. Milken began lending to it, and now valued at $4.5 billion in inexpensive mail-order pharmaceuticals; Barnes & Noble-B. Dalton, now the nation's largest bookseller; Hasbro, the world's largest toy maker; Circus Circus and Mirage, reshaping the skyline and bringing family themes to Las Vegas resorts; Chrysler and American Motors; and TLC-Beatrice, the international food conglomerate that was the source of the nation's largest black fortune. It was owned by the late Reginald Lewis, a close Milken associate.

Now many of Mr. Milken's investments are household names and in retrospect seem obvious winners. But at the time Mr. Milken was bitterly assaulted in the financial press for nearly all his major deals. When he began financing takeovers, the hostility reached a hysterical pitch, and politicians and prosecutors entered the fray. Yet the most reviled ventures often yielded the best results. One unsuccessful raid on Disney by Saul Steinberg galvanized a restructuring of the company that increased its worth elevenfold. In essence, these takeovers of the 1980s reversed the disastrous conglomerate movement of the 1970s.

Listening to the laments of entrenched management, however, the courts and Congress finally acted to bring the entire movement to an abrupt halt by enacting the Orwellian Financial Institutions Reform, Recovery, and Enforcement Act (FIRREA) and other legislation that forced savings and loans, banks, and insurance companies to sell off their high-yield securities. Under this assault, the market finally crashed in 1989, and Mr. Milken's critics were sure that the bonds would never revive. Indeed, many analysts warned that in a recession, such highly leveraged firms as McCaw, TCI, and NewsCorp would go bankrupt.

The recession came on schedule. But for two years in a row, high-yield bonds—led by Mr. Milken's—have been America's best fixed-income investment. While investors in blue-chip IBM lost some $70 billion in market value in five years, holders of so-called junk gained $100 billion.

Fully Vindicated

Economist GLENN YAGO has demonstrated that if the relatively few S&Ls with large junk positions had been allowed to keep them, they would have earned hundreds of millions on their holdings and would have imposed no costs on the government. For example, the West Coast Columbia Savings & Loan would have made about $1 billion on its junk portfolio and remained in business at no cost to the federal government.

In 1993 we can say that Michael Milken's portfolio of companies, both debt and equity, has fully vindicated him. His alleged infractions of parking codes and such seem utterly picayune beside his monumental contributions to the nation's wealth, well-being, and competitiveness.

The man whose indefatigable services to his community exceeded all others during the 1980s finds himself bound to perform 5,400 hours of so-called community service under the supervision of social workers. America does not need federal boondoggles disguised as social spending or "investments" in "infrastructure." Mr. Milken has already financed the key components of America's infrastructure for the information age. To consummate his vision, it is now necessary for the government to get out of the way and allow these private firms to collaborate in linking the separate networks that Mr. Milken helped create during the 1980s' decade of enterprise.

The Liberty Manifesto

P. J. O'Rourke

THE CATO INSTITUTE has an unusual political cause—which is no political cause whatsoever. We are here tonight to dedicate ourselves to that cause, to dedicate ourselves, in other words, to . . . nothing.

We have no ideology, no agenda, no catechism, no dialectic, no plan for humanity. We have no "vision thing," as our ex-president would say, or, as our current president would say, we have no Hillary.

All we have is the belief that people should do what people want to do, unless it causes harm to other people. And that had better be clear and provable harm. No nonsense about secondhand smoke or hurtful, insensitive language, please.

I don't know what's good for you. You don't know what's good for me. We don't know what's good for mankind. And it sometimes seems as though we're the only people who don't. It may well be that, gathered right here in this room tonight, are all the people in the world who don't want to tell all the people in the world what to do.

This is because we believe in freedom. Freedom—what this country was established upon, what the Constitution was written to defend, what the Civil War was fought to perfect.

Freedom is not empowerment. Empowerment is what the Serbs have in Bosnia. Anybody can grab a gun and be empowered. It's not entitlement. An entitlement is what people on welfare get, and how free are they? It's not an endlessly expanding list of rights—the "right" to education, the "right" to health care, the "right" to food and housing. That's not freedom; that's dependency. Those aren't rights, those are the rations of slavery—hay and a barn for human cattle.

There is only one basic human right, the right to do as you damn well please. And with it comes the only basic human duty, the duty to take the consequences.

So WE ARE HERE tonight in a kind of antimatter protest—an unpolitical undemonstration by deeply uncommitted inactivists. We are part of a huge invisible picket line that circles the White House twenty-four hours a day. We are participants in an enormous non-march on Washington—millions and millions of Americans *not* descending upon the nation's capital in order to demand *nothing* from the United States government. To demand nothing, that is, except the one thing which no government in history has been able to do—leave us alone.

There are just two rules of governance in a free society: mind your own business, and keep your hands to yourself.

Bill, keep your hands to yourself. Hillary, mind your own business.

We have a group of incredibly silly people in the White House right now, people who think government works. Or that government *would* work, if you got some real bright young kids from Yale to run it.

We're being governed by dorm room bull session. The Clinton administration is over there right now pulling an all-nighter in the West Wing. They think that, if they can just stay up late enough, they can create a healthy economy and bring peace to former Yugoslavia.

The Clinton administration is going to decrease government spending by increasing the amount of money we give to the government to spend.

Health care is too expensive, so the Clinton administration is putting a high-powered corporate lawyer in charge of making it cheaper. (This is what I always do when I want to spend less money—hire a lawyer from Yale.) If you think health care is expensive now, wait until you see what it costs when it's free.

The Clinton administration is putting together a program so that college graduates can work to pay off their school tuition. As if this were some genius idea. It's called *getting a job*. Most folks do that when they get out of college, unless, of course, they happen to become governor of Arkansas.

And the Clinton administration launched an attack on people in Texas because those people were religious nuts with guns. Hell, this country was *founded* by religious nuts with guns. Who does Bill Clinton think stepped ashore on Plymouth Rock? Peace Corps volunteers? Or maybe the people in Texas were attacked because of child abuse. But, if child abuse was the issue, why didn't Janet Reno teargas Woody Allen?

YOU KNOW, if government were a product, selling it would be illegal.

Government is a health hazard. Governments have killed many more people than cigarettes or unbuckled seat belts ever have.

Government contains impure ingredients—as anybody who's looked at Congress can tell you.

On the basis of Bill Clinton's 1992 campaign promises, I think we can say government practices deceptive advertising.

And the merest glance at the federal budget is enough to convict the government of perjury, extortion, and fraud.

There, ladies and gentlemen, you have the Cato Institute's program in a nutshell: government should be against the law.

Term limits aren't enough. We need jail.

George Will's Baseball— A Conservative Critique

Donald Kagan

BASEBALL, more than any other sport, has inspired good writing from important authors and gained serious attention from thoughtful people. From Ring Lardner's ignorant and mean-spirited "busher," Jack Keefe, to Mark Harris's intelligent and warm-hearted southpaw Henry Wiggen, to Bernard Malamud's mythical Arthurian hero, the "natural" Roy Hobbs, writers have used baseball and its players to say something about the world and the people in it. How someone sees the game and its players reveals the kind of person he is and what he values.

My friend Bart Giamatti was a student and explicator of epic poetry before he became president of Yale University, president of baseball's National League, and commissioner of baseball. He viewed the game as an epic, whose elements were simple and primordial: a man stood on a hill and hurled a rock at another man, who waited below with a tree trunk in his hands. (Malamud had a similar vision, in which the bat was "like a caveman's ax.") So it must have been from the time of the Stone Age. A dramatically heroic and potentially tragic confrontation stands at the heart of this most poetic game.

From a more classical perspective Giamatti regarded baseball as a kind of Homeric *Odyssey.* The batter is its hero. He begins at home, but his mission is to venture away from it, encountering various unforeseeable dangers. At each station opponents scheme to put him out by strength or skill or guile. Should they succeed he dies on the bases, defeated. If his own heroic talents are superior, however, he completes the circuit and returns victorious to home, there to be greeted with joy by the friends he left behind. But Giamatti knew the *Iliad,* too, and as a long-time Red Sox fan he believed that the tragic epic best corresponded to baseball; thus he observed that the game "was meant to break your heart."

That is not how George Will sees it. Educated at Connecticut's Trinity College and at Oxford and Princeton, the holder of a doctorate in political theory, a former professor himself and the son of a professor, he has become a Pulitzer Prize–winning columnist and a political commentator on national television, and he has earned a reputation as the most thoughtful and urbane of conservative journalists. His best-selling book *Men at Work** clearly shows his characteristic analytic intelligence, a witty and graceful writing style, a deep knowledge of baseball and its history, and a love for the game and the men who work at it in the major leagues. It is not a book, however, for those who look to the game for the celebration of that heroic greatness that can inspire and elevate the rest of us to admire a natural excellence that we ourselves can achieve only in dreams. His book is not for humanists, poets, or hero worshipers—but for systems analysts, social scientists, and computer programmers.

As we would expect from its author, it is no mere narrative account but makes a powerful argument. Supported by a formidable array of statistics and testimony from current participants, Will rejects the widespread assertion that baseball today is a degenerate perversion of the great game that once was. Critics point to the dilution of talent caused by the expansion from sixteen to twenty-six teams, and to the unseasoned and untutored players who still must learn the rudiments of the game when they are brought too soon to the majors to fill out the added rosters. They complain of the absence of the great dynastic championship teams that we knew in better times, the decline of hitting (the most difficult and most exciting part of the game), the shortage of great players—in short, the mediocrity of baseball today.

Will dismisses these complaints as the usual crabbing of elders,

---

* George F. Will. *Men at Work: The Craft of Baseball.* Macmillan Publishing, 1990.

almost as old as baseball itself. To him "the national pastime is better then ever in almost every way and is getting better every year." For this conclusion he offers three major reasons:

1. The games are getting closer. The powerful 1988 American League champion Oakland Athletics scored only 180 runs more than their opponents for a per-game average margin of victory of 1.1 runs. The great Yankees of 1927 had an advantage more than twice that size—2.45 runs, and the Yankees of 1939 defeated their rivals by an average of 2.67 runs per game.

2. Competition for the championships is becoming more equal. No team has won the World Series for two consecutive years since the Yankees of 1977 and 1978. Since then there has been tremendous volatility: in the eleven seasons from 1979 through 1989 nine different teams won the American League pennant, and seven won in the National League. Compare this with the dynasties that dominated the past: the New York Giants won four pennants in a row from 1921 through 1924; the Brooklyn Dodgers won six out of ten from 1947 through 1956, and the Los Angeles team that has usurped their name won three of four from 1963 through 1966. The greatest dynasty of all, of course, was created by the New York Yankees. From 1921 through 1928 they won six of eight pennants; from 1936 through 1943 they won seven of eight; from 1947 through 1964 they won fifteen of eighteen (winning four consecutive pennants once and five in a row twice during that last stretch).

3. The culminating reason for the superiority of the modern game is that it is smarter; now, as never before, intelligence is the decisive element in the game.

The very name of his book is ominous for Will's approach to the subject: *Men at Work: The Craft of Baseball.* It is not a game but a *craft;* the participants do not play, they *work.* "Baseball was evolving from lower forms of activity about the time the colonies were evolving into a nation, and baseball became a mode of work—as distinct from a pastime—remarkably soon after the nation got going." The participants succeed at their craft as men do at any other, by means of hard work and intelligent study. Will knows, of course, that baseball players need physical ability and natural talent, but he mentions these as little as possible. In his view baseball has progressed and improved because intelligence and knowledge have come to the fore, aided by advances in technology. Charts, computers, and videotapes have made it possible to acquire and organize information better than ever before and therefore to use it more effectively and decisively. "Games are won by a combination of informed aggression and prudence based on information."

As George Orwell once put it, only an intellectual could believe that. This is the fantasy of a smart, skinny kid who desperately wants to believe that brains count more than the speed, power, and reckless courage of the big guys who can play, but it is also the dominant message of this book. More puzzling than this bizarre prejudice is Will's defense of the modern game against its detractors. As a conservative, a self-proclaimed Tory, he might be expected to be a *laudator temporis acti,* a praiser of the past even beyond justice. An admirer of a nobler time should look askance at the use of the designated hitter and other specialists who demean the all-roundedness esteemed by both the principle of aristocracy and liberal education.

Decline and Fall

ONE NEED NOT BE A CONSERVATIVE, however, to be appalled by what has happened to baseball. Aesthetically, the decline is evident. Baseball was meant to be played on nature's green grass in the sunshine. Bart Giamatti liked to point out that "paradise" derives from an Old Persian word that meant "enclosed park or green." Baseball responds to "a vestigial memory of an enclosed green space as a place of freedom or play." For Will, of course, it is a place of work—hard, dangerous, and exacting. Most modern baseball fields suit Will's vision better, for they are anything but parks, not to mention paradise. Many of them have replaced the grass with a surface hard as a pool table, whose covering has seams that sometimes come undone. In some of them the sky is shut out, turning the game into an indoor sport, like bowling and roller derby. The fields tend to be uniform and standardized, lacking the delightful peculiarities that real ball-parks like Ebbets Field, Griffith Stadium, Crosley Field, and the Polo Grounds used to have. The modern stadia seem fake, manufactured, unnatural. They are noisy, distracting, and offensive places, where scoreboards ceaselessly blare rock music and show cartoons. They sound military charges, tell the fans when to cheer, and produce mechanized rhythmic noise that used to be supplied rarely, spontaneously, and at appropriate times by the collision of human palms. Everything possible is done to turn the spectator's attention from the game.

This may well be necessary, because the game has become much more boring. In the 1940s the Yankees began their games at three o'clock in the afternoon, and they were generally over by five. On June 25, 1990, a day picked at random, omitting a twelve-inning game that lasted four hours and fifteen minutes, twelve games were played in the major leagues. The quickest lasted over two and a half hours, the longest over three and a half; the average was two hours and forty-three minutes. This is not because there is more scoring today: the highest scoring team in 1987 averaged 5.5 runs per game; the figure in 1941 was 5.6.

The percentage of elapsed time that involves significant action in a baseball game is always small, but it has become intolerably so. Part of the increased dead time results from a prodigal use of relief pitchers unknown in better days. Much of the rest consists of pitchers holding the ball or throwing to first to limit the running game that is the modern substitute for the most difficult part of the game and its life's blood—hitting. As Ted Williams neatly put it: "When you're coming towards the park and you're two blocks away, and you hear a tremendous cheer, that isn't because someone has thrown a strike. That's because someone has hit the ball." The threat posed by batters who can hit with consistency and power is what gives the game excitement and drama, and what provides the danger that alone makes great pitching and fielding impressive. Baseball was not meant to be a track meet, but the new fields—with their distant fences that make home runs into outs, and their hard surfaces that produce singles out of ordinary ground balls—are turning it into one.

Nor is the argument from equality compelling, for modern baseball is so equal because it is mediocre. The critics' complaints are sound; the quality of play is diminished everywhere, and no team can stock itself with enough talent to establish itself as a dynasty. Instead, an equality of incompetence reigns. The last time when great dynasties flourished was the 1950s, when the Yankees dominated the American League and the Dodgers controlled the National League almost as completely, challenged most successfully by an impressive Giants team. This is precisely the period that Will particularly scorns. Home runs, he tells us,

> began to drive out other forms of offense. When home runs became the center of baseball's mental universe, the emphasis shifted away from advancing runners. The new emphasis was on just getting runners on base to wait for lightning to strike. The major league teams of the 1950s were like the American automobiles of the 1950s. There was not much variety or subtlety. . . . The stolen base was like the foreign car: It was considered cute and fun and not quite serious, and was not often seen. . . .
>
> The wonder is that baseball took such a wrong turn in . . . the 1950s. Yes, that was a conservative decade. The Eisenhower years have been characterized as "the bland leading the bland." Bland was fine in politics. . . . But baseball is entertainment and bland entertainment is not fun. . . . It was insufficiently entertaining because it was not sufficiently intelligent.

That is an extraordinary passage to be written by a conservative and a baseball fan. Consider the contempt for "wait[ing] for lightning to strike." That is just what thrilled fans did in the 1920s and 1930s, as they watched the Yankees of Ruth, Gehrig, and Lazzeri, waiting for their legendary "five o'clock lightning." Whatever else may be said of American cars of the fifties, they had size and power;

the foreign car of the day was the Volkswagen Beetle, a tiny simulacrum of an automobile, miserably cramped and powerless.

In Defense of the Fifties

THE FIFTIES were when the first great black players—Jackie Robinson, Willie Mays, Roy Campanella, Don Newcombe, Henry Aaron, Frank Robinson, and Ernie Banks—came into their own and raised the quality and excitement of the game to a new level. All the thrills offered by baseball were present in abundance. If you like hitting you could have enjoyed watching Stan Musial, Williams, Aaron, Mays, Duke Snider, Mickey Mantle, Yogi Berra, and Roberto Clemente. If pitching is to your taste you could have seen Bob Feller, Warren Spahn, Early Wynn, Whitey Ford, and a host of other outstanding hurlers. If defense is what you want, the fifties were graced with such brilliant shortstops as Pee Wee Reese, Phil Rizzuto, and Luis Aparicio. Stealing bases, to be sure, was an appropriately minor part of the game, but no one who saw Willie Mays run the bases will ever forget it, and the thrill of watching Jackie Robinson steal home cannot be matched.

In the fifties these great players were not scattered about one or two to a side, as at best they are today, but were often collected in one place to make a great team. At their peak, the Dodgers terrified everyone with a lineup that included Robinson, Snider, Campanella, Gil Hodges, and Carl Furillo; and the 1951 Yankees could field a team that included Joe DiMaggio, Mantle, Berra, and Johnny Mize, who averaged 353 career home runs apiece. Great pitching staffs, with a depth not equalled in our time, were also assembled. The same Yankees had three pitchers (Allie Reynolds, Vic Raschi, and Eddie Lopat), each of whom averaged almost eighteen victories a season from 1950 through 1952; in 1953 they were joined by Ford, who won eighteen that year. The Cleveland staff of the same era—which included Feller, Wynn, Bob Lemon, and Mike Garcia—was even more impressive.

But even though pitching is generally conceded to be between 75 and 90 percent of the game, these Indians won only one pennant, in 1954, when they won 111 out of the 154 games (162 are played today) to beat out the Yankees, who won "only" 103. The Dodgers and Yankees faced stiff competition in the fifties, and there were tight pennant races. In fact, the 1950s witnessed two of the most thrilling pennant races and the single most miraculous game in the history of baseball. In 1950 the Phillies won the pennant by beating the Dodgers at Ebbets Field on the last day of the season on a tenth-inning home run by Dick Sisler. In 1951 the Giants came from thirteen games behind on August 11 to tie the Dodgers on the last day of the regular season. With the Giants trailing 4–2 in the bottom of the ninth inning of the third and final game of the playoffs, Bobby Thomson hit a three-run homer to win the game. It was the only time ever that the pennant was decided by the last pitch of the season.

Why does Will think that such a glorious era was dull? It was a time of heroic greatness and consistent excellence, when dynasties were challenged by other dynasties. The war between the Yankees and Dodgers extended from 1947 through 1956, a decade—the very length of the war between the Greeks and Trojans. It is true that most of the action took place in New York City among the Dodgers, Giants, and Yankees, and that Will is devoted to the Chicago Cubs. But in the twelfth century B.C. all the action was at Troy, and you didn't have to root for Troy or Argos or Ithaca to appreciate the show. Of course, the Cubs haven't won a pennant since 1945 or a World Series since Teddy Roosevelt was president; no doubt such lengthy frustration makes a man disgruntled and causes him to lose his judgment.

How else can we explain Will's failure to appreciate the lost grandeur of baseball in the fifties? For the last time the national game held its place as part of nature, timeless and regular as Newton's universe. In the beginning God created sixteen major-league baseball teams, eight in the National League and eight in the American. Baseball was played on natural grass and mostly in the daytime. Each team played every other team in its league twenty-two times a season, eleven games at home and eleven away; the seventy-seven games at home and seventy-seven away made for a perfectly symmetrical season. The Yankees ruled this world as the Olympian gods ruled theirs. The mighty Dodgers and Giants challenged their supremacy as the Titans and Giants challenged the Olympians, and to no more avail. The Yankees ruled with steadiness, serenity, and justice, and only the unworthy gnashed their teeth in envy and prayed for chaos to shatter the unwelcome order.

Then, at last, the forces of disorder held sway. The Yankees, a pale copy of the great teams, won their last pennant of the era in 1964. Then came Götterdämmerung: burning cities at home, frustrating and divisive wars abroad, one president forced not to seek reelection and another to resign his office, debasement of the schools and universities, the rise of a drug culture, the collapse of sexual decorum and restraint.

If, in a future age, Western civilization should come to an end, some perceptive scholar will point with certainty to the era that marked the beginning of its decline. The first clear sign came in 1953, when the Boston Braves moved to Milwaukee; the next year the St. Louis Browns became the Baltimore Orioles. Beginning in 1961 new teams were added, and in 1969 each league was divided into two divisions. The Dark Ages had begun. It is not clear that we shall ever see a Renaissance. It boggles the mind that a serious thinker who passes for a conservative could applaud such a decline.

Overrating Intelligence

WHAT MUST LIE behind Will's assessment is his passionate delusion that intelligence, not power, controls the modern degenerate game. Certainly, the men he admires most in the game today all rely on intelligence and on the new informational tools to enhance their success.

The heart of Will's book is a study of four such men: the manager Tony La Russa of Oakland, the pitcher Orel Hershiser of Los Angeles, the batter Tony Gwynn of San Diego, and the shortstop Cal Ripken of Baltimore. The choices are by no means obvious. It is true that managers like Casey Stengel, John McGraw, and Leo Durocher are no longer around, but it is most unlikely that Will would have chosen them if they were. No more did he choose the Cardinals' Whitey Herzog, the Dodgers' Tom Lasorda, or the Tigers' Sparky Anderson, highly successful managers who resemble those past greats in their blue-collar, extroverted, nonintellectual styles. Instead he chose La Russa, a fine manager who is greatly respected and has had remarkable success with two different teams, and who perfectly fits Will's model of the intellectual in baseball. He is the fifth manager in major-league history to hold a law degree, and, as Will points out, the other four are in the Hall of Fame.

La Russa's Athletics have won the last three American League championships chiefly because they have the best hitters and pitchers in the league, but La Russa plays and talks a brainy game. It is the game that Will loves, in which runners aggressively take extra bases, and managers engage in intellectual warfare by stealing the enemy's signs and making complicated calculations. Will recounts that La Russa once precisely timed an opposing pitcher's natural delivery to the plate at 1.6 seconds, one-fifth of a second more than a good runner needs to steal second base. La Russa inserted a speedy pinch runner on first to take advantage of the opportunity. The pitcher adjusted to the danger by hurrying some of his deliveries, at the paradoxical cost of losing speed on those pitches. La Russa carefully decided when the next delivery would be slow and signaled the runner to steal. He guessed wrong, but the runner was still safe, although according to the calculation he should have been out. Now Oakland had an advantage, for the runner could score from second on a mere single. On the other hand, the pitcher no longer needed to worry about a stolen base, so he pitched naturally at his highest efficiency. "The tricky stuff was over. Now it was pitcher against the hitter. The pitcher won. Henderson hit a fly ball caught by the left fielder. Texas won."

However technically sophisticated and intelligent La Russa's strategy might have been, it was confounded by the performance of the pitcher and the batter, which was not intellectual but physical. Besides, it is not even clear that La Russa's strategy was smart. It was based on anticipating the pitching pattern, which he got wrong, only to be saved by the sheer speed of the runner. Was he wise to order a steal at all, and thus to take the pressure off the pitcher? Might La Russa not have done better to keep the runner on first, and to compel a fat pitch that the batter could have demolished? It is not possible to know, as is true of all such decisions. The dictates of inside baseball are like maxims; different ones prescribe mutually exclusive courses of action. "A stitch in time saves nine," but "haste makes waste." In the same way, it is good for a pitcher to throw over to first to keep the runner close, but it is bad to do so too often, for that wears him out and distracts his attention from the batter. How often is too often? It depends. Clever managers always tell you about their shrewd moves that worked out, and blame the players' faulty execution for their failures. But by far the most important element in the contest is not intelligence but the natural ability of the players—a point that Will does not make.

Will's preferred game is as old as the hills; it dominated baseball in the era of the dead ball, when power hitting was rare. In recent years it has been most closely associated with Gene Mauch, who managed four different teams over twenty-six years, winning much admiration but no league championships, chiefly because he lacked hitters like Oakland's Rickey Henderson, Carney Lansford, Mark McGwire, and Jose Canseco, and pitchers like Dave Stewart, Bob Welch, and Dennis Eckersley. It is a game meant to compensate for lack of talent, but even so, natural ability, speed, strength, and skill are more important to its success than anything else. In the words of Whitey Herzog, whose speedy, light-hitting Cardinals won three pennants playing that game: "When I managed Kansas City I wasn't too smart because I didn't have a closer. I got smarter in St. Louis because I've had Bruce Sutter, Todd Worrell, and Ken Dayley." Today only Dayley is left, and by the last week of the season he had only four wins and two saves. It is no accident, as the Stalinists used to say, that the Cardinals finished last this year and that Herzog is no longer managing.

Will's favorite pitcher, Orel Hershiser, has achieved wonderful things, including breaking the record for consecutive scoreless innings and taking his team to the world championship in 1988. He is a worthy subject of attention for the student of baseball, but by no means the most obvious. As Will points out, no one in baseball history has had a more sensational first five years than the Mets' Dwight Gooden. He has great speed, an outstanding curve, and remarkable control. He is great strikeout artist and has one of the best winning percentages ever, much better than Hershiser's. Gooden has the best chance of breaking an assortment of pitching records before he is through, yet Will is more interested in Hershiser. The reason he gives is that Hershiser has done something very rare: he is "pitching with steady success in his thirties." That is, indeed, a fine achievement, but the Texas Rangers' Nolan Ryan is still pitching with astonishing success at the age of forty-two! (Hershiser, who turned thirty-two in September, had no success whatever this year, because of a sore arm.) Ryan has struck out more batters and thrown more no-hitters than any pitcher who ever played in the major leagues, won his three hundredth victory this past season, and led the league in strikeouts. Yet Will chose Hershiser, and his real reason is clear. Gooden, Ryan, and Boston's Roger Clemens are hard throwers, "naturals," whose success plainly comes from their extraordinary physical abilities. None is very talkative about his skills, which is why Will is less interested in them than in the articulate Dodger, whose success "is more an achievement of mind than muscle."

The story is the same with Baltimore's Cal Ripken. He is a very good hitter; after his first six years in the majors he had a batting average of .283 and 160 home runs, easily the best among active shortstops, with no serious competition. (Some perspective on the pitiful decline of hitting in today's game is provided by the fact that in 1941 seven of the sixteen major-league shortstops had a combined batting average of .299, and this was no fluke. Their combined career average, covering 110 years of play, was .297.*) He is also the modern iron man of baseball, having played in more consecutive games than anyone except Lou Gehrig. By dint of hard work and ceaseless study he has learned to position himself so as to compensate for his lack of

---

* I owe this observation to Michael Seidel's splendid book *Streak: Joe DiMaggio and the Summer of '41* (New York: McGraw-Hill, 1988), 13.

extraordinary speed and agility. He is a fine fielder, but he happens to be a contemporary of Ozzie Smith, whom Will rightly calls "the most elegant shortstop of his era, and perhaps the finest fielder ever." Why, then, is Ripken his chosen subject? Again because Smith is a "natural," blessed with the skills and talents that make him superb. Ripken, on the other hand, is the intellectual's shortstop, relying on thought and knowledge for success. He was voted the "smartest defensive player" by his peers and says of himself, "I'm not blessed with the kind of range a lot of shortstops have. The way I have success, I guess, is by thinking."

The Hitter as Antihero

PERHAPS THE STRANGEST of Will's choices, however, is his batter, Tony Gwynn. In general, Will seems to prefer defense to offense, citing with approval the sportswriter Tom Boswell's observation that defense is "the cognoscenti corner of baseball." If he must have offense, Will prefers running to hitting. If he must have hitting, he prefers thought and finesse to power. Thus it is Gwynn's cerebral approach to batting that explains Will's selection. No student of the art of hitting is more dedicated than Gwynn, whose quest to perfect his style is such that he is distressed at hitting a home run with an imperfect swing, and pleased by a hard-hit out when the ball went where he intended it. He is the first National Leaguer to win three consecutive batting titles since the great Stan Musial won his third straight in 1952, and his .370 average in 1988 is the highest since Musial's .376 in 1948.

But Gwynn, unlike Musial, is a singles hitter. Compared with the outstanding hitters in the game he lacks power, as revealed in home-run totals and slugging average, and the dominant hitter's chief contribution, runs batted in. To be sure, there are few Musials in the game today, but there are at least two batters who clearly have a better claim to greatness than Gwynn: the veteran George Brett of the Kansas City Royals and the Yankees' Don Mattingly, Gwynn's baseball contemporary. The statistics in the following table make Gwynn's inferiority clear:

Table: Career Batting Statistics (through the 1989 season)

	Gwynn	Brett	Mattingly	Musial
Batting average	.332	.310	.323	.331
Slugging average	.443	.501	.520	.559
Runs batted in*	59	82	102	93
Home runs*	6	17	23	23

Sources: The Sporting News Official Baseball Register (1990 edition), Barry Siegel, ed. (The Sporting News, 1990); The Baseball Encyclopedia (7th edition), Joseph L. Reichler, ed. (Macmillan Publishing, 1988).
*Average per full season.

Will's choice of Gwynn instead of Brett or Mattingly crystallizes the shortcomings of his approach to the game. Bemoaning Gwynn's failure to win recognition in spite of his high average, Will complains, "What has all this earned Gwynn? He is called 'the West Coast Wade Boggs.' That is because Gwynn practices his craft at the wrong end of the continent." No, that is because both Gwynn and the Red Sox's high-average hitter have failed to provide the kind of heroic leadership by performance that carries a team to victories and championships, the combination of power and timeliness that drives in runs and inspires teammates.

This year, in an extraordinary departure from the tight-lipped protectiveness usual in the game, Gwynn's teammates have expressed their disappointment. One of the Padres complained that Gwynn "cares only about his hits. . . . He doesn't care about this team." Another objected to Gwynn's decision to bunt with two men on and nobody out:

If you sacrifice, you can protect your average, but what that does is put the pressure on the other guy. Tony has a chance to be a game-breaking player. We expect him to take his chance and hit. If you sacrifice, the pressure goes to the next guy, and the next guy and the next guy, and they think now they have to get a hit. And when you have to do that, your chances of doing it are going down the toilet, and so are your chances of winning.

A third said, "You like to see a No. 3 hitter with 100 RBI. Tony has the potential to do that. He can drive the ball. He's the type of player who can lead a team to a championship, and he knows that. If I was hitting .350 and there were runners on first or second and they see me bunt and they say to me why don't you hit away, it makes a lot of sense."

Gwynn defends himself as follows: "This is a game based on numbers. It's not based on character or heart or work ethic. It's the numbers. At contract time people say, 'Did you hit .300?' The people want to see numbers on the board. I'm a high-average hitter. Some hit for power. Some move a runner over. Some hit for average. I try to do what I am capable of doing, whether people like it or not."* That is not the voice of Roy Hobbs, Malamud's fictional "natural," who literally knocked the cover off the ball in his first at bat in the majors, and whose goal was to be "the best there ever was in the game"; nor is it the voice of the real-life Ted Williams, who said at the age of twenty, "All I want out of life is that when I walk down the street folks will say, 'There goes the greatest hitter that ever lived.'" Gwynn's is the voice of our times, of the antihero who knows his limitations and accepts them, who shuns the burden of leadership, who goes his own way and "does his own thing," who is satisfied with well-rewarded competence and does not seek greatness. And that is what Will likes about Gwynn: "'Stay within yourself is baseball's first commandment.' . . . A player's reach should not exceed his grasp." If Mighty Casey came to bat at a crucial moment today, George Will would want him to punch a grounder through the right side to move the runner to third and leave things up to the next batter.

It would not be fair to suggest that Will has no place for the heroic; it is just that he understands heroism in a peculiarly modern and constricted way. He endorses the novelist John Updike's view

---

* The preceding quotations appear in Peter Richmond's "Trouble in Paradise," the *National Sports Daily*, 25 June 1990, 36–39. Richmond is not persuaded by Will's account of Gwynn: "Traditionally, Gwynn's talents have been viewed by the baseball community at large with the clinical detachment we afford the chemist's feats. When columnist George Will devoted 100 pages of his recent book to Gwynn he glorified only the deeds that could be measured in quantifiable units, and managed to avoid characterization of the man entirely—a test-tube profile, and, in retrospect, quite naive."

that baseball heroism "comes not from flashes of brilliance, but . . . from 'the players who always *care*,' about themselves and their craft," and adds his own observation that "those who pay the price of excellence in any demanding discipline are heroes."

In his famous essay about Ted Williams's final game Updike spoke of his hero's "hard blue glow of high purpose." For him "Williams is the classic ballplayer of the game on a hot August weekday before a small crowd, when the only thing at stake is the tissue-thin difference between a thing done well and a thing done ill." Such heroism is aesthetic more than it is moral. The game in question was meaningless, for the Red Sox were out of the pennant race. The "high purpose" was entirely personal and made no contribution to a practical or elevated goal. Williams wanted to end his career with a home run. He did so and sat out the team's last few games on the road. In his nineteen brilliant years with the Red Sox they won one pennant and no World Series. In the ten key games of his career—seven in the Series and the other three in which a Red Sox victory would have brought a league championship—Williams hit .232 and made no important contribution. Like Tony Gwynn, but with infinitely greater power and talent, he was a keen student of the game, a tireless perfectionist who refused to swing at a pitch out of the strike zone or to change his style to meet particular situations. What he did he did beautifully and with meticulous care. His last game was a fitting end to the career of a great hitter and stylist—but not of a hero.

Will's concept is less aesthetic but more democratically modern: everyone is a potential hero, provided that he cares for his craft and works hard to perfect it. That definition flatters us ordinary people, but it also badly diminishes the status of the meritorious, establishing a kind of affirmative-action heroism. It is not what people have sought for millennia in their heroes, who instead are expected to perform great and wondrous deeds, so marvelous that they verge on the magical. Heroes must far outdo ordinary mortals, to the point where their actions give rise to song, story, and legend. Heroes do not, however, perform their deeds for themselves alone; instead their deeds are vital to those who rely on them. Achilles is heroic because even other heroes cannot match his speed and strength, without which the

Greeks cannot take Troy; Odysseus is heroic because he surpasses all others in cleverness, without which his men will die and never reach home.

True Heroism

BABE RUTH was a true baseball hero, because his achievements dwarfed all others'. When he hit fifty-nine home runs in 1921, the next best slugger had twenty-four; when he hit his seven hundredth homer, only two others had over three hundred. Even more important, throughout his career his hitting brought victory and championships to his team. Legends sprang up of Ruth's vast appetite for food and drink and women, of his visits to dying children and the fulfillment of his promises to hit home runs for them, of his pointing to the place in the stands where he would drive the next pitch for a home run (and then hitting it there). Will remarks that "[i]t is inconceivable that a protean figure like Babe Ruth could burst upon baseball today," and he is glad of it. He scolds Ruth for his bad habits (the faults of a hero can be as gigantic as his virtues) and concludes that such great superiority in performance could not exist today—not because of the general mediocrity of today's game, but because today's players "are generally bigger and stronger and faster, and they know more about a game that rewards *knowing* [emphasis in the original]."

But the more important point is that none of today's players is likely to match the achievements or epic status of such real heroes as Ruth or Joe DiMaggio. Will is impressed by DiMaggio's commitment to excellence and his knowledge of the game. The one specific achievement that he singles out for praise, however, is that DiMaggio was never thrown out going from first to third! That is what he finds noteworthy about a man who was one of the great batters and fielders of all time, who led his team to ten pennants and to victories in nine World Series in his thirteen years as a player, and who holds what is generally agreed to be the most remarkable and unapproachable baseball record of all time—a hitting streak of fifty-six consecutive games.

That streak is the subject of Michael Seidel's recent book, which displays a better understanding of baseball heroism: "The individual effort required for a personal hitting streak is comparable to what heroic legend calls the *aristeia,* whereby great energies are gathered for a day, dispensed, and then regenerated for yet another day, in an epic wonder of consistency." DiMaggio's exploits, moreover, had meaning not for himself alone, but carried and inspired his companions, as the deeds of epic heroes do. During his great streak Johnny Sturm, Frank Crosetti, and Phil Rizzuto, none of them normally great hitters, each enjoyed a lesser streak of his own. At the beginning of DiMaggio's streak the Yankees were in a terrible slump, five and a half games out of first place. At its end they had destroyed the will of the opposition, were safely in first place, and on their way to clinching the pennant on September 4 (the earliest date in history), and finishing twenty games ahead of the next best team.

But there is more still to true heroism: the qualities of courage, suffering, and sacrifice. These DiMaggio displayed most strikingly in 1949. Before the season he had a bone spur removed from his heel (as with Achilles, a vulnerable spot). The pain was great enough to keep him out of the lineup until the end of June, when the Yankees went to Boston for a three-game series against the team that they had to beat. DiMaggio blasted four home runs in three games, batting in nine runs as New York swept the series. The importance of that manifestation of *aristeia* was very clear at the end of the season, when the Red Sox came into Yankee Stadium for the two final games. Had they won even one of the three played in June, the championship would have been theirs already; instead the Red Sox had to win one of the remaining two. DiMaggio had missed the last couple of weeks, felled by a case of viral pneumonia. Once again, the ailing warrior returned to the field of battle. Weak as he was, he managed two hits and led his mates to victory. The next day, the staggering DiMaggio managed to run out a triple and to last until the ninth inning (when weakness and leg cramps finally forced him from the field). The inspired Yankees won the game and the championship.

That is the sort of thing Ernest Hemingway had in mind when he told of the old fisherman in *The Old Man and the Sea,* who struggled in a life-and-death battle with the greatest fish he had ever seen, despite a body cramped with pain and a wounded hand: "I think the great Joe DiMaggio would be proud of me today. I had no bone spurs. But the hands and the back hurt truly." Nor was this the end. In the sad, confused 1960s, when heroism seemed only myth, Simon and Garfunkel caught America's longing for a true hero: "Where have you gone, Joe DiMaggio? A nation turns its lonely eyes to you."

No one ever thought that DiMaggio's greatness came chiefly from intelligence, care, and hard work. Millions of people have those admirable qualities without significant result. Heroes arise by means of natural talents that are beyond the rest of us; the secret of their success is mysterious and charismatic. As Toots Shor put it:

> There never was a guy like DiMaggio in baseball. The way people admired him, the way they admire him now. Everybody wanted to meet Joe, to touch him, to be around him—the big guys too. I'm not just talking about fans coming into the joint. Joe was a hero, a real legitimate hero. I don't know what it takes to be a hero like Joe. You can't manufacture a hero like that. It just has to be there, the way he plays, the way he works, the way he is.

George Will set out to write a antiromantic book about baseball, and he succeeded. In so doing, however, he has missed what baseball is all about. Baseball without romance and heroism is like *Hamlet* without poetry or the Prince of Denmark—just words. We care about baseball not because we enjoy watching working men try hard to improve their craft, or because we seek models for aesthetic appreciation, but because we keep hoping that some hero or team of heroes will come along and do something wonderful and magical, something never done before, something neither we nor any other player could do. Will concludes his book with the words of Malamud in *The Natural*: "When we are without heroes we 'don't know how far we can go,'" but he has curtailed the quotation. The original reads: "Without heroes we're all plain people and don't know how far we can go." His heroes are just like the rest of us, who concentrate their intelligence, work hard, and apply themselves to reach a level that is somehow within the reach of anyone with intelligence and discipline. In hard times, however, and all times are in some way hard, we need greater and more potent heroes—to tell us not what all of us can do but what only the best of us can do. Their doing so inspires the rest of us to do the best we can. What we need are heroes like Malamud's Roy Hobbs:

> He belonged [the sportswriters wrote] with the other immortals, a giant in performance. . . . He was a throwback to a time of true heroes, not of the brittle, razzle dazzle boys that had sprung up around the jack rabbit ball—a natural not seen in a dog's age, and weren't they the lucky ones he had appeared here and now to work his wonders before them.

Cracking That Post-Soviet Market

David Brooks

Y OU SEE THE LAPTOP EXPLORER stranded in the waiting rooms of obscure post-Soviet airports. Once a normal Western business-man, he was dispatched to seize the Tremendous Opportunities created by the fall of communism. So he sits on a pile of lug-gage, tapping away maniacally on his laptop, his pupils strangely dilated, his once-proud wingtips scuffed and fraying, his stained anorak pulled tightly around his chest. His plane has been delayed thirty-six hours for lack of fuel, but he can't return to the local In-tourist hotel because he cursed at one of the floor ladies after she ac-cused him of stealing a toilet; the one in his room had already been pinched by the time he checked in.

Shell-shocked men and women spend their days hacking through the post-Soviet wilderness in search of a near-mythical creature, an honest joint-venture partner. Many modern Diogenes have come this way before: Take the American company that put up money for the construction of a building in Moscow but returned to find nothing but a construction shed on the lot and the Russian partners driving Mercedes cars. And then there was the European agricultural concern that dispatched $1 million in top-quality seed to its Ukrainian part-ner, only to receive a letter to the effect of "Thanks for the gift. We now consider our relationship at an end."

They had contracts, of course. But this is the land of no legal re-course. (They should have signs at the airports: Welcome to Ukraine. You Have No Legal Recourse.) Some companies have tried to get around the shambles of the post-Soviet legal structure by writing into contracts that disputes will be settled according to the corporate laws of a third country, such as Sweden. Decisions make interesting reading, but little more. There's no enforcement mechanism in the former Soviet Union.

Judge the Person

THE RULE HERE is that it makes no sense to judge the deal, or the contract; just judge the person. But an honest face is hard to find. Companies often visit eighty or one hundred local enterprises before selecting a joint-venture partner. These sorts of meetings are not always thrilling. The conversational style of post-Soviet businessmen over fifty years of age consists mostly of rambling monologues on the speaker's glorious accomplishments—updated versions of the way Nikita Khrushchev used to boast about the success of the most recent five-year plan. These agenda-busting speeches are interrupted only by histrionic ultimatums, bizarre conspiracy theories, and impassioned pleas for money:

MODERN KHRUSHCHEV: If you give us $50 million, we will make the finest widgets on earth.
LAPTOP EXPLORER: That's a lot of money.
MODERN KHRUSHCHEV: OK, give us $5 million. . . . What about $250,000? . . . One Volvo?"

After this sort of fruitful exchange, there will be a long dinner, and the Laptop Explorer will be able to enjoy his fourteenth successive meal of caviar and rolled meat. There will be little conversation but plenty of toasts, growing increasingly sentimental as the night wears on, so that by the end there will be hugging and crying and the Laptop Explorer will wake up the next morning still feeling where his partner's razor stubble rubbed his cheek the night before.

"We are the last of the idealists," writes Russian businessman Sergei Protosov in an article intended for Western investors. "I do not suppose this thought has even occurred to you as you sipped your gin at those conservative business parties in the West where everyone has an identical smile and the guests swap business cards and talk shop."

Boy is he wrong. What does he think brings Western businessmen to his rathole of a country? The comfortable living? The easy deal-making? It is precisely what he calls the idealism, but which really is the unfathomableness of it all.

Executives back home at the head offices seldom find themselves surrounded by thugs in sweatsuits who are threatening to burn down the corporate headquarters unless they get a cut of the quarterly profits. In the former Soviet Union, this is a rite of passage. The Westerner has to sense whether these are just random hoodlums wandering in off the street or members of a real criminal organization, aspiring security guards, or gunpowder freaks.

Laptop Explorers insist they don't pay such people off. But in the past few weeks things have gotten ugly. A British businessman was stabbed to death by several assailants in his room in one of Moscow's fancier hotels. The director of a Russian-American restaurant was shot in the head by a masked assassin. On July 21, seven men with machine guns and pistols opened fire on the showroom of an Italian-Russian car dealership that had spurned a protection threat. Security guards shot back, and before the battle was over four people were dead and an Alfa-Romeo was riddled with bullets.

Two sorts of Western businesses can survive in this environment, the big AT&T-style behemoths that make the ground shake when they walk and the one-person companies that hope they are too small to be noticed.

Dave Zeigler is one of the latter. He ran an employment agency for eight years in Hemet, California, but one day got a workers' comp bill for $75,000 and decided it was time to close shop and head east. When he first arrived in Kiev, Mr. Zeigler chased the sorts of export deals that are the stuff of fantasy for post-Soviet prospectors. Everything fell through, and after eleven months of earning not a kopek, Mr. Zeigler took his guitar out to the city's main square and began singing country and western tunes, pulling in 6,000 Ukrainian coupons. He figured that he'd made enough mistakes to qualify as a consultant, and now arranges housing and gives advice to companies doing business in Kiev.

Primarily, he corrects the mistakes of clients who behave normally: people who put their addresses on their business cards, who put up a sign to announce their presence, who broadcast a success, who don't realize that an apartment offered for $1,500 a month might be available for one-fifth that. He's also a fountain of scuttlebutt.

The Laptop Explorers tend to take great pleasure in rudimentary accomplishments: taking delivery on a shipment of modular furniture from the West, making contact with the last of the dozen or so agencies that hold "exclusive" rights to a piece of property, successfully buying back a piece of machinery from the people who stole it from them.

Some Go Native

SOMETIMES YOU MEET AN EXPLORER who's gone native. His wingtips have been exchanged for construction boots; he wears a concrete-colored Soviet shirt under a soiled sweater. He hints at the dark forces all around, and when the discussion gets serious he breaks out in poem or song—just like the locals. "You know these Russians designed a space station with almost no computers," he repeats, for combating Western condescension has become his pastime.

Perhaps he will never be able to return to the West, to be one more vice president along a corridor, working in conditions that make sense. Possibly he will venture ever deeper into the wilderness in pursuit of subsidiary agreements. Then, in a $3-a-night Intourist hotel room in a formerly closed Soviet city, he will have one last delirious fantasy of a Western-style salad bar crammed with fresh vegetables, and his body, broken by hard travel, will shut down and he will be dead.

The standard bribe for expediting a burial in the former Soviet Union is about $7.

Part 5

RESPONSIBILITIES

I Dodged the Draft,
and I Was Wrong

Mark Helprin

I AM FREQUENTLY ASKED how it is that I, an American, served in the Israeli Army and Air Force, and not in the military of my own country.

The first part of the question is easy to answer. I point out the long tradition of Americans serving in the armed forces of allies—the Lafayette Escadrille, Faulkner in the Canadian Royal Air Force, e.e. cummings and John Dos Passos in the Norton-Harjes Ambulance Corps, the Eagle Squadron, the Flying Tigers. I mention that before I served under another flag I reported to the Department of State and formally swore an oath of loyalty to the United States and to defend the Constitution. And I remind my questioners that Israel fought not only armies trained and equipped by the Soviet Union, but, sometimes, Soviet soldiers themselves. In that period, the United States and Israel worked very closely together.

To the second part of the question, I reply that though the men in my family have served, since our arrival in this country, with Pershing in Mexico, in the First World War, and so many in the Second World War that the welcome home had to be held in a hotel, that despite this tradition in which I was certain I would have a place, I did not serve.

If you think that it is easy to stand here in front of thousands of officers and future officers of the United States Army and explain this, think again. But just as the heart of your profession is your willingness to give your lives in defense of your country, even, as the case has been, as you are mocked, reviled, and dismissed by those for whom you will die, the heart of my profession is to convey the truth.

Let me try to convey, then, what I have come to believe is the truth of a time that was over before many of you were born. I do so not to gain approval or to attain an end, but in service of illumination and memory.

My conduct in the Vietnam era can be expressed by stating that although in the Israeli Army I later had, but for corrective lenses, a perfect physical rating for combat, here I was officially, legally, and properly 4-F. If I were Bill Clinton, I would take ten thousand words to explain this and say nothing, but I'm not Bill Clinton, and I can get to the heart of it in eight: What I did was called dodging the draft.

I thought Vietnam was so much the wrong place to fight and that the conduct of the war was so destructive in human terms and of American power, prestige, and purpose that I was justified in staying out. What the existence of the reeducation camps and the boat people, and the triumph of containment have taught me is that my political assessment was not all that I thought it was. I have also come to believe that, even if it had been, I still would not have been released from honoring the compact under which I had lived until that moment, and which I then broke. I did not want to participate in a war the conduct of which was often morally ambiguous. Now I understand that this was precisely my obligation.

So you can imagine what I felt when I came to a passage in David McCullough's *Truman,* explaining how Truman had volunteered in the First World War: "He turned thirty-three the spring of 1917, which was two years beyond the age limit set by the new Selective Service Act. He had been out of the National Guard for nearly six years. His eyes were far below the standard requirements for any of the armed services. And he was the sole supporter of his mother and sister. As a farmer, furthermore, he was supposed to remain on the farm. . . . So Harry might have stayed where he was for any of several reasons. That he chose to go . . . was his own doing entirely."

Truman had five unimpeachable reasons not to serve, and he

tossed them to the wind. Had he tossed them at my class at Harvard, I assure you, they would have been fought over like five flawless versions of the Hope Diamond.

His actions were all the more impressive when it is remembered that the First World War was far more brutal than the war in Vietnam, far more costly, and far more senseless. At least the war in Vietnam was fought in the context of a policy of containment that later was to triumph. Even were Vietnam not the best place to make a stand, it was the fact that a stand was made that mattered.

In contrast, the First World War was fought almost entirely for nothing. Though it is true that the country was more enthusiastic about it, that just drives home the fact, as did Vietnam, that you simply cannot know how things will turn out, and that a war may be right or wrong, opportune or inopportune, the proper time and place to make a stand, or it may not be, but that this is something to be determined in national debate and not in the private legislatures of each person with a draft card.

I am absolutely certain that in not serving I was wrong. I began to realize this in 1967, when I served briefly in the British Merchant Navy. In the Atlantic we saw a lot of American warships, and every time we did I felt both affection and pride. One of the other sailors, a seaman named Roberts, was a partisan of the Royal Navy and maintained that it was more powerful than our own. As I was a regular reader of the Proceedings of the United States Naval Institute, and had almost memorized *Jane's Fighting Ships,* I quickly, let us say, blew his arguments out of the water.

And then, in riposte, he asked why I was not in uniform. I answered with the full force of the rationalizations so painstakingly developed by the American intellectual elite. Still, he kept coming at me. Although he was not an educated man, and although I thought I had him in a lock, the last thing he said broke the lock. I remember his words exactly. He said: "But they're your mates."

That was the essence of it. Although I did not modify my position until it was too late, I began to know then that I was wrong. I thought, mistakenly, perhaps just for the sake of holding my own in an argument, that he was saying, "My country, right or wrong," but it was not what he was saying at all. Only my sophistry converted the many virtues of his simple words from something I would not fully understand until much later.

Neither a man nor his country can always pick the ideal quarrel, and not every war can be fought with moral surety or immediacy of effect. It would be nice if that were so, but it isn't. Any great struggle, while it remains undecided and sometimes even afterward, unfolds not in certainties but in doubts. It cannot be any other way. It never has been.

In the Cambridge Cemetery are several rows of graves in which rest the remains of those who were killed in Vietnam. On one of the many days of that long war, I was passing by as a family was burying their son. I stopped, in respect. I could not move. And they looked at me, not in anger, as I might have expected, but with love. You see, they had had a son.

Soon thereafter, not understanding fully why, I was on my way to the Middle East, in a fury to put myself on the line. And though I did, it can never make up for what I did not do. For the truth is that each and every one of the Vietnam memorials in that cemetery and in every other—those that are full, those that are empty, and those that are still waiting—belongs to a man who may have died in my place. And that is something I can never put behind me.

I want you to know this so that perhaps you may use it. For someday you may find yourself in a terrible place, about to die from a wound that is too big for a pressure bandage, or you may find yourself in an enemy prison, facing years of torture, or you may find yourself, more likely, as I did, in a freezing rain-soaked trench, at four o'clock in the morning, listening to your heart beat like thunder as you stare into the hallucinatory darkness of a field sown with mines. You may speak to yourself out loud, asking, why am I here? I could have been someplace else. I could have done it another way. I could have been home.

If that should happen to you, your first comfort will be your God, and then you will have—believe me—the undying image of your family, and then duty, honor, country. These will carry you through.

But if, after you have run through them again and again, you have time and thought left, then perhaps you will think of me, and this day at the beginning of your careers. I hope it will be encouragement. For that I was not with you, in my time, at Khe Sanh, and Da Nang, and Hue, and all the other places, is for me now, looking back, a great surprise, an even greater disappointment, and a regret that I will carry to my grave.

A New Approach
to Welfare Reform: Humility

James Q. Wilson

WE ARE ENTERING THE LAST YEARS of the twentieth century with every reason to rejoice and little inclination to do so, despite widespread prosperity, a generally healthy economy, the absence of any immediate foreign threat, and extraordinary progress in civil rights, personal health, and school enrollment. Despite all this and more, we feel that there is something profoundly wrong with our society.

That communal life is thought to be deficient in many respects, plagued by crime, drug abuse, teenage pregnancy, welfare dependency, and the countless instabilities of daily life. What these problems have in common in the eyes of most Americans is that they result from the weakening of the family.

Having arrived at something approaching a consensus, we must now face the fact that we don't know what to do about the problem. The American people are well ahead of their leaders in this regard. They doubt very much that government can do much of anything at all. They are not optimistic that any other institution can do much better, and they are skeptical that there will be spontaneous regeneration of decency, commitment, and personal responsibility.

I do not know what to do either. But I think we can find out, at least to the degree that feeble human reason is capable of understanding some of the most profound features of our condition.

The great debate is whether, how, and at what cost we can change lives. If not the lives of this generation, then of the next. There are three ways of framing the problem.

First, the structural perspective: Owing to natural social forces, the good manufacturing jobs that once existed in inner-city areas have moved to the periphery, leaving behind decent men and women who are struggling to get by without work that once conferred both respect and money. Their place is now taken by streetwise young men who find no meaningful work, have abandoned the search for work, and scorn, indeed, the ethic of work.

Second is the rationalist perspective: Welfare benefits, including not only Aid to Families with Dependent Children (AFDC), but also Medicaid, subsidized housing, and food stamps, have become sufficiently generous as to make the formation of stable two-parent families either irrational or unnecessary. These benefits have induced young women wanting babies and a home of their own to acquire both at public expense, and have convinced young men, who need very little convincing on this score, that sexual conquest need not entail any personal responsibilities.

Third is the cultural perspective: Child rearing and family life as traditionally understood can no longer compete with or bring under prudent control a culture of radical self-indulgence and oppositional defiance, fostered by drugs, television, video games, street gangs, and predatory sexuality.

Now, a visitor from another planet hearing this discourse might say that obviously all three perspectives have much to commend them, and, therefore, all three ought to be acted upon. But the public debate we hear tends to emphasize one or another theory and thus one or another set of solutions. It does this because people, or at least people who are members of the political class, define problems so as to make them amenable to those solutions that they favor for ideological or moral reasons. Here roughly is what each analysis pursued separately and alone implies:

1. Structural solutions. We must create jobs and job-training programs in inner-city areas, by means either of tax-advantaged enterprise zones or government-subsidized employment pro-

grams. As an alternative, we may facilitate the relocation of the inner-city poor to places on the periphery where jobs can be found and, if necessary, supplement their incomes by means of the earned-income tax credit.

2. Rationalist solutions. Cut or abolish AFDC, or, at a minimum, require work in exchange for welfare. Make the formation of two-parent households more attractive than single parenthood, and restore work to prominence as the only way for the physically able to acquire money.

3. Cultural solutions. Alter the inner-city ethos by means of private redemptive movements, supported by a system of shelters or group homes in which at-risk children and their young mothers can be given familial care and adult supervision in safe and drug-free settings.

Now, I have my own preferences in this menu of alternatives, but it is less important that you know what these preferences are than that you realize that I do not know which strategy would work, because so many people embrace a single strategy as a way of denying legitimacy to alternative ones and to their underlying philosophies.

Each of those perspectives, when taken alone, is full of uncertainties and inadequacies. These problems go back, first of all, to the structural solution. The evidence that links family dissolution with the distribution of jobs is, in fact, weak. Some people—such as many recent Latino immigrants in Los Angeles—notice that jobs have moved to the periphery from the city and board buses to follow the jobs. Other people notice the very same thing and stay home to sell drugs.

Now, even if a serious job mismatch does exist, it will not easily be overcome by enterprise zones. If the costs of crime in inner-city neighborhoods are high, they cannot be compensated for by very low labor costs or very high customer demand. Moreover, employers in scanning potential workers will rely, as they have always relied, on the most visible cues of reliability and skill—dress, manner, speech, and even place of residence. No legal system, no matter how much we try to enforce it, can completely or even largely suppress these cues, because they have substantial economic value.

Second, let's consider some of the inadequacies of the rational strategy. After years of denying that the level of welfare payments had any effect on childbearing, many scholars now find that states with higher payments tend to be the ones in which more babies are born to welfare recipients; and when one expands the definition of welfare to include not only AFDC but Medicaid, food stamps, and subsidized housing, increases in welfare were strongly correlated with increases in illegitimate births from the early 1960s to about 1980. At that point, the value of the welfare package in real dollars flattened out, but the illegitimacy rate continued to rise.

Moreover, there remain several important puzzles in the connection between welfare and childbearing. One is the existence of great differences in illegitimacy rates across ethnic groups facing similar circumstances. Since the Civil War at least, blacks have had higher illegitimacy rates than whites, even though federal welfare programs were not invented until 1935.

These days, it has been shown that the illegitimacy rate among black women is more than twice as high as among white women, after controlling for age, education, and economic status. David Hayes Bautista, a researcher at UCLA, compared poor blacks and poor Mexican Americans living in California. He found that Mexican-American children are much more likely than black children to grow up in a two-parent family, and that poor Mexican-American families were only one-fifth as likely as black ones to be on welfare.

Even among blacks, the illegitimacy rate is rather low in states such as Idaho, Montana, Maine, and New Hampshire, despite the fact that these states have rather generous welfare payments. And the illegitimacy rate is quite high in many parts of the Deep South, even though these states have rather low welfare payments.

Clearly, there is some important cultural or at least noneconomic factor at work, one that has deep historical roots and that may vary with the size of the community and the character of the surrounding culture.

Finally, the cultural strategy. Though I have a certain affinity for it, it has its problems, too. There are many efforts in many cities by public and private agencies, individuals, and churches to persuade young men to be fathers and not just impregnators, to help drug addicts and alcoholics, to teach parenting skills to teenage mothers. Some have been evaluated, and a few show signs of positive effects. Among the more successful programs are the Perry Pre-School Project in Ypsilanti, Michigan; the Parent Child Development Center in Houston; the Family Development Research Project in Syracuse, New York; and the Yale Child Welfare Project in New Haven, Connecticut. All of these programs produce better behavior, lessened delinquency, more success in school.

The Manhattan Institute's Myron Magnet (author of *The Dream and the Nightmare: The Sixties' Legacy to the Underclass*) and I have both endorsed the idea of requiring young unmarried mothers to live in group homes with their children under adult supervision as a condition of receiving public assistance. I also have suggested that we might revive an institution that was common earlier in this century but has lapsed into disuse of late—the boarding school, sometimes mistakenly called an orphanage, for the children of mothers who cannot cope. At one time such schools provided homes and education for more than a hundred thousand young people in large cities.

Though I confess I am attracted to the idea of creating wholly new environments in which to raise the next generation of at-risk children, I must also confess that I do not know whether it will work. The programs that we know to be successful, like the ones mentioned above, are experimental efforts led by dedicated men and women. Can large versions of the same thing work when run by the average counselor, the average teacher? We don't know. And even these successes predated the arrival of crack on the streets of our big cities. Can even the best program salvage people from that viciously destructive drug? We don't know.

There is evidence that such therapeutic communities as those run by Phoenix House, headquartered in New York, and other organizations can salvage people who remain in them long enough. How do we get people to stay in them long enough? We don't know.

Now, if these three alternatives or something like them are what is available, how do we decide what to do? Before trying to answer that question, let me assert three precepts that ought to shape how we formulate that answer.

The first precept is that our overriding goal ought to be to save the children. Other goals—such as reducing the costs of welfare, discouraging illegitimacy, preventing long-term welfare dependency, getting even with welfare cheats—may all be worthy goals, but they are secondary to the goal of improving the life prospects of the next generation.

The second precept is that nobody knows how to do this on a large scale. The debate has begun about welfare reform, but it is a debate, in large measure, based on untested assumptions, ideological posturing, and perverse principles. We are told by some that worker training and job placement will reduce the welfare rolls, but we now know that worker training and job placement have so far had only a very modest effect. And few advocates of worker training tell us what happens to children whose mothers are induced or compelled to work, other than to assure us that somebody will supply day care.

The third precept that should guide us is that the federal government cannot have a meaningful family policy for the nation, and it ought not to try. Not only does it not know and cannot learn from experts what to do, whatever it thinks it ought to do, it will try to do in the worst possible way. Which is to say, uniformly, systematically, politically, and ignorantly.

Now, the clear implication of these three precepts, when applied to the problem we face now, is that we ought to turn the task and the money for rebuilding lives, welfare payments, housing subsidies, the whole lot, over to cities and states and private agencies, subject to only two conditions. First, they must observe minimum but fundamental precepts of equal protection, and second, every major new initiative must be evaluated by independent observers operating in accordance with accepted scientific canons.

Some states or counties in the regime may end AFDC as we know it. Others may impose a mandatory work requirement. A few may require welfare recipients to turn their checks over to the group homes in which the recipients must reside or the boarding schools that their children must attend. Some may give the money to private agencies that agree to supply parent training, job skills, and preschool education. Some may move welfare recipients out of the inner city and to the periphery.

Any given state government may do no better than Washington, but the great variety of the former will make up for the deadening uniformity of the latter. And within the states, the operating agencies will be at the city and county level, where the task of improving lives and developing character will be informed by the proximity of government to the voices of ordinary people.

A Nation of Cowards

Jeffrey R. Snyder

OUR SOCIETY has reached a pinnacle of self-expression and respect for individuality rare or unmatched in history. Our entire
popular culture—from fashion magazines to the cinema—
positively screams the matchless worth of the individual and
glories in eccentricity, nonconformity, independent judgment, and
self-determination. This enthusiasm is reflected in the prevalent notion that helping someone entails increasing that person's "self-
esteem"; that if a person properly values himself, he will naturally be
a happy, productive, and, in some inexplicable fashion, responsible
member of society.

And yet, while people are encouraged to revel in their individuality and incalculable self-worth, the media and the law enforcement
establishment continually advise us that, when confronted with the
threat of lethal violence, we should not resist, but simply give the at-
tacker what he wants. If the crime under consideration is rape, there
is some notable waffling on this point, and the discussion quickly
moves to how the woman can change her behavior to minimize the
risk of rape, and the various ridiculous, nonlethal weapons she may
acceptably carry, such as whistles, keys, mace, or that weapon which
really sends shivers down a rapist's spine, the portable cellular phone.

Now how can this be? How can a person who values himself
so highly calmly accept the indignity of a criminal assault? How
can one who believes that the essence of his dignity lies in his self-
determination passively accept the forcible deprivation of that self-
determination? How can he, quietly, with great dignity and poise,
simply hand over the goods?

The assumption, of course, is that there is no inconsistency. The advice not to resist a criminal assault and simply hand over the goods is founded on the notion that one's life is of incalculable value, and that no amount of property is worth it. Put aside, for a moment, the outrageousness of the suggestion that a criminal who proffers lethal violence should be treated as if he has instituted a new social contract: "I will not hurt or kill you if you give me what I want." For years, feminists have labored to educate people that rape is not about sex, but about domination, degradation, and control. Evidently, someone needs to inform the law enforcement establishment and the media that kidnapping, robbery, carjacking, and assault are not about property.

Crime is not only a complete disavowal of the social contract, but also a commandeering of the victim's person and liberty. If the individual's dignity lies in the fact that he is a moral agent engaging in actions of his own will, in free exchange with others, then crime always violates the victim's dignity. It is, in fact, an act of enslavement. Your wallet, your purse, or your car may not be worth your life, but your dignity is; and if it is not worth fighting for, it can hardly be said to exist.

The Gift of Life

ALTHOUGH DIFFICULT for modern man to fathom, it was once widely believed that life was a gift from God, that to not defend that life when offered violence was to hold God's gift in contempt, to be a coward, and to breach one's duty to one's community. A sermon given in Philadelphia in 1747 unequivocally equated the failure to defend oneself with suicide:

> He that suffers his life to be taken from him by one that hath no authority for that purpose, when he might preserve it by defense, incurs the Guilt of self murder since God hath enjoined him to seek the continuance of his life, and Nature itself teaches every creature to defend itself.

"Cowardice" and "self-respect" have largely disappeared from public discourse. In their place we are offered "self-esteem" as the bellwether of success and a proxy for dignity. "Self-respect" implies that one recognizes standards and judges oneself worthy by the degree to which one lives up to them. "Self-esteem" simply means that one feels good about oneself. "Dignity" used to refer to the self-mastery and fortitude with which a person conducted himself in the face of life's vicissitudes and the boorish behavior of others. Now, judging by campus speech codes, dignity requires that we never encounter a discouraging word and that others be coerced into acting respectfully, evidently on the assumption that we are powerless to prevent our degradation if exposed to the demeaning behavior of others. These are signposts proclaiming the insubstantiality of our character, the hollowness of our souls.

It is impossible to address the problem of rampant crime without talking about the moral responsibility of the intended victim. Crime is rampant because the law-abiding, each of us, condone it, excuse it, permit it, submit to it. We permit and encourage it because we do not fight back, immediately, then and there, where it happens. Crime is not rampant because we do not have enough prisons, because judges and prosecutors are too soft, because the police are hamstrung with absurd technicalities. The defect is there, in our character. We are a nation of cowards and shirkers.

Do You Feel Lucky?

IN 1991, when then Attorney General Richard Thornburgh released the FBI's annual crime statistics, he noted that it is now more likely that a person will be the victim of a violent crime than that he will be in an auto accident. Despite this, most people readily believe that the existence of the police relieves them of the responsibility to take full measures to protect themselves. The police, however, are not personal bodyguards. Rather, they act as a general deterrent to crime, both by their presence and by apprehending criminals after the fact. As numerous courts have held, they have no legal obligation to protect anyone in particular. You cannot sue them for failing to prevent you from being the victim of a crime.

Insofar as the police deter by their presence, they are very, very good. Criminals take great pains not to commit a crime in front of them. Unfortunately, the corollary is that you can pretty much bet your life (and you are) that they won't be there at the moment you actually need them.

Should you ever be the victim of an assault, a robbery, or a rape, you will find it very difficult to call the police while the act is in progress, even if you are carrying a portable cellular phone. Nevertheless, you might be interested to know how long it takes them to show up. Department of Justice statistics for 1991 show that, for all crimes of violence, only 28 percent of calls are responded to within five minutes. The idea that protection is a service people can call to have delivered and expect to receive in a timely fashion is often mocked by gun owners, who love to recite the challenge. "Call for a cop, call for an ambulance, and call for a pizza. See who shows up first."

Many people deal with the problem of crime by convincing themselves that they live, work, and travel only in special "crime-free" zones. Invariably, they react with shock and hurt surprise when they discover that criminals do not play by the rules and do not respect these imaginary boundaries. If, however, you understand that crime can occur anywhere at any time, and if you understand that you can be maimed or mortally wounded in mere seconds, you may wish to consider whether you are willing to place the responsibility for safeguarding your life in the hands of others.

Power and Responsibility

IS YOUR LIFE WORTH PROTECTING? If so, whose responsibility is it to protect it? If you believe that it is the police's, not only are you wrong—since the courts universally rule that they have no legal obligation to do so—but you face some difficult moral quandaries. How can you rightfully ask another human being to risk his life to protect yours, when you will assume no responsibility yourself? Because that is his job and we pay him to do it? Because your life is of incalculable value, but his is only worth the $30,000 salary we pay him? If you believe it reprehensible to possess the means and will to use lethal force to repel a criminal assault, how can you call upon another to do so for you?

Do you believe that you are forbidden to protect yourself because the police are better qualified to protect you, because they know what they are doing but you're a rank amateur? Put aside that this is equivalent to believing that only concert pianists may play the piano and only professional athletes may play sports. What exactly are these special qualities possessed only by the police and beyond the rest of us mere mortals?

One who values his life and takes seriously his responsibilities to his family and community will possess and cultivate the means of fighting back, and will retaliate when threatened with death or grievous injury to himself or a loved one. He will never be content to rely solely on others for his safety, or to think he has done all that is possible by being aware of his surroundings and taking measures of avoidance. Let's not mince words: He will be armed, will be trained in the use of his weapon, and will defend himself when faced with lethal violence.

Fortunately, there is a weapon for preserving life and liberty that can be wielded effectively by almost anyone—the handgun. Small and light enough to be carried habitually, lethal, but unlike the knife or sword, not demanding great skill or strength, it truly is the "great equalizer." Requiring only hand-eye coordination and a modicum of ability to remain cool under pressure, it can be used effectively by the old and the weak against the young and the strong, by the one against the many.

The handgun is the only weapon that would give a lone female jogger a chance of prevailing against a gang of thugs intent on rape, a teacher a chance of protecting children at recess from a madman intent on massacring them, a family of tourists waiting at a midtown subway station the means to protect themselves from a gang of teens armed with razors and knives.

But since we live in a society that by and large outlaws the carrying of arms, we are brought into the fray of the Great American Gun War. Gun control is one of the most prominent battlegrounds in our current culture wars. Yet it is unique in the halfheartedness with which our conservative leaders and pundits—our "conservative elite"—do battle, and have conceded the moral high ground to liberal gun-control proponents. It is not a topic often written about, or written about with any great fervor, by William F. Buckley or Patrick Buchanan. As drug czar, William Bennett advised President Bush to ban "assault weapons." George Will is on record as recommending the repeal of the Second Amendment, and Jack Kemp is on record as favoring a ban on the possession of semiautomatic "assault weapons." The battle for gun rights is one fought predominantly by the common man. The beliefs of both our liberal and conservative elites are in fact abetting the criminal rampage through our society.

Selling Crime Prevention

B Y ANY RATIONAL MEASURE, nearly all gun-control proposals are hokum. The Brady Bill, for example, would not have prevented John Hinckley from obtaining a gun to shoot President Reagan; Hinckley purchased his weapon five months before the attack, and his medical records could not have served as a basis to deny his purchase of a gun, since medical records are not public documents filed with the police. Similarly, California's waiting period and background check did not stop Patrick Purdy from purchasing the "assault rifle" and handguns he used to massacre children during recess in a Stockton schoolyard; the felony conviction that would have provided the basis for stopping the sales did not exist, because Mr. Purdy's previous weapons violations were plea-bargained down from felonies to misdemeanors.

In the mid-sixties there was a public service advertising campaign targeted at car owners about the prevention of car theft. The purpose of the ad was to urge car owners not to leave their keys in their cars. The message was, "Don't help a good boy go bad." The implication was that, by leaving his keys in his car, the normal, law-abiding car owner was contributing to the delinquency of minors who, if they just weren't tempted beyond their limits, would be "good." Now, in those days people still had a fair sense of just who was responsible for whose behavior. The ad succeeded in enraging a goodly portion of the populace and was soon dropped.

Nearly all of the gun-control measures offered by Handgun Control, Inc. (HCI) and its ilk embody the same philosophy. They are founded on the belief that America's law-abiding gun owners are the source of the problem. With their unholy desire for firearms, they are creating a society awash in a sea of guns, thereby helping good boys go bad, and helping bad boys be badder. This laying of moral blame for violent crime at the feet of the law-abiding, and the implicit absolution of violent criminals for their misdeeds, naturally infuriates honest gun owners.

The files of HCI and other gun-control organizations are filled with proposals to limit the availability of semiautomatic and other firearms to law-abiding citizens, and barren of proposals for apprehending and punishing violent criminals. It is ludicrous to expect that the proposals of HCI, or any gun-control laws, will significantly curb crime. According to Department of Justice and Bureau of Alcohol, Tobacco and Firearms (ATF) statistics, fully 90 percent of violent crimes are committed without a handgun, and 93 percent of the guns obtained by violent criminals are not obtained through the lawful purchase and sale transactions that are the object of most gun-control legislation. Furthermore, the number of violent criminals is minute in comparison to the number of firearms in America—estimated by the ATF at about 200 million, approximately one-third of which are handguns. With so abundant a supply, there will always be enough guns available for those who wish to use them for nefarious ends, no matter how complete the legal prohibitions against them, or how draconian the punishment for the acquisition or use. No, the gun-control proposals of HCI and other organizations are not seriously intended as crime control. Something else is at work here.

The Tyranny of the Elite

GUN CONTROL is a moral crusade against a benighted, barbaric citizenry. This is demonstrated not only by the ineffectualness of gun control in preventing crime, and by the fact that it focuses on restricting the behavior of the law-abiding rather than apprehending and punishing the guilty, but also by the execration that gun-control proponents heap on gun owners and their evil instrumentality, the NRA. Gun owners are routinely portrayed as uneducated, paranoid rednecks fascinated by and prone to violence, that is, exactly the type of person who opposes the liberal agenda and whose moral and social "reeducation" is the object of liberal social policies. Typical of such bigotry is New York Gov. Mario Cuomo's famous characterization of gun owners as "hunters who drink beer, don't vote, and lie to their wives about where they were all weekend." Similar vituperation is rained upon the NRA, characterized by Sen. Edward Kennedy as the "pusher's best friend," lampooned in political cartoons as standing for the right of children to carry firearms to school, and, in general, portrayed as standing for an individual's God-given right to blow people away at will.

The stereotype is, of course, false. As criminologist and constitutional lawyer Don B. Kates, Jr., and former HCI contributor Dr. Patricia Harris have pointed out, "Studies consistently show that, on the average, gun owners are better educated and have more prestigious jobs than non-owners. . . . Later studies show that gun owners are *less* likely than non-owners to approve of police brutality, violence against dissenters, etc."

Conservatives must understand that the antipathy many liberals have for gun owners arises in good measure from their statist utopianism. This habit of mind has nowhere been better explored than in *The Republic*. There, Plato argues that the perfectly just society is one in which an unarmed people exhibit virtue by minding their own business in the performance of their assigned functions, while the government of philosopher-kings, above the law and protected by armed guardians unquestioning in their loyalty to the state, engineers, implements, and fine-tunes the creation of that society, aided and abetted by myths that both hide and justify their totalitarian manipulation.

The Unarmed Life

WHEN COLUMNIST CARL ROWAN preaches gun control and uses a gun to defend his home, when Maryland governor William Donald Schaefer seeks legislation year after year to ban semiautomatic "assault weapons" whose only purpose, we are told, is to kill people, while he is at the same time escorted by state police armed with large-capacity 9 mm semiautomatic pistols, it is not simply hypocrisy. It is the workings of that habit of mind possessed by all superior beings who have taken upon themselves the terrible burden of civilizing the masses and who understand, like our Congress, that laws are for other people.

The liberal elite know that they are philosopher-kings. They know that the people simply cannot be trusted; that they are incapable of just and fair self-government; that left to their own devices, their society will be racist, sexist, homophobic, and inequitable—and the liberal elite know how to fix things. They are going to help us live the good and just life, even if they have to lie to us and force us to do it. And they detest those who stand in their way.

The private ownership of firearms is a rebuke to this utopian zeal. To own firearms is to affirm that freedom and liberty are not gifts from the state. It is to reserve final judgment about whether the state is encroaching on freedom and liberty, to stand ready to defend that freedom with more than mere words, and to stand outside the state's totalitarian reach.

The Florida Experience

THE ELITIST DISTRUST of the people underlying the gun control movement is illustrated beautifully in HCI's campaign against a new concealed-carry law in Florida. Prior to 1987, the Florida law permitting the issuance of concealed-carry permits was administered at the county level. The law was vague, and, as a result, was subject to conflicting interpretation and political manipulation. Permits were issued principally to security personnel and the privileged few with political connections. Permits were valid only within the county of issuance.

In 1987, however, Florida enacted a uniform concealed-carry law which mandates that county authorities issue a permit to anyone who satisfies certain objective criteria. The law requires that a permit be issued to any applicant who is a resident, at least twenty-one years of age, has no criminal record, no record of alcohol or drug abuse, no history of mental illness, and provides evidence of having satisfactorily completed a firearms safety course offered by the NRA or other competent instructor. The applicant must provide a set of fingerprints, after which the authorities make a background check. The permit must be issued or denied within ninety days, is valid throughout the state, and must be renewed every three years, which provides authorities a regular means of reevaluating whether the permit holder still qualifies.

Passage of this legislation was vehemently opposed by HCI and the media. The law, they said, would lead to citizens shooting each other over everyday disputes involving fender benders, impolite behavior, and other slights to their dignity. Terms like "Florida, the Gunshine State" and "Dodge City East" were coined to suggest that the state, and those seeking passage of the law, were encouraging individuals to act as judge, jury, and executioner in a "Death Wish" society.

No HCI campaign more clearly demonstrates the elitist beliefs underlying the campaign to eradicate gun ownership. Given the qualifications required of permit holders, HCI and the media can only believe that common, law-abiding citizens are seething cauldrons of homicidal rage, ready to kill to avenge any slight to their dignity, eager to seek out and summarily execute the lawless. Only lack of immediate access to a gun restrains them and prevents the blood from flowing in the streets. They are so mentally and morally deficient that they would mistake a permit to carry a weapon in self-defense as a state-sanctioned license to kill at will.

Did the dire predictions come true? Despite the fact that Miami and Dade County have severe problems with the drug trade, the homicide rate fell in Florida following enactment of this law, as it did in Oregon following enactment of similar legislation there. There are, in addition, several documented cases of new permit holders successfully using their weapons to defend themselves. Information from the Florida Department of State shows that, from the beginning of the program in 1987 through June 1993, 160,823 permits have been issued, and only 530, or about 0.33 percent of the applicants, have been denied a permit for failure to satisfy the criteria, indicating that the law is benefiting those whom it was intended to benefit—the law-abiding. Only 16 permits, *less than 1/100th of 1 percent,* have been revoked due to the postissuance commission of a crime involving a firearm.

The Florida legislation has been used as a model for legislation adopted by Oregon, Idaho, Montana, and Mississippi. There are, in addition, seven other states (Maine, North and South Dakota, Utah, Washington, West Virginia, and, with the exception of cities with a population in excess of 1 million, Pennsylvania) which provide that concealed-carry permits must be issued to law-abiding citizens who satisfy various objective criteria. Finally, no permit is required at all in Vermont. Altogether, then, there are thirteen states in which law-abiding citizens who wish to carry arms to defend themselves may do so. While no one appears to have compiled the statistics from all of these jurisdictions, there is certainly an ample database for those seeking the truth about the trustworthiness of law-abiding citizens who carry firearms.

Other evidence also suggests that armed citizens are very responsible in using guns to defend themselves. Florida State University criminologist Gary Kleck, using surveys and other data, has determined that armed citizens defend their lives or property with firearms against criminals approximately 1 million times a year. In 98 percent of these instances, the citizen merely brandishes the weapon or fires a warning shot. Only in 2 percent of the cases do citizens actually shoot their assailants. In defending themselves with their firearms, armed citizens kill 2,000 to 3,000 criminals each year, three times the number killed by the police. A nationwide study by

Kates, the constitutional lawyer and criminologist, found that only 2 percent of civilian shootings involved an innocent person mistakenly identified as a criminal. The "error rate" for the police, however, was 11 percent, over five times as high.

It is simply not possible to square the numbers above and the experience of Florida with the notions that honest, law-abiding gun owners are borderline psychopaths itching for an excuse to shoot someone, vigilantes eager to seek out and summarily execute the lawless, or incompetent fools incapable of determining when it is proper to use lethal force in defense of their lives. Nor upon reflection should these results seem surprising. Rape, robbery, and attempted murder are not typically actions rife with ambiguity or subtlety, requiring special powers of observation and great book-learning to discern. When a man pulls a knife on a woman and says, "You're coming with me," her judgment that a crime is being committed is not likely to be in error. There is little chance that she is going to shoot the wrong person. It is the police, because they are rarely at the scene of the crime when it occurs, who are more likely to find themselves in circumstances where guilt and innocence are not so clear-cut, and in which the probability for mistakes is higher.

Arms and Liberty

C LASSICAL REPUBLICAN PHILOSOPHY has long recognized the critical relationship between personal liberty and the possession of arms by a people ready and willing to use them. Political theorists as dissimilar as Niccolò Machiavelli, Sir Thomas More, James Harrington, Algernon Sidney, John Locke, and Jean-Jacques Rousseau all shared the view that the possession of arms is vital for resisting tyranny, and that to be disarmed by one's government is tantamount to being enslaved by it. The possession of arms by the people is the ultimate warrant that government governs only with the consent of the governed. As Kates has shown, the Second Amendment is as much a product of this political philosophy as it is of the American experience in the Revolutionary War. Yet our conservative elite has abandoned this aspect of republican theory. Although our conservative pundits recognize and embrace gun owners as allies in other arenas, their battle for gun rights is desultory. The problem here is not a statist utopianism, although goodness knows that liberals are not alone in the confidence they have in the state's ability to solve society's problems. Rather, the problem seems to lie in certain cultural traits shared by our conservative and liberal elites.

One such trait is an abounding faith in the power of the word. The failure of our conservative elite to defend the Second Amendment stems in great measure from an overestimation of the power of the rights set forth in the First Amendment, and a general undervaluation of action. Implicit in calls for the repeal of the Second Amendment is the assumption that our First Amendment rights are sufficient to preserve our liberty. The belief is that liberty can be preserved as long as men freely speak their minds; that there is no tyranny or abuse that can survive being exposed in the press; and that the truth need only be disclosed for the culprits to be shamed. The people will act, and the truth shall set us, and keep us, free.

History is not kind to this belief, tending rather to support the view of Hobbes, Machiavelli, and other republican theorists that only people willing and able to defend themselves can preserve their liberties. While it may be tempting and comforting to believe that the existence of mass electronic communication has forever altered the balance of power between the state and its subjects, the belief has certainly not been tested by time, and what little history there is in the age of mass communication is not especially encouraging. The camera, radio, and press are mere tools and, like guns, can be used for good or ill. Hitler, after all, was a masterful orator, used radio to very good effect, and is well known to have pioneered and exploited the propaganda opportunities afforded by film. And then, of course, there were the Brownshirts, who knew very well how to quell dissent among intellectuals.

Polite Society

IN ADDITION TO BEING ENAMORED of the power of words, our conservative elite shares with liberals the notion that an armed society is just not civilized or progressive, that massive gun ownership is a blot on our civilization. This association of personal disarmament with civilized behavior is one of the great unexamined beliefs of our time.

Should you read English literature from the sixteenth through nineteenth centuries, you will discover numerous references to the fact that a gentleman, especially when out at night or traveling, armed himself with a sword or a pistol against the chance of encountering a highwayman or other such predator. This does not appear to have shocked the ladies accompanying him. True, for the most part there were no police in those days, but we have already addressed the notion that the presence of the police absolves people of the responsibility to look after their safety, and in any event the existence of the police cannot be said to have reduced crime to negligible levels.

It is by no means obvious why it is "civilized" to permit oneself to fall easy prey to criminal violence, and to permit criminals to continue unobstructed in their evil ways. While it may be that a society in which crime is so rare that no one ever needs to carry a weapon is "civilized," a society that stigmatizes the carrying of weapons by the law-abiding—because it distrusts its citizens more than it fears rapists, robbers, and murderers—certainly cannot claim this distinction. Perhaps the notion that defending oneself with lethal force is not "civilized" arises from the view that violence is always wrong, or the view that each human being is of such intrinsic worth that it is wrong to kill anyone under any circumstances. The necessary implication of these propositions, however, is that life is not worth defending. Far from being "civilized," the beliefs that counterviolence and killing are always wrong are an invitation to the spread of barbarism. Such beliefs announce loudly and clearly that those who do not respect the lives and property of others will rule over those who do.

In truth, one who believes it wrong to arm himself against criminal violence shows contempt of God's gift of life (or, in modern parlance, does not properly value himself), does not live up to his responsibilities to his family and community, and proclaims himself mentally and morally deficient, because he does not trust himself to behave responsibly. In truth, a state that deprives its law-abiding citizens of the means to effectively defend themselves is not civilized but barbarous, becoming an accomplice of murderers, rapists, and thugs and revealing its totalitarian nature by its tacit admission that the disorganized, random havoc created by criminals is far less a threat than are men and women who believe themselves free and independent, and act accordingly.

While gun control proponents and other advocates of a kinder, gentler society incessantly decry our "armed society," in truth we do not live in an armed society. We live in a society in which violent criminals and agents of the state habitually carry weapons, and in which many law-abiding citizens own firearms but do not go about armed. Department of Justice statistics indicate that 87 percent of all violent crimes occur *outside* the home. Essentially, although tens of millions own firearms, we are an unarmed society.

Take Back the Night

CLEARLY THE POLICE AND THE COURTS are not providing a significant brake on criminal activity. While liberals call for more poverty, education, and drug treatment programs, conservatives take a more direct tack. George Will advocates a massive increase in the number of police and a shift toward "community-based policing." Meanwhile, the NRA and many conservative leaders call for laws that would require violent criminals serve at least 85 percent of their sentences and would place repeat offenders permanently behind bars.

Our society suffers greatly from the beliefs that only official action is legitimate and that the state is the source of our earthly salvation. Both liberal and conservative prescriptions for violent crime suffer from the "not in my job description" school of thought regarding the responsibilities of the law-abiding citizen, and from an overestimation of the ability of the state to provide society's moral moorings. As long as law-abiding citizens assume no personal responsibility for combating crime, liberal and conservative programs will fail to contain it.

Judging by the numerous articles about concealed-carry in gun magazines, the growing number of products advertised for such purpose, and the increase in the number of concealed-carry applications in states with mandatory-issuance laws, more and more people, including growing numbers of women, are carrying firearms for self-defense. Since there are still many states in which the issuance of permits is discretionary and in which law enforcement officials routinely deny applications, many people have been put to the hard choice between protecting their lives or respecting the law. Some of these people have learned the hard way, by being the victim of a crime, or by seeing a friend or loved one raped, robbed, or murdered, that violent crime can happen to anyone, anywhere at any time, and that crime is not about sex or property but life, liberty, and dignity.

The laws proscribing concealed-carry of firearms by honest, law-abiding citizens breed nothing but disrespect for the law. As the Founding Fathers knew well, a government that does not trust its honest, law-abiding, taxpaying citizens with the means of self-defense is not itself worthy of trust. Laws disarming honest citizens proclaim that the government is the master, not the servant, of the people. A federal law along the lines of the Florida statute—overriding all contradictory state and local laws and acknowledging that the carrying of firearms by law-abiding citizens is a privilege and immunity of citizenship—is needed to correct the outrageous conduct of state and local officials operating under discretionary licensing systems.

What we certainly do not need is more gun control. Those who call for the repeal of the Second Amendment so that we can really begin controlling firearms betray a serious misunderstanding of the Bill of Rights. The Bill of Rights does not *grant* rights to the people, such that its repeal would legitimately confer upon government the powers otherwise proscribed. The Bill of Rights is the list of the fundamental, inalienable rights, endowed in man by his Creator, that define what it means to be a free and independent people, the rights that must exist to ensure that government governs only with the consent of the people.

At one time this was even understood by the Supreme Court. In *United States v. Cruikshank* (1876), the first case in which the Court had an opportunity to interpret the Second Amendment, it stated that the right confirmed by the Second Amendment "is not a right granted by the constitution. Neither is it in any manner dependent upon that instrument for its existence." The repeal of the Second Amendment would no more render the outlawing of firearms legitimate than the repeal of the due process clause of the Fifth Amendment would authorize the government to imprison and kill people at will. A government that abrogates any of the Bill of Rights, with or without majoritarian approval, forever acts illegitimately, becomes tyrannical, and loses the moral right to govern.

This is the uncompromising understanding reflected in the warning that America's gun owners will not go gently into that good, utopian night: "You can have my gun when you pry it from my cold, dead hands." While liberals take this statement as evidence of the retrograde, violent nature of gun owners, we gun owners hope that liberals hold equally strong sentiments about their printing presses, word processors, and television cameras. The republic depends upon fervent devotion to all our fundamental rights.

The Coming White Underclass

Charles Murray

EVERY ONCE IN A WHILE the sky really is falling, and this seems to be the case with the latest national figures on illegitimacy. The unadorned statistic is that, in 1991, 1.2 million children were born to unmarried mothers, within a hair of 30 percent of all live births. How high is 30 percent? About four percent points higher than the black illegitimacy rate in the early 1960s that motivated Daniel Patrick Moynihan to write his famous memorandum on the breakdown of the black family.

The 1991 story for blacks is that illegitimacy has now reached 68 percent of births to black women. In inner cities, the figure is typically in excess of 80 percent. Many of us have heard these numbers so often that we are inured. It is time to think about them as if we were back in the mid-1960s with the young Moynihan and asked to predict what would happen if the black illegitimacy rate were 68 percent.

Impossible, we would have said. But if the proportion of fatherless boys in a given community were to reach such levels, surely the culture must be *Lord of the Flies* writ large, the values of unsocialized male adolescents made norms—physical violence, immediate gratification, and predatory sex. That is the culture now taking over the black inner city.

But the black story, however dismaying, is old news. The new trend that threatens the United States is white illegitimacy. Matters have not yet quite gotten out of hand, but they are on the brink. If we want to act, now is the time.

In 1991 707,502 babies were born to single white women, representing 22 percent of white births. The elite wisdom holds that this phenomenon cuts across social classes, as if the increase in Murphy Browns were pushing the trend line. Thus, a few months ago, a Census Bureau study of fertility among all American women got headlines for a few days because it showed that births to single women with college degrees doubled in the last decade to 6 percent from 3 percent. This is an interesting trend, but of minor social importance. The real news of that study is that the proportion of single mothers with less than a high school education jumped to 48 percent from 35 percent in a single decade.

These numbers are dominated by whites. Breaking down the numbers by race (using data not available in the published version), women with college degrees contribute only 4 percent of white illegitimate babies, while women with a high-school education or less contribute 82 percent. Women with family incomes of $75,000 or more contribute 1 percent of white illegitimate babies; while women with family incomes under $20,000 contribute 69 percent.

The National Longitudinal Study of Youth, a Labor Department study that has tracked more than ten thousand youths since 1979, shows an even more dramatic picture. For white women below the poverty line in the year prior to giving birth, 44 percent of births have been illegitimate, compared with only 6 percent for women above the poverty line. White illegitimacy is overwhelmingly a lower-class phenomenon.

This brings us to the emergence of a white underclass. In raw numbers, European-American whites are the ethnic group with the most people in poverty, most illegitimate children, most women on welfare, most unemployed men, and most arrests for serious crimes. And yet whites have not had an "underclass" as such, because the whites who might qualify have been scattered among the working class. Instead, whites have had "white trash" concentrated in a few streets on the outskirts of town, sometimes a skid row of unattached white men in the large cities. But these scatterings have seldom been large enough to make up a neighborhood. An underclass needs a critical mass, and white America has not had one.

But now the overall white illegitimacy rate is 22 percent. The figure in low-income, working-class communities may be twice that. How much illegitimacy can a community tolerate? Nobody knows, but the historical fact is that the trend lines on black crime, dropout from the labor force, and illegitimacy all shifted sharply upward as the overall black illegitimacy rate passed 25 percent.

The causal connection is murky—I blame the revolution in social policy during that period, while others blame the sexual revolution, broad shifts in cultural norms, or structural changes in the economy. But the white illegitimacy rate is approaching that same problematic 25 percent region at a time when social policy is more comprehensively wrongheaded than it was in the mid-1960s, and the cultural and sexual norms are still more degraded.

The white underclass will begin to show its face in isolated ways. Look for certain schools in white neighborhoods to get a reputation as being unteachable, with large numbers of disruptive students and indifferent parents. Talk to the police; listen for stories about white neighborhoods where the incidence of domestic disputes and casual violence has been shooting up. Look for white neighborhoods with high concentrations of drug activity and large numbers of men who have dropped out of the labor force. Some readers will recall reading the occasional news story about such places already.

As the spatial concentration of illegitimacy reaches critical mass, we should expect the deterioration to be as fast among low-income whites in the 1990s as it was among low-income blacks in the 1960s. My proposition is that illegitimacy is the single most important social problem of our time—more important than crime, drugs, poverty, illiteracy, welfare, or homelessness because it drives everything else. Doing something about it is not just one more item on the American policy agenda, but should be at the top. Here is what to do:

In the calculus of illegitimacy, the constants are that boys like to sleep with girls and that girls think babies are endearing. Human societies have historically channeled these elemental forces of human behavior via thick walls of rewards and penalties that constrained the overwhelming majority of births to take place within marriage. The past thirty years have seen those walls cave in. It is time to rebuild them.

The ethical underpinning for the policies I am about to describe is this: Bringing a child into the world is the most important thing that most human beings ever do. Bringing a child into the world when one is not emotionally or financially prepared to be a parent is wrong. The child deserves society's support. The parent does not.

The social justification is this: A society with broad legal freedoms depends crucially on strong nongovernmental institutions to temper and restrain behavior. Of these, marriage is paramount. Either we reverse the current trends in illegitimacy—especially white illegitimacy—or America must, willy-nilly, become an unrecognizably authoritarian, socially segregated, centralized state.

To restore the rewards and penalties of marriage does not require social engineering. Rather, it requires that the state stop interfering with the natural forces that have done the job quite effectively for millennia. Some of the changes I will describe can occur at the federal level; others would involve state laws. For now, the important thing is to agree on what should be done.

I begin with the penalties, of which the most obvious are economic. Throughout human history, a single woman with a small child has not been a viable economic unit. Not being a viable economic unit, neither have the single woman and child been a legitimate social unit. In small numbers, they must be a net drain on the community's resources. In large numbers, they must destroy the community's capacity to sustain itself. Mirabile dictu, communities everywhere have augmented the economic penalties of single parenthood with severe social stigma.

Restoring economic penalties translates into the first and central policy prescription: to end all economic support for single mothers. The AFDC (Aid to Families with Dependent Children) payment goes to zero. Single mothers are not eligible for subsidized housing or for food stamps. An assortment of other subsidies and in-kind benefits disappear. Since universal medical coverage appears to be an idea whose time has come, I will stipulate that all children have medical coverage. But with that exception, the signal is loud and unmistakable: From society's perspective, to have a baby that you cannot care for yourself is profoundly irresponsible, and the government will no longer subsidize it.

How does a poor young mother survive without government support? The same way she has since time immemorial. If she wants to keep a child, she must enlist support from her parents, boyfriend, siblings, neighbors, church, or philanthropies. She must get support from somewhere, anywhere, other than the government. The objectives are threefold.

First, enlisting the support of others raises the probability that other mature adults are going to be involved with the upbringing of the child, and this is a great good in itself.

Second, the need to find support forces a self-selection process. One of the most shortsighted excuses made for current behavior is that an adolescent who is utterly unprepared to be a mother "needs someone to love." Childish yearning isn't a good enough selection device. We need to raise the probability that a young single woman who keeps her child is doing so volitionally and thoughtfully. Forcing her to find a way of supporting the child does this. It will lead many young women who shouldn't be mothers to place their babies for adoption. This is good. It will lead others, watching what happens to their sisters, to take steps not to get pregnant. This is also good. Many others will get abortions. Whether this is good depends on what one thinks of abortion.

Third, stigma will regenerate. The pressure on relatives and communities to pay for the folly of their children will make an illegitimate birth the socially horrific act it used to be, and getting a girl pregnant something boys do at the risk of facing a shotgun. Stigma and shotgun marriages may or may not be good for those on the receiving end, but their deterrent effect on others is wonderful—and indispensable.

What about women who can find no support but keep the baby anyway? There are laws already on the books about the right of the state to take a child from a neglectful parent. We have some 360,000 children in foster care because of them. Those laws would still apply. Society's main response, however, should be to make it as easy as possible for those mothers to place their children for adoption at infancy. To that end, state governments must strip adoption of the nonsense that has encumbered it in recent decades.

The first step is to make adoption easy for any married couple who can show reasonable evidence of having the resources and stability to raise a child. Lift all restrictions on interracial adoption. Ease age limitations for adoptive parents.

The second step is to restore the traditional legal principle that placing a child for adoption means irrevocably relinquishing all legal rights to the child. The adoptive parents are parents without qualification. Records are sealed until the child reaches adulthood, at which time they may be unsealed only with the consent of biological child and parent.

Given these straightforward changes—going back to the old way, which worked—there is reason to believe that some extremely large proportion of infants given up by their mothers will be adopted into good homes. This is true not just for flawless blue-eyed blond infants but for babies of all colors and conditions. The demand for infants to adopt is huge.

Some small proportion of infants and larger proportion of older children will not be adopted. For them, the government should spend lavishly on orphanages. I am not recommending Dickensian barracks. In 1993, we know a lot about how to provide a warm, nurturing environment for children, and getting rid of the welfare system frees up lots of money to do it. Those who find the word "orphanages" objectionable may think of them as twenty-four-hour-a-day preschools. Those who prattle about the importance of keeping children with their biological mothers may wish to spend some time in a patrol car or with a social worker seeing what the reality of life with welfare-dependent biological mothers can be like.

Finally, there is the matter of restoring the rewards of marriage. Here, I am pessimistic about how much government can do and optimistic about how little it needs to do. The rewards of raising children within marriage are real and deep. The main task is to shepherd children through adolescence so that they can reach adulthood—when they are likely to recognize the value of those rewards—free to take on marriage and family. The main purpose of the penalties for single parenthood is to make that task easier.

One of the few concrete things that the government can do to increase the rewards of marriage is make the tax code favor marriage and children. Those of us who are nervous about using the tax code for social purposes can advocate making the tax code at least neutral.

A more abstract but ultimately crucial step in raising the rewards of marriage is to make marriage once again the sole legal institution through which parental rights and responsibilities are defined and exercised.

Little boys should grow up knowing from their earliest memories that if they want to have any rights whatsoever regarding a child that they sire—more vividly, if they want to grow up to be a daddy— they must marry. Little girls should grow up knowing from their earliest memories that if they want to have any legal claims whatsoever on the father of their children, they must marry. A marriage certificate should establish that a man and a woman have entered into a unique legal relationship. The changes in recent years that have blurred the distinctiveness of marriage are subtly but importantly destructive.

Together, these measures add up to a set of signals, some with immediate and tangible consequences, others with long-term consequences, still others symbolic. They should be supplemented by others based on a reexamination of divorce laws, and their consequences.

That these policy changes seem drastic and unrealistic is a peculiarity of our age, not of the policies themselves. With embellishments, I have endorsed the policies that were the uncontroversial law of the land as recently as John Kennedy's presidency. Then, America's elites accepted as a matter of course that a free society such as America's can sustain itself only through virtue and temperance in the people, that virtue and temperance depend centrally on the socialization of each new generation, and that the socialization of each generation depends on the matrix of care and resources fostered by marriage.

Three decades after that consensus disappeared, we face an emerging crisis. The long, steep climb in black illegitimacy has been

calamitous for black communities and painful for the nation. The reforms I have described will work for blacks as for whites, and have
been needed for years. But the brutal truth is that American society
as a whole could survive when illegitimacy became epidemic within
a comparatively small ethnic minority. It cannot survive the same
epidemic among whites.

The Moral Origins of the Urban Crisis

William J. Bennett

"**A** CHAOS OF LEVITY AND FEROCITY" is how Edmund Burke described the French Revolution. He could just as well have been talking about south-central Los Angeles last week, when Americans watched the nation's second-largest city descend into social anarchy.

The postmortem has begun. We are now in the midst of a debate about the legacy of the Great Society and the contemporary urban crisis. It is dominating the national conversation and the presidential campaign. That is appropriate; the broader issues raised by Los Angeles are the real substance of politics: justice, right and wrong, and how we should live together. The economy and jobs may be the engine of society, but what happened in L.A. is about its soul.

On one side of the debate are the guardians of the old order: the so-called civil rights leadership, Left-leaning social analysts, and the architects and defenders of the Great Society. Their response to the L.A. riots was as predictable as it was misguided: The solution to the problems of the urban underclass is a massive infusion of new federal money. But as George Mason University professor Walter Williams has pointed out, the money spent on poverty programs since the 1960s "could have bought the entire assets of the Fortune 500 companies and virtually all the U.S. farm land. And what did it do? The problems still remain and they are even worse."

Despite a Great Society effort now well into its third decade—at the cost of more than $2.5 trillion—the life of many inner-city residents has never been worse, for blacks especially. Today blacks comprise almost half of the prison population. The homicide rate for black males aged fifteen to twenty-four has increased by 40 percent since the mid-1980s and is now the leading cause of death for that age group. Forty percent of those murdered in the United States are black men killed by other black men. Sixty-five percent of all black babies are born to unwed mothers; the number is as high as 80 percent in many inner cities.

Instead of facing up to the facts and offering constructive alternatives, the familiar critics have resorted to what they know best: reflexively and mindlessly bashing the Reagan and Bush administrations. According to AFL-CIO President Lane Kirkland, what happened in Los Angeles "is symptomatic of more than a decade of policies that favor the rich and privileged while ignoring and injuring the disadvantaged and their communities." These supposed "champions of the poor" keep recycling the same stale, failed proposals of the past. They are increasingly irrelevant to the debate.

Republicans, on the other hand, are wrong to decry all Great Society programs. As Charles Krauthammer wrote several years ago, the Great Society experienced some successes. But he pointed out that the crisis of modern liberalism comes from the realization that its remedies have reached the limits of their success. Many of the problems we now face—particularly those plaguing the underclass—have proved remarkably resistant to Great Society cures. The real problem is the degree to which the Great Society program, taken as a whole, promoted a culture of dependency and rewarded (unintentionally) bad behavior. According to historian Gertrude Himmelfarb:

> After making the most arduous attempt to objectify the problem of poverty, to divorce poverty from any moral assumptions and conditions, we are learning how inseparable the moral and material dimensions of that problem are. And after trying to devise social policies that are scrupulously neutral and "value free," we are finding these policies fraught with moral implications that have grave material and social consequences.

Republicans properly believe in limited government. But we also believe in essential government. And the first responsibility of government is the security of the citizenry. It is scandalous that the police were not on the streets of Los Angeles, en masse, to protect innocent life and prevent a small uprising from turning into a conflagration.

Order must permeate our cities every day. Not a harsh law and order that excuses police brutality, but the lawful order of a civil society—the kind of environment and treatment that residents in affluent suburbs insist on, and usually get. We seek order for what it makes possible—enterprise and work, play and study, stability and domestic tranquility; in short, civilized life.

When I was director of the Office of National Drug Control Policy, I met with citizens in one of the most drug-ridden areas in south-central Los Angeles. It had been home to a violent drug gang, and the residents had seen their share of drug dealing and drive-by shootings. So the police tried something unusual. They barricaded parts of the neighborhood and operated street patrols in cooperation with neighborhood watch groups. Crime within the barricaded area was down 12 percent over the previous year; drive-by shootings were down 85 percent. And crime figures outside the zones were also down, suggesting that Operation Cul-de-Sac (as it was referred to) hadn't simply pushed crime beyond the wall. Neighborhood residents were enthusiastic supporters of the police operation. The L.A. police department canvassed 563 people before erecting the barricades; 558 of them approved of police intervention.

Something else happened as well: School attendance in the neighborhood went up. According to the principal of Jefferson High School, 150 to 200 more students were back in school once a police presence was established. The police provided the basic protection so that parents felt better about sending their children to school. Personal security is a necessary condition of democracy—in south-central Los Angeles as well as Bel Air.

The most immediate problem facing inner-city residents is crime. John J. DiIulio, Jr., of Princeton University has written that the essential difference between the middle class and many of those who reside in urban neighborhoods is that the middle class "can avoid what the underclass cannot escape; we can drive quickly past the crime-torn streets where they must walk, live, and cope." We will not see families, neighborhoods, schools, churches, or local economies flourish in communities where predatory street criminals are in control.

We have heard a lot in recent days about the "root causes" of civil disorder. Unfortunately most of the "root cause" theorists do not go deep enough; their nostrums do not address the source of much of the urban violence. When the American people watched in horror as stores were burned and looted and people were dragged from their vehicles and beaten to death, they were seeing in part the results of a disastrous twenty-five-year social experiment—boys growing up in a nihilistic culture without the presence of their fathers, few positive male role models, terrible schools, and feckless churches—in other words, few civilized influences. We should not be shocked when these boys do not grow up to be good and decent men.

President Bush stands at a domestic crossroad. Out of last week's tragedy and ruin there is also opportunity. He has the attention of the nation. The president needs to lay out a clear, principled response to our urban crisis—one that is responsible, realistic, and humane. First, he should vigorously embrace his own urban agenda based on the rule of law, a more effective criminal justice system, support for school choice as a means of better education, reversal of the destructive incentives of the welfare culture, and an "empowerment" agenda, including strong support for market-oriented solutions, urban enterprise zones, tenant ownership, and the rest of Secretary Jack Kemp's plan. We need to tear down the economic barriers that keep the underclass in poverty.

Second, President Bush must remain firm. He should resist calls for a "new Marshall Plan for the cities" (read: federal guilt money). That will simply give us more of the same. Third, he should strongly condemn those who have implied that riotous behavior and murder can be excused because of a lack of federal funds or because of the troubling verdict in the Rodney King case. The blame for riots and killings rests with the rioters and killers. To suggest otherwise undermines the efforts of decent, law-abiding parents and their children, the majority of whom did not participate in riots. At a time when we most need to affirm belief in individual responsibility, civic duty, and obedience to the law, we are hearing too much from putative political and religious leaders who are themselves morally exhausted. We cannot raise children to be good without forcefully condemning what is bad.

Fourth, the president must focus the nation's attention on irreducible realities. There is a tendency on both sides to exaggerate the impact—for good or ill—of government programs. Block grants and enterprise zones cannot rebuild a shattered moral order. What happened in the streets of Los Angeles is, at bottom, not about economic poverty. For parts of that city, the road to disaster has been paved by a corrosive popular culture, educational failure, moral and spiritual depletion, and the breakdown of our most critical institution—the family. Cultural problems demand cultural solutions. We will not see an end to urban despair and violence unless we attend to this hard truth.

Part 6

CONFRONTATIONS

A Soldier of the Not Great War

Mark Helprin

MR. PRESIDENT, Haiti is on an island, and its navy, which was built mainly in Arkansas, is well characterized by the International Institute for Strategic Studies as "Boats only." The Haitian gross national product is little more than half of what Americans spend each year on greeting cards, its defense forces outnumbered five to one by the corps of lawyers in the District of Columbia.

With other than a leading role in world military affairs, the Haitian army has retreated into a kind of relaxed confusion in which it is also the fire department, captains can outrank colonels, and virtually no one has ever seen combat. Which raises the question, why has the leading superpower placed Haiti at the center of its political universe?

Mr. President, in trumpeting this gnatfest at a hundred times the volume of the Normandy invasion you have invited challenges from all who would take comfort at the spectacle of the United States in full fluster over an object so diminutive as to be a source of wonder.

Anyone considering a serious challenge to the United States has been reassured that we have no perspective in international affairs, that we act not in regard to our basic interests but in reaction to sentiment and ideology, that we can be distracted by the smallest matter and paralyzed by the contemplation of force, that we have become timid, weak, and slow. This is what happens when the leaders of the world's most powerful nation take a year to agonize over Haiti. This is what happens when the elephant ignores the jackals and gravely battles a fly.

Given that Haiti is a nation doomed to perpetual harmlessness, that it is not allied to any great power, that it does not export an ideology, that it does not have an ideology, and that it is of no economic consequence to any nation except perhaps the Dominican Republic, you strained to justify intervention the way a prisoner with his hand stretched through the bars strains for a key just out of his reach.

In your recent address you mentioned rape three times, the killing of children three times, and the words "dictator" or "tyrant" eighteen times. If we must act "when brutality occurs close to our shores," why not now invade Cuba, or Colombia, or the South Bronx, or Anacostia? Every year in the United States we are subject to more than one hundred thousand reported rapes and twenty thousand homicides. How do rape and murder in Haiti, no numbers supplied, justify U.S. intervention? And if they do, where were we in Rwanda?

Is it possible that having no idea whatsoever about the balance of power among nations, the workings of the international system, and the causes and conduct of war, you are directing the foreign relations of the United States of America in accord with the priorities of feminism, environmentalism, and political correctitude? Why not invade Saudi Arabia because of the status of women there, Canada because they kill baby seals, Papua New Guinea because it doesn't have enough wheelchair ramps?

Haitian illegal immigrants (did you not mention AIDS because it would offend the Haitians, or some other group?) have been to some extent motivated by the embargo and are a minute proportion of the total that seek our shores. If it is so that the best way to deal with a country that spills over with souls is to invade it, *qué viva* Mexico? Should the U.K. invade Pakistan; France, Algeria; and Hong Kong, Vietnam? For that matter, why have you not hastened forward to Havana? In fact, the history of Great-Power interventions shows that conquest does not prevent but, rather, facilitates population transfers.

Your desire to wipe out the expenditure of $14 million a month to maintain the leaky embargo that you put in place was not consonant with your robust urge to spend elsewhere, and was a rather dainty pretext. Fourteen million dollars is what we in this country spend on "sausages and other prepared meats" every seven hours. If you truly believe, Mr. President, that "restoring Haiti's democratic government will help lead to more stability and prosperity in our region," then you, sir, have more voodoo than they do. The entire Haitian gross national product is worth but three hours of our own. Were it to grow after intervention by 10 percent and were the United States to reap fully one half the benefit, we would surge ahead another nine minutes' worth of GNP. This is not exactly high-stakes geopolitics.

Why, then, Haiti? Why are your subordinates suddenly so Churchillian? Clearly, in a real crisis they would be so worked up that all their bulbs would burst. The nations towed along for the ride (Poles? Jordanians?) seemed not to know whether to be embarrassed by the stupidity of the task or amused by the peculiarity of their bedfellows. This the secretary of state described as "a glowing coalition." Never in the history of the English language has such an inept phrase been launched with such forced enthusiasm to miss so little a target. Granted, the vice president's "modalities of departure" did much to inspire the nation to a frenzy of war.

Why Haiti? Because, like the father in Joyce's story, "Counterparts," who bullies his son because he cannot fight his bullying boss, what you do in Haiti says less about Haiti than about North Korea, Europe, and the Middle East, where the real challenges lie, and where you cannot act because you do not have a lamp to go by and you have forced your own military to its knees.

Why Haiti? Because you have been unable to say no to the Black Caucus as it stands like the candlestick on the seesaw of your grandiose legislation, and because you are a liberal and in race you see wisdom, or lack of wisdom; qualification, or lack of qualification; virtue, or lack of virtue. And because the Black Caucus is way too tight with Father Aristide.

Why Haiti? Because you have no more sense of what to do or where to turn in a foreign policy crisis than a moth in Las Vegas at 2:00 A.M. You should not have singled out Haiti in the first place, but once you did you should not have spent so much time and so much capital on it, blowing it out of all proportion, so that this, this Gulf Light, this No-Fat Desert Storm, is your Stalingrad. Six weeks and it should have been over, even including an invasion, about which the world would have learned only after it had begun. All communications with the Haitian regime should have been in private, leaving them the flexibility to capitulate without your having to distract Jimmy Carter from his other good works.

Though you and your supporters made a marriage of convenience with the principles of presidential war powers, your new position is miraculously correct; while that of the Republicans who also switched sides in the question is not. You did have the legal authority to invade Haiti. What you did not have was the moral authority. Despite what you have maintained during the first 46/48 of your life, the decision was yours, but your power was merely mechanical.

Like your false-ringing speech, the dry bones of your authority had none of the moral flesh and blood that might otherwise have invigorated even a senseless policy. The animation that you have failed to lend to this enterprise was left to the soldiers in the field, who with the greatest discipline and selflessness would have taken on the task that, generations ago, you refused. I wonder if your view of them has really changed. In your philosophy they must have been pawns then, and they must be pawns now: The only thing that has been altered is your position.

Though it is fair to say that I differ with your policy, if our soldiers had gone into combat I would have been behind them 100 percent, and I hope that, despite the orders in Somalia, you would have been too. This is a lesson that you might have learned earlier but did not, the truth of which you now embrace only because you have become president of the United States. You are the man who will march only if he is commander in chief. Yours, Mr. President, has been a very expensive education. And, unfortunately, every man, woman, and child in this country is destined to pay the bill for your training not because it is so costly but because it is so achingly incomplete.

Those Who Don't Get It

Andrew Ferguson

The following memo has been passed along by Andrew Ferguson, a senior writer at Washingtonian *magazine. Any relation to any actual memo circulating in Washington newsrooms is purely coincidental.*

From: XXX   XXX, Managing Editor, The XXXX XXXXXX.
To: Political Reporters
Re: Covering the New Congress

I KNOW the last several days have been difficult for you. Soon you will bid adieu to many good friends on the Hill—men and women who were always there with that pointed quote, that special document to round out our stories and bring our readers the fairest, most informed congressional coverage possible.

But now is no time for tears, frankly. Literally thousands of new Republicans will be moving here to take positions on the Hill, and we have a big task ahead as we transition to this much less familiar environment.

The purpose of this memo is to make your transition as painless as possible.

What are congressional Republicans? In a nutshell, that's the question I've heard from many of you over the last week. It's a fair one. All across Washington, from Georgetown on one side to Cleveland Park on the other, neighbors have been asking the same thing. Our librarians have been very helpful (see profile of Everett Dirksen attached). And I have done some research of my own.

My information is admittedly sketchy. I have a call in to Elliot Richardson, an old tennis partner who is himself a Republican, and hopefully he'll be able to flesh out some details. What follows is the information I've gleaned from several casual conversations, including my lunch earlier this week with Dave Gergen.

(Incidentally, Dave indicated in the strongest possible terms that contrary to erroneous reports last year, he has always been a Republican and is "damn proud of it." Some of these erroneous reports appeared in our own paper. We have got to be more careful, people.)

Here, then, are the results of my reporting.

The days when moderates like George Mitchell controlled the Hill are gone, at least for now. Most of the new Republican congresspersons and staffers are adherents of the right-wing philosophy of "conservatism." Conservatism can be traced to such right-wing thinkers as Franco, Pinochet, and William F. Buckley, Jr. Conservatism, in brief, calls for dismantling the entire government while simultaneously controlling the most intimate decisions of a person's life. Contradictory? Sure: like cutting taxes, increasing defense, and balancing the budget, all at the same time! Let's make sure our readers understand the impossibility of doing this.

Several sources emphasized that in reporting our stories, we should take care not to call staffers or congresspersons on Sunday morning, when the vast majority of Americans stay home to watch Brinkley. But apparently many Republicans "go to church." Some of you will be familiar with churches in Cleveland Park for their marvelous chamber music concerts. Our new Republican friends, however, go to church for "services"—patriarchal rituals that date back to the early 1900s or even earlier. This also has something to do with "turning back the clock," another right-wing tenet of conservatism.

Over the years you have been able to develop relations with congressional sources through your kids' schools—at soccer games, Earth Day ceremonies, Condom Fairs, and the like. But beware! I'm told that many of the new Republicans will be sending their kids to "public schools" in the suburbs, where they don't even charge tuition. As one waggish source put it to me, "Half these clowns have never heard of Sidwell Friends or Georgetown Day!" Good news for you as parents; bad news for you as reporters, who will have to create new avenues of informal communication.

Again, not easy: Many of the Republicans will be living in Virginia, the state across the Potomac from Bethesda (see map attached). These suburbs are usually 1980s-style wastelands of tract houses—"one step up from the trailer park," another source quips—that have destroyed irreplaceable historic landscapes. If there's sufficient interest, the paper will be happy to arrange a bus tour. They must be seen to be believed.

This won't be news to some of you. It's been my pleasure to entertain members of our staff at my farm in the Shenandoah Valley, which is also in Virginia. As you drove out you may have noticed that instead of Volvos and Camrys many of the natives drove old cars, "pickup" trucks, and vans. The men wear their baseball caps oddly—with the bill turned forward, instead of backward in the more conventional manner. Often the women look as if their fitness-center memberships were canceled years ago. Oblivious to the population crisis, these people sometimes parent more than two children (and then complain about condoms in the schools!). All of them own guns.

I mention this because you've heard Gingrich talk of the "ordinary Americans" that he and his congresspersons supposedly represent. My sources indicate that this is a ruse. Historically, Republicans have been controlled by the "haves" in the war against minorities, women, gays, and other "have-nots." There is a great deal of documentation for this. I suggest you consult books by Sidney Blumenthal and Haynes Johnson. Their understanding of Republicans sets a lofty goal all of us should aspire to.

So let's get to work. In this new era our job remains the same: to comfort the afflicted and afflict the comfortable. When it comes to choosing between a self-satisfied, out-of-touch elite and ordinary Americans, I think we all know where we stand.

A Conservative Looks at Liberalism

William Kristol

I
N BILL CLINTON'S America, liberalism is everywhere dominant and
altogether bankrupt.

By "liberalism" I mean post-1960s liberalism: a movement
committed in politics to further expansion of the welfare state,
and in social matters to an agenda of individual autonomy and "liberation." Liberalism in this sense pervades the key institutions of
American society.

Thus, liberals have reclaimed control of the executive branch, and
will soon once again take over the federal judiciary. Liberals continue
to dominate Congress and most state and local governments; they
rule virtually unchallenged over our educational institutions and our
cultural and philanthropic organizations; they shape most of the
products of the mass media, journalism, book publishing, and Hollywood. Liberalism is powerful in our churches and synagogues; and
even the world of business is by no means generally hostile or imper-
vious to the enlightened doctrines of the Left. Furthermore, government at all levels grows ever bigger and more intrusive—except with
regard to sexual morality, where the ethos of individual liberation
proceeds apace.

The election of Bill Clinton is, of course, the capstone in the arch.
Until now, even as post-1960s liberalism was taking control of the
institutions of American society, the great limit to its success was its
failure to capture the presidency. A national majority, mobilized in
good part in reaction to liberalism, repeatedly elected conservative
presidents (including even, it could be argued, Jimmy Carter) who
stood as barriers to liberal supremacy. Now the tenuous balance of

power is gone. Vice President Al Gore announced on election night that "We are the children of modern America." It is those children of modern America, having been formed by the late 1960s and having completed their long march through the institutions, who now govern America.

And yet, with all its apparent success, liberalism still fails to command the loyalty of the vast majority of Americans. Liberal possession of the commanding heights of American society is not matched by occupation of the ground below.

For two decades, more Americans have considered themselves conservative than liberal. From 1980 on, in polls taken by CBS News/ *New York Times,* no more than 23 percent of the American public have identified themselves as liberals, and in January 1993 that figure stood at 18 percent. (The number identifying themselves as conservatives has averaged around 33 percent, with another 40 percent or so calling themselves moderates.) Even in the presidential race of 1992, the two *non*liberal candidates received 57 percent of the vote, while Clinton, the one liberal, ran as "a new kind of Democrat"—that is, a not-so-liberal Democrat. In 1992, moreover, over the opposition of the liberal establishment, measures limiting the terms of legislators passed in all fourteen states in which they were on the ballot.

Polls confirm not only that the American people do not consider themselves liberals, but also that they reject most core liberal beliefs. Contemporary liberalism insists upon a latitudinarian view of the family, and it abhors the idea of "family values"; but on election day 1992, as measured in exit polls, the American people, by 70 to 25 percent, wanted government to encourage "traditional family values" rather than "tolerance of nontraditional families."

Or again, as the Clinton administration has demonstrated, contemporary liberalism inclines toward higher taxes and bigger government; yet the American people today, by 55 to 36 percent, would rather pay less in taxes and receive fewer government services than pay more taxes in return for more services.

Finally, contemporary liberalism stands or falls by a faith in the efficacy of big government; but popular distrust of government is at an all-time high. In 1972, 74 percent of Americans had at least a "fair amount" of confidence in the federal government; today, that figure has fallen to 42 percent. And in January of this year, by 69 to 22 percent, Americans agreed that the federal government creates more problems than it solves.

CONTEMPORARY LIBERALISM, then, has not captured the hearts and minds of the American people. Indeed, its resort to the machinery of political correctness—the attempt to impose sanctions on views contrary to liberal dogma—has been driven in part by just this failure to capture those hearts and minds.

Ordinarily, such a failure need not be permanent. A confident and determined liberal elite might well expect to overcome popular hesitations or even resistance; it has done so in the past. But this brings us to the greater vulnerability of contemporary liberalism: beneath its smugness and self-righteousness, liberalism is undergoing a crisis of faith.

The liberal crisis of faith has sources that are profound, and an exploration of them is beyond my purposes here; but the *fact* of the crisis is, I think, undeniable.

Think back to contemporary liberalism's older (though quite different) cousin, postwar American liberalism. The liberals of the 1950s and 1960s were confident that government could fine-tune the economy. They were confident that enlightened government action could virtually do away with racism and poverty. (After signing one piece of Great Society legislation, President Lyndon B. Johnson proclaimed that "the days of the dole are numbered.") The more "philosophic" liberals were convinced that a rationalist humanism could supplant religious belief as the source of decency and morality. And liberals then also believed that international cooperation and "alliances for progress" would soon replace antiquated and retrograde forces like nationalism and ethnic tribalism.

Do today's liberals truly have faith in any of these propositions?

COMPARE, too, the inaugural addresses of John F. Kennedy and Bill Clinton: where the one is assertive, the other is plaintive. In

1961, President Kennedy hailed "a new generation of Americans" who would gladly "bear the burden of a long twilight struggle" against tyranny, poverty, disease, and war, and who would support the use of American military power, where necessary, "to assure the survival and the success of liberty." In 1993, President Clinton, by contrast, identified "the urgent question of our time" as "whether we can make change our friend and not our enemy."

In short, the older liberalism was confident of progress; contemporary liberalism seeks merely to keep up with "change," and seems rather doubtful as to whether it can handle even that rather uninspiring task.

But this loss of confidence does not need to be inferred; it has been openly proclaimed by none other than Hillary Rodham Clinton, the high priestess of contemporary liberalism. In her now-famous speech at the University of Texas this past April, Mrs. Clinton virtually declared liberalism's bankruptcy: "We are in a crisis of meaning. . . . We lack at some core level meaning in our individual lives and meaning collectively. . . . We need a new politics of meaning. . . . We need a new definition of civil society."

"Who is 'we'?" one is tempted to ask. But it is clear enough that in the first instance Mrs. Clinton means "we liberals." A confident liberalism once knew that the last thing "we" need is the vaguely feel-good, vaguely illiberal mishmash that goes by the name of the "politics of meaning." Today's attempt to reach for so sodden a life preserver is testimony to the fact that contemporary liberalism no longer knows what to believe.

Or consider the fate of the work of the Harvard philosophy professor John Rawls. In 1971 Rawls published *A Theory of Justice,* a book hailed at the time as the definitive theoretical defense of the liberal welfare state, and hence as a book for the ages. Does anyone now read *A Theory of Justice?*

Rawls has just brought out a new book, *Political Liberalism,** in which he modifies his argument of twenty years ago. In 1971 in constructing his theory of justice, Rawls thought it reasonable to assume a "well-ordered society" in which there would be broad agreement on

---

* Columbia University Press, 1993.

basic moral beliefs. Today, Rawls has abandoned this assumption as "unrealistic." Instead, he now tries to construct a political conception of justice that will, as he writes, be able to accommodate incompatible and even irreconcilable moral and religious doctrines.

Yet this bow to philosophical multiculturalism makes an already thin conception of justice thinner still. So meager a gruel cannot provide sustenance for a vigorous political movement. Nor can the job be done by such other stopgaps as deconstruction, critical race theory in law, or any of the increasingly exotic forms of feminism.

Liberalism today derives what energy it has from currents that are so far out of the mainstream (the radical gay-rights movement, the voting-rights arguments of Lani Guinier) that it must seek to keep them in check, while finding itself unable to explain exactly what is wrong with them. And if this is where liberalism gets its energy, its real political strength now rests almost entirely on the self-interest of individuals and groups who are dependent on government, and who have a material stake in liberal policies and doctrines.

Despite the mounds of writing and beehives of activity, then, liberalism is in a deep crisis. All of the churning at the periphery conceals the hollowness at the core. True, liberals can still intimidate those who might launch serious assaults against them; they do not hesitate to enforce compliance with their dogmas, or to root out heresy wherever it rears its politically-incorrect head. Yet even Mrs. Clinton has found it necessary to say, in a recent interview, that she is a "conservative" on values. Today's liberalism, in other words, hardly dares govern in its own name.

To WHAT can the condition of liberalism in the United States today be compared? Mutatis mutandis, and with all necessary distinctions duly registered: to the condition of Communism in the Soviet Union about fifteen years ago. Needless to say, American liberalism and Soviet Communism are worlds apart, politically and morally; but there is a certain structural similarity in their respective situations.

In the old Soviet Union, Communism was utterly dominant and, it soon turned out, utterly hollow. Marxism lacked the support of the people; and the Communist administrative class, the nomenklatura, had lost faith in the doctrines that justified its rule. But this did not lessen its desire to hang on to power. As Leonid Brezhnev is alleged to have said in 1968, "Don't talk to me about 'socialism.' What we have, we hold."

So it is in America. Our liberal nomenklatura clings to power, even though its god, too, has failed. Liberalism justifies its continuing hold on power by massive psychological denial. Thus, we are constantly reassured that all is well, or that all will be well once the liberal project is completed. As the liberal nomenklatura would have it, the public schools, for example, need only a bit more money, or a bit more multiculturalism. In the meantime, real, deep educational reform continues to be opposed—not because there are convincing intellectual arguments against it, but because too many teachers and administrators have a huge material interest in the status quo.

So, too, with race. Liberal policies like affirmative action have made race relations in this country worse, not better. Yet the liberal nomenklatura tells us that the solution is more and more of the same.

And so, again, with crime. Like the rest of us, liberals profess to be appalled by the crime rate, but they act as if police brutality were a more serious problem than the epidemic of lawlessness and violence, and they disparage the notion of building more prisons, the one certain way to cut the crime rate by keeping repeat offenders off the streets.

All this is due not so much to cynicism on the part of the liberal nomenklatura as to something more powerful, something closer to self-deception. But how long can such a situation persist? Liberals are now beginning to acknowledge, for example, that Dan Quayle was right about family breakup, but most liberals adamantly refuse to draw the implications—that is, to rethink the meaning and consequences of sexual "liberation" and of the tendency to devalue the traditional family. Yet ideas have consequences. Once a real rethinking begins, in this and countless other areas, the whole structure of liberal doctrine could crumble with great speed. Indeed, the unarticulated sense that "it" could happen here—that glasnost, as it were, could open the floodgates to real change—may well account for the remarkable intransigence in the face of new ideas manifested by the ideologists of contemporary liberalism.

This intransigence cannot be sustained forever. The liberal nomenklatura may hang on for a longer rather than a shorter time; the "prerevolutionary" situation can persist for a while. But an elite that has lost confidence in itself cannot long govern a society that has lost confidence in that elite.

One could object that the crisis of liberalism is nothing new; it became particularly evident in the late 1960s, when the liberalism of that period, incapable of standing up to assaults upon it from the radical Left, instead succumbed to them, thereby embarking on the long slide which has brought things to their present pass. Nor is liberalism's inner loss of confidence new, either. As Harvey Mansfield of Harvard presciently noted fifteen years ago: "From having been the aggressive doctrine of vigorous, spirited men, liberalism has become hardly more than a trembling. . . . Who today is called a liberal for strength and confidence in defense of liberty?" Finally, predictions of the demise of liberalism have also been around for a long time. So what is different now?

One difference stems from the very fact that post-1960s liberalism is now in total command. For twenty of the last twenty-four years, Republicans held the White House. Republican control of the presidency served to mask the dominance of liberalism over the society and even over major sectors of the polity. With Clinton in power, liberalism now has no excuse, and also no exit. In this sense, the election of Bill Clinton may yet prove to be, for liberals, a deeply Pyrrhic victory.

Another difference stems from the collapse of the Soviet Union and more broadly of Marxism. As long as it existed, Soviet Communism forced some sort of reality check on liberalism, reminding it that there *were* enemies to the Left. But now liberalism truly has no enemies to the Left. Is there *any* aspect of feminism, environmentalism, or multiculturalism that is clearly beyond the pale of contemporary liberalism? The collapse of Marxism has removed the last barrier to the tendency within liberalism to push liberal doctrines to destructive extremes.

CONSERVATIVE thought, for its part, may be revived and even radicalized by the dominance of contemporary liberalism. Where once some conservatives were content to call attention to the limits of modern social policy, or to worry that, in practice, liberal policies weakened the social institutions upon which their success depended, now conservatives increasingly have the opportunity to call into question the very purposes and premises of liberal policy, and to debate how best to reconstruct the institutions of a free society.

Similarly, where once conservatives saw themselves as trying to slow down the progress of history in order to husband the moral capital of an earlier time, of a world that had been lost, now conservatives might see themselves as creating moral capital for a world that needs to be remade.

Indeed, most conservatives once secretly feared that history was "progressing" in a liberal direction, and that this progress could not be fundamentally reversed. Liberalism's loss of confidence could release conservatism from the debilitating fear. With secular humanism now exposed as the opiate of the elite, conservatives might now even dare to see in the modern "quest for meaning" the seeds of an authentic revival of religious belief.

This bold new conservatism has not yet come into being, let alone arrived at the point of taking control of the Republican party as liberalism has done with the Democrats. But if, once upon a time, conservatives felt a Burkean responsibility to uphold sound social habits and traditional customs against liberal debunking, now it is liberalism that constitutes the old order, dictating "correct" habits and permissible customs, while conservatives can become the exponents of light and air, of free and open debate, of demystification and even of political and intellectual liberation. The bankruptcy of liberalism invites the possibility of a new, governing conservatism.

Such a conservatism is needed, but that does not mean it will come forth. It is not inevitable that the liberal crack-up will be followed by some sort of conservative renewal or reconstruction. After all, to return to our earlier analogy, the jury is still very much out on what will succeed Communism in the former Soviet Union and Eastern Europe—chaos, varieties of neofascism, or decent civil societies.

Comparable alternatives obtain here. And it is also possible that the liberal American nomenklatura will be able to hang on longer than one might expect, successfully beating back popular insurgencies from below and the loss of confidence from within. No outcome is preordained.

For conservatives, the immediate task is to contain liberalism and its depredations. But containment is not enough. In the end, the conservative task is not to contain contemporary liberalism but to transcend it.

Brickbats and Broomsticks

P. J. O'Rourke

WE ARE HERE TONIGHT to celebrate the twenty-fifth anniversary of the *American Spectator*—the magazine, the men and women, the way of life.

But we are also here to celebrate something else—our return to political opposition. Let's be honest with ourselves. What a relief to be on the attack again. No more gentle sparring with the administration. No more striking with the flat of our sword. No more firing blanks. Ladies and gentlemen, we have game in our sights. Clinton may be a disaster for the rest of the nation, but he is meat on our table.

What a joy to be able to turn to the helmsman of our good ship *Spectator* and say, "Captain Bob, bring the guns down to deck level and load with grapeshot."

So stand warned, Boy Clinton . . . Mr. Bill . . . Wet Willie . . . You and your "Presidential Partner" . . . President Clinton and First Person Hillary . . . Pudge and Ruffles. (If the Fathers of the Christian church had known these two, divorce would not only be permitted; it would be a sacrament.) Anyway, stand warned the pair of you. We're going to laugh you out of office. We did it to the Carters, and we'll do it to you.

So we're here tonight not just to congratulate ourselves for writing and reading and founding and editing and—most important—contributing lots of money to the *American Spectator*. We are also here to work ourselves into a delicious battle frenzy. Let us take our text from that great paean to individual rights, *Animal House*. I quote the ultimate paleo-conservative hero, Bluto, as played by John Belushi: "Take no prisoners!"

Y OU KNOW, some people think we lost this election. *We* didn't lose it. Some people we know . . . people we like personally . . . people whose politics we can just barely tolerate . . . *They* lost this election. We've been in opposition for four years already. And opposition is where we belong. Being opposed to government is what defines true conservatism. We know that government doesn't work even when the most brilliant people in the world—us—run it. We know government is an ineffective and morally unacceptable means of delivering life's benefits.

Clinton doesn't know this. Clinton thinks Americans can vote themselves richer, vote themselves smarter, vote themselves taller. He probably thinks some inches can be voted off his own waistline.

We know people have free will and responsibility for their own actions. Clinton thinks people are victims. Victims of a Republican administration—you remember how George Bush liked to sneak out of the White House at night and sell crack and get teenage girls pregnant.

We believe in God. Clinton believes in going to church. And Clinton's staff believes that Twelve Step programs are the only way that God manifests himself in the modern world.

We believe in freedom and we know that there is no freedom without economic liberty. Clinton has never had a real job in his life. And won't have another after 1996.

T HE CLINTON PEOPLE like to say that they are "nonideological." Let me translate. It means that they don't know right from wrong. The Clinton people claim to be "pragmatists." And I agree. Because pragmatism is a fancy term for "don't know *can't* from *shouldn't*."

Well, the American voters elected Clinton. But one of the many good things about being conservatives is that we never have to feel betrayed by the common people. Sure, they voted for Clinton—that's what made them so common.

Another great advantage of conservatism is that we don't have to fill this evening with sanctimonious twaddle and self-righteous blather. Think of the dreadful dinners that liberals will be sitting through for the next four years. . . . Yes, welcome to the 1990s. Let us all salute (and be sensitive to the needs of) the shiftless, the feckless, the senseless, the worthwhileness-impaired, the decency-challenged, and the differently moraled. And hello to their leaders—progressive, committed, and filled to the nose holes with enormous esteem for themselves.

BUT THAT'S their problem. Our problem, on the *American Spectator's* silver anniversary, is to lead the straying nation. To lead our straying nation, not forward—we're conservatives—but back. Back to that lost golden age of yore—the eighties.

The eighties, when Communist dictators were losing their jobs, not presidents of American and General Motors. When Bill Clinton was only a microscopic polyp in the colon of American politics and Hillary was still in flight school—hadn't even soloed on her broom. Back when health care was a tummy tuck, not an unalienable right. When, if you wanted a better environment, you went to Laura Ashley. When sleeping with the president meant you'd attended a cabinet meeting.

Let us return to that glad epoch when we knew the proper order of words in our language—"free alcohol" not "alcohol-free." When we preferred a Shining City on a Hill to a whining Hill all over Clarence Thomas. When the Malcolm who mattered was Forbes. When tax cuts were in bloom. And Clinton was in Flowers.

The Greatest Cold War Myth of All

Charles Krauthammer

"**W**E LOOK BACK to that era now, and we long for a—I even made a crack the other day. I said, 'Gosh, I miss the cold war.' It was a joke, I mean, I don't really miss it, but you get the joke."

—President Clinton, interview with the *Washington Post,* October 15, 1993.

It is not really a joke. It is an alibi. When the Clinton Administration runs into trouble abroad—debacle in Somalia, humiliation in Haiti, dithering over Bosnia—it likes to preface its list of extenuations with: Of course, we no longer have the easy divisions of the cold war to make things clear and crisp and simple. Things are so much harder now.

So clear and crisp and simple? Curious. During the cold war, especially during its last two decades, liberals claimed that things were not so simple, that only ideologues and dimwits—Ronald Reagan, for example—insisted on seeing the world through the prism of the cold war.

Now they tell us how clear and clarifying it was. "We had an intellectually coherent thing," said Clinton of the cold war era. "The American people knew what the rules were and when we did whatever." How about when we did Vietnam? Vietnam, fought under the theory of containment enunciated first by Harry Truman in 1947, was the quintessential cold war engagement. It was also the most divisive.

At the time, Bill Clinton called it "a war I opposed and despised with a depth of feeling I have reserved solely for racism in America."

Yet it was prosecuted by two successive administrations. In the 1972 election, the winner by landslide was Richard Nixon, war president. Same war. Clinton had a clarity of vision about the war no less certain than Nixon's—only diametrically opposed.

Vietnam rent the nation because it presented the basic dilemmas of the cold war period: Was containment the paramount American foreign-policy goal? Was it worth the risk of military intervention? Where? At what cost? There were no easy answers. There was certainly none of the unanimity that nostalgics now pretend there was.

To hear the blather about cold war consensus, one would think that the 1980s never happened. At every turn, on every issue for which there presumably was one simple, knee-jerk, anti-Soviet answer—the MX, El Salvador, Nicaragua, Grenada, "Euromissile" deployment—there was deep division. And practically every time, liberals, so wistful now for the easy choices of yore, made the wrong choice.

In the late 1970s, for example, the Soviets aggressively deployed medium-range Euromissiles designed to intimidate and neutralize Western Europe. It was a clear-cut challenge. The correct response was equally clear-cut: a NATO counterdeployment of comparable medium-range missiles.

Reagan and Thatcher and Kohl pulled it off. But not without enormous resistance from Western liberals and leftists. In America the resistance took the form of a nuclear-freeze movement that would have frozen Soviet missiles in place and frozen NATO's out.

Where were the Democrats on this one? They forced a nuclear-freeze resolution through the House of Representatives, 278 to 149. Their central idea—if one can speak of a hysteria in terms of ideas—was that Reagan was blinded by his cold war anti-Sovietism. The real enemy, they insisted, was not Communism but the nuclear weapons themselves.

Similarly on the other great cold war issue, Third World revolution: The real enemy, the Democrats protested, was not Communism but deprivation. In the great debates over El Salvador and Nicaragua, liberals insisted that to see these conflicts in cold war, East-West terms was again to miss the point.

"If Central America were not racked with injustices, there would be no revolution," said the Democrats in a 1983 televised address opposing military aid to El Salvador. "There would be nothing for the Soviets to exploit. But unless those oppressive conditions change, that region will continue to seethe with revolution—with or without the Soviets."

As history has demonstrated: wrong. No one would dare claim that in Central America poverty and injustice are gone. But the region no longer seethes with revolution. What happened? Injustice did not disappear. The Soviets did, and with them the sinews and romance of socialist revolution.

The evil empire was the enemy. That was the central tenet of American cold warriors. Liberals deplored such talk as crude Manichaeism. Now, after twenty years of deriding anticommunists for being blinded by the Soviet threat, they wistfully recall how the Soviet threat brilliantly illuminated the foreign-policy landscape— and lament how obscure it all is with the lodestar gone. Ah, the Golden Age when everything was easy and we all joined hands in the cold war battles of Vietnam and Nicaragua and the Euromissiles.

Yesterday, cold warrior was a liberal epithet. Today everyone pretends to have been one. My father, who had a Frenchman's appreciation for cynicism, had a term for this kind of after-battle résumé revision. *Maquis d'après-guerre:* resistance fighter, postwar.

Voice of America:
Why Liberals Fear Me

Rush Limbaugh

T HERE ARE TIMES in one's life that despite all the blood, toil, tears, and sweat expended in the pursuit of excellence, one really should lean back, light up a good cigar, take a sip of an adult beverage, and just savor the moment. My friends, this is one of those times.

Thirty years after the inauguration of Lyndon Johnson's Great Society; twenty-five years after Woodstock; two decades after Richard Nixon's resignation; and two years after Democrats secured control of the White House and both chambers of Congress, modern liberalism—exhausted and confused—is on the run. Three decades after Ronald Reagan's brilliant enunciation of conservative ideals at the end of the 1964 campaign, he told me "Now that I've retired from active politics, I don't mind that you've become the number one voice for conservatism in our country." And liberal fear is palpable.

Target Numero Uno

T HUS CAME THE SIZZLING summer onslaught against me. "He's a showman, a showoff, and a jerk," wrote one pundit. "Chief propagandist for the revolution," said another. "A self-serving, hate-mongering liar," railed one writer. "A tool-shed-sized hate monger," said another. "Rush Limbaugh's ideology makes him a political dinosaur, which puts him on the endangered species list," wrote one critic. "Judge for yourself about that slabhead, Rush Limbaugh," said another.

The assault came from every corner of liberalism—from the White House and the *Washington Post,* from *The New York Times* and the *New Yorker,* from the *Nation* and the *New Republic,* from *Time* magazine and the *Los Angeles Times,* from C-SPAN and CNN, from *U.S. News & World Report* and *USA Today,* and from National Public Radio, the National Organization for Women, and the National Education Association (I'm leaving many out, but you get the picture). In the month that followed President Clinton's June attack on me, I was mentioned in 1,450 stories, including the *South China Morning Post* and *Agence France Presse,* as tracked by a media database service.

Liberals have, in fact, elevated me to the role of leading political figure. Target Numero Uno. It is a role I have never sought. My goal has always been to host the most-listened-to radio and television shows in history and, in turn, charge confiscatory advertising rates. But as it happens, not only am I a performer, I am also effectively communicating a body of beliefs that strikes terror into the heart of even the most well entrenched liberals, shaking them to their core.

The interesting question is, Why? Why do liberals fear me? I am not a distinguished member of Congress. I am not running for president. I do not control billions of dollars in taxpayer money. I can enact no policy, law, or regulation to affect a single American citizen's behavior. So why the high level of liberal emotion? This would seem to me to be a legitimate area of inquiry to be pursued by members of the mainstream media—but their own animus has prevented them from solid analysis of the phenomenon. Yet again, I must do their job for them.

First, liberals fear me because I threaten their control of the debate. These are the facts: Twenty million people a week listen to my radio program on 659 stations nationwide, on short wave and Armed Forces Radio worldwide, while several million more watch my television show on 250 stations nationally. I am on the air seventeen-and-a-half hours a week. Add to that 6 million copies sold of my two books, *The Way Things Ought To Be* and *See, I Told You So,* and 475,000 monthly subscribers to *The Limbaugh Letter* after just two years in business.

What I do in this rather large *oeuvre* (a little literary lingo, there) is hard for pundits to peg. Media sages have not to this point been confronted with a conservative who is both commentator and entertainer. A conservative who traffics in satire, of all things—mostly liberal turf until now. A conservative who dares poke fun at liberal sacred cows, and who does so with relish, optimism, and good cheer. A conservative whose expression of core beliefs is unabashed, unapologetic, unembarrassed—and who has the best bumper music on the air.

How do I attract so many people? First, I approach my audience with enormous respect. I am absolutely convinced that the country contains vast numbers of intelligent, engaged citizens who are hungry for information and inspiration. These are people who play by the rules, who are working hard to raise their families, to strengthen their communities, to do the right thing—and to enthusiastically enjoy life in the process. They are proud to be counted among those who believe in God, American ideals, morality, individual excellence, and personal responsibility.

These are the people who are constantly told: "You are the problem. You aren't compassionate enough, you don't pay enough taxes, your selfishness and greed [which is how the desire to look after one's own family and improve one's lot in life is always defined] are destroying the country." These are the people whose most heartfelt convictions have been dismissed, scorned, and made fun of by the mainstream media. I do not make fun of them. I confirm their instincts, with evidence taken directly from pages of the daily papers and from television news programs. I explain what is actually in legislation. I quote what our esteemed members of Congress and the mainstream media actually say. I detail and analyze news stories (many of which don't get national play except on my programs) that demonstrate the absurdity of liberal policies.

"I Am Equal Time"

I HAVE NOT ATTRACTED and kept my audience by being a blowhard, a racist, a sexist, a hatemonger. Those who make such charges insult the intelligence of the American people. If I were truly what my critics claim, I would have long ago, deservedly, gone into oblivion. The fact is, my audience knows I constantly champion rugged individualism. One of the most oft-heard phrases on my shows is this: "I want a great America made up of great individuals, an America where everyone is unshackled to be the best he can be." This is the philosophy that sends liberals into fits—because they know a country made of strong, self-reliant individuals does not need them at all.

My tools are not "right-wing demagoguery," as is so often charged. My tools are evidence, data, and statistics. Economic analysis. Cultural criticism. Political comment. I demonstrate. I illustrate. I provide my audience with information that the mainstream media refuses to disseminate. And I do so in an entertaining, enjoyable way. That is why I always say my views and commentary don't need to be balanced by equal time. I *am* equal time. And the free market has proved my contention.

Despite claims from my detractors that my audience is comprised of mind-numbed robots, waiting for me to give them some sort of marching orders, the fact is that I am merely enunciating opinions and analysis that support what they already know. Thousands of listeners have told me, on the air, in faxes, letters, and by computer e-mail, that *I* agree with *them.* Finally, they say, somebody in the media is saying out loud what they have believed all along.

This hard evidence that huge numbers of ordinary Americans have privately rejected the tenets of liberalism is a genuine threat to the decades-long liberal dominance of American institutions. Conservatives—who have been shut out of the debate in the arena of ideas for a generation—are finally understanding the stunning truth that they are not alone. The marginalization of conservative ideas, a successful liberal tactic for thirty years, is over. Most Americans are, in fact, conservative. They may not always vote that way, but they live their lives that way. This fact has been successfully hidden from the population. Until now.

Don't Ignore Him

BEYOND MERE JEALOUSY that their territory has been horned-in on, the political and cultural significance of this phenomenon has finally begun to dawn on liberals. One of the first signs of panic occurred back in the Outlook section of the *Washington Post* last February. In "Day of the Dittohead," David Remnick opined: "Nearly all the hype about Limbaugh winds up on the entertainment pages. And yet there is very little in the press to suggest that he is, above all, a sophisticated propagandist, an avatar of the politics of meanness and envy. Limbaugh's influence is hard to gauge," Remnick continued. "But attention must be paid . . . the left-wing media and the 'arts and croissants crowd,' as Limbaugh puts it, ignore him at their peril."

President Clinton picked up this fretful refrain in Atlanta on May 3, amidst sagging poll numbers and embarrassing headlines ranging from Whitewater to Paula Jones. "You [have] got to understand in the rural South where you've got Rush Limbaugh and all this right-wing extremist media just pouring venom at us every day and nothing to counter that, we need an election to get the facts out," claimed the president on CNN. A few weeks later, the president was back on the warpath during an interview aboard *Air Force One* with St. Louis radio station KMOX. "The Republicans and the Far Right in this country have their own media networks. We don't have anything like that. They have extra organized political action groups that we can't match, and they have the Republican Party's fund-raising apparatus, which has been strengthened by having had the White House for all but four in the [past] twenty years." (For the record, Bill Clinton had spoken at a $3.5 million Democratic fund-raiser thirty-six hours before. But I digress.)

"I think there is too much cynicism and too much intolerance . . . look at how much of talk radio is a constant, unremitting drumbeat of negativism and cynicism," the president continued, explaining that he was newly determined "to be aggressive." He then added, "After I get off the radio with you today, Rush Limbaugh will have three hours to say whatever he wants, and I won't have any opportunity to respond, and there's no truth detector. You won't get on afterward and say [what] was true and what wasn't."

The pundits didn't quite know what to make of that. Yes, they agreed, Rush Limbaugh is a blemish on the American political landscape. Still, the president's performance was odd. The response of *The New York Times* editorial page was blistering: "Whining and public self-pity are not presidential-scale attributes." The *Washington Post*'s Mary McGrory concurred: "His remarks were soggy with self-pity. . . . Self-pity is exhaustion's little sister and follows her everywhere. Clinton should read what was said about our most saintly president, Abraham Lincoln, and stop whining." Even London's *Sunday Telegraph* could not resist commenting: "To get into a barnyard scrap with right-wing talk show hosts like Rush Limbaugh does little for the dignity of the Oval Office."

Reign of Error?

THE PRESIDENT'S TIRADE on KMOX occurred on June 24. On June 28, a left-wing media attack-dog group released a "report" entitled Limbaugh's "Reign of Error." "From AIDS to ozone, from Whitewater to the Bible, Limbaugh seems to be able to dissemble and deceive on virtually any subject," read the press release issued by the misnamed Fairness and Accuracy in Reporting (FAIR) and picked up by the Associated Press.

According to FAIR, I am guilty of forty-three instances of "sloppiness, ignorance, or fabrication." The *National Review* recently came to my defense: "Considering that Mr. Limbaugh has logged over 4,000 hours on the air, 43 mistakes would be a pretty good record: how does FAIR's record compare?" But members of the mainstream media, looking for a way to justify their animosity toward me and slavishly devoted to the agenda if not the person of Bill Clinton, could not resist FAIR's seduction.

One charge spread like wildfire because it seemed to best illustrate the premise that I invent stories with abandon and lie about my sources. In January of this year, I mentioned on my radio show a report that the private school that Chelsea Clinton attends had assigned its eighth graders to write a paper on "Why I Feel Guilty Being White." I cited CBS as my source. FAIR's report implied that I made this up out of whole cloth. In an advertisement on *The New York Times* editorial page, FAIR claimed this was an example of a "groundless assertion." Ellen Hume, on CNN's "Reliable Sources," had a field day.

> I don't respect someone who is clearly telling myths and pretending that he's got facts behind him. Occasionally [Limbaugh will] do something like say that the Sidwell Friends School had some test for Chelsea—some essay Chelsea Clinton had to write about why I don't like being white, or why I'm embarrassed to be white, and then he cites a source like CBS News. That simply isn't true. None of that was true. So where is this coming from . . . and where do you draw the line at a mistake, which we all make, and a deliberate distortion of the fact to pander to myths that people wish were true?

I did not fabricate this story, as I explained in a column in *USA Today*. CBS Morning Resource, a wire service for radio talk-show hosts run by the CBS Radio Network, reported the story on January 6, 1994. An Ohio radio station brought the CBS wire story to my attention. *Playboy* magazine and *Heterodoxy* magazine had both already published the story, and in fact were the sources of the CBS wire story. Sidwell later denied that the incident occurred, and I accepted its word and said so on my radio program. But I refused to accept FAIR's suggestion that I made up the story or lied about CBS as its source.

The following week on "Reliable Sources," Ellen Hume admitted her mistake.

> In deference to Rush, I would like to make a clarification, which is that there was a story that he put out on the radio, that Chelsea Clinton had to write some essay about how she hates being white. This was not a true story. Rush, as far as I know, never apologized for

broadcasting it, but he did say he got it from CBS. *It turns out that the bad guy here was CBS, not Rush.* They had a tip sheet that actually put the story out, so I say, Rush, you're off the hook on that one. (Emphasis mine.)

The media makes mistakes about me all the time. One columnist claimed I call Hillary Rodham Clinton a feminazi. I do no such thing. Another said I blame the falling dollar on welfare and feminazis. I never have. Still another pundit claimed my radio show is carried on more than 1,400 stations. Not yet true, but inevitable. What is undeniable is that my critics—from the president to his left-wing political allies and devotees in the mainstream media—are quick to judge what I say as outrageous, fabricated, and deceptive because I am effective, and they are panic-stricken by my ability to challenge the current terms of political debate.

The second reason liberals fear me is that I represent middle America's growing rejection of the elites. Americans are increasingly convinced they have been deceived by the so-called "professionals" and "experts"—particularly, but not exclusively, in the media. Seeing themselves as sacrosanct, the self-important media elite have adopted a religious zeal toward their business—which they actually consider a "mission." I pointed this out in my first book, but the situation has gotten both worse and more transparent. The *Washington Post*'s advertising campaign for new subscribers states bluntly, "If you don't get it, you don't get it." Fortunately, most Americans don't get it. Meanwhile, *The New York Times Magazine* promotes itself as "What Sunday Was Created For," which might amuse the Creator, whom, I suspect, had something very different in mind when He did the creating. But that's just it. What you have here is the arrogance of power. And that is why so many people are looking elsewhere, and increasingly to me.

Of course, it is not just the media elites that Americans are rejecting. It is the medical elites, the sociology elites, the education elites, the legal elites, the science elites—the list goes on and on—and the ideas this bunch promotes through the media. Americans have been told our health care lags behind the rest of the industrialized world;

it doesn't. They were told drugs are safe; they aren't. They were told free sex is liberating; it isn't. They were told massive welfare spending would help people get back on their feet; it hasn't. They were told that without government intervention on behalf of environmentalist wackos, the world would come to an end; it won't. They were told that religious people are dangerous to the country; they aren't.

An assistant managing editor for one regional newspaper actually wrote, "I despise the Rush Limbaugh show," throwing the pretense of journalistic objectivity to the winds. Most aren't so explicit, but their work reeks with animosity for my audience and me. The FAIR report, in fact, is interesting precisely because it is far more an elitist attack on my core beliefs than a critique of my accuracy. FAIR was launched in 1987 with seed money from the New World Foundation, whose chairman that year was none other than Hillary Rodham Clinton. Its board of advisers include some of America's best-known leftists and feminists, from Ed Asner to Gloria Steinem. Its mission is to expose right-wing bias in the media. That's right—I'm not making this up—right-wing bias: The group attacked the ABC miniseries *Amerika* for being too harsh on communists.

Hook, Line, and Sinker

ALONG THE WAY, FAIR has developed quite a track record for inaccuracy. In 1988 FAIR charged that a Texas reporter had attempted suicide because his paper (*Beaumont Enterprise*) refused to print an article about toxic waste. The truth was that the paper ran an entire series of articles, which won a journalism prize. The reporter hadn't tried to kill himself; he accidentally wounded himself with a handgun.

In 1993, FAIR promoted the myth that domestic violence soars on Super Bowl Sunday, flooding abuse telephone hotlines with calls and crowding emergency rooms with wives beaten to a pulp by football-crazed husbands. The story was picked up by media outlets all over the country. There was just one problem; it wasn't true. In fact, *Washington Post* reporter Ken Ringle debunked the story and detailed FAIR's role in the hoax in a widely praised article of January 31, 1993. The next day, the *San Francisco Examiner* reported: "Jeff Cohen, executive director of FAIR, acknowledged that he could not find a specific study to back up his group's claim."

What was disturbing, though not surprising, was that anyone in the mainstream media took FAIR's assault on me seriously, given the group's obvious bias and history of error. But since FAIR was repeating so many elitist liberal myths as facts, many in the mainstream media could not tell the difference. Take health care, for example. Not surprising given the current debate, FAIR attacked my view on health care, a charge quickly picked up by the Associated Press. I'm quoted as saying: "If you have any doubts about the status of American health care, just compare it with that in other industrialized nations." FAIR responded: "The United States ranks 16th in life expectancy and 21st in infant survival among industrialized nations, according to the CIA's 1993 *World Fact Book.*"

The truth is, I was right. The Associated Press bought FAIR's charge hook, line, and sinker, but the evidence supporting my claim was there for the asking—in the *New Republic,* no less. Elizabeth Mc-Caughey, then a fellow at the Manhattan Institute, in her article, "No Exit," answered this myth directly:

> The [Clinton] Administration often cites two statistics—America's relatively high infant mortality rate and its lower life expectancy—to support the need for the Clinton health bill. But these have almost nothing to do with the quality of American medical care. Both statistics reflect the epidemic of low-birth-weight babies born to teenage and drug-addicted mothers, as well as the large numbers of homicides in American cities and drug-related deaths. In fact, if you're seriously ill, the best place to be is in the United States. Among all industrialized nations, the United States has the highest cure rates for stomach, cervical, and uterine cancer, the second-highest cure rate for breast cancer, and is second to none in treating heart disease.

The real issue at stake in the health-care debate, as I have pointed out relentlessly on my programs, has been personal liberty. I examined for my audience the actual contents (a novel approach, I realize) of the Clinton health-care plan and its various Democratic incarnations, I pointed out the strictures, fines, penalties—including jail time—included in the president's plan. I ran the numbers. I detailed projections of the economic effects of the proposal on small business. I examined the history of government-run health care worldwide. I examined the history of government-run programs in the United States. Information citizens needed to make informed decisions, don't you think? Yet the interest of the mainstream media was merely to champion the Clinton plan, and "give the Clintons credit" for "raising the issue."

I welcome scrutiny. I gladly defend my opinions, my analysis, and the evidence I cite for them. But my contention is that this administration's policies do not, except on programs like mine, receive the kind of scrutiny regularly aimed at me. And the emphasis is clearly skewed. I cannot raise your taxes. I cannot regulate your business out of existence. I cannot affect your behavior in any way, shape or form—nor do I wish to. I merely seek to persuade. You are free to turn me off; you can ignore me. But you cannot tune in to another administration, or turn off the one we have. It is their ideas, their assertions, their policies that cry out for careful analysis and scrutiny.

Next, let's go to the issue of condoms. *The New York Times* sold FAIR advertising space on its editorial page to make this charge: "Rush's groundless assertions on issues of public importance include . . . condom users have a one-in-five AIDS risk." This distorts even FAIR's own study, which quotes me as saying, "The worst of all this is the lie that condoms really protect against AIDS. The condom failure rate can be as high as 20 percent. Would you get on a plane—or put your children on a plane—if one in five passengers would be killed on the flight? Well, the statistic holds for condoms, folks." That, of course, is distinctly different from saying that condom users have a one-in-five AIDS risk. In addition, though liberals are loath to admit it, I am right about the ineffectiveness of condoms. A 1993 study by Susan C. Weller for the University of Texas Medical Branch found that "Although contraceptive research indicates that condoms are 87 percent effective in preventing pregnancy, results of HIV transmission studies indicate that condoms may reduce risk of HIV infections by approximately 69 percent," adding that condom "efficacy may be much lower than commonly assumed." Weller's study concludes: "It is a disservice to encourage the belief that condoms will prevent sexual transmission of HIV."

Ideological Fiction

OR TAKE WOMEN'S ISSUES. The *Los Angeles Times* couldn't resist citing FAIR's attack on my views on contemporary feminism. I'm quoted as saying: "Women were doing quite well in this country before feminism came along." FAIR's response: "Before feminism, women couldn't even vote." The fact is, the objectives and tactics of militant feminism bear little resemblance to the women's suffrage movement. The true backlash in this country is against militant feminism, yet another sign of victory. The largest women's organization in the country, for example, is not the National Organization for Women, with just 250,000 members. It is, instead, Concerned Women for America, a conservative group, with over 600,000 members. And even liberal women are having second thoughts. Wrote columnist Marilyn Gardner in the *Christian Science Monitor* (not exactly a conservative rag):

> Every revolution has its losing side. In the sexual revolution, evidence continues to mount that the supposed winners—liberated women—are in some cases turning out to be the losers. Instead of the freedom and equality they thought they had achieved, too many find themselves shackled by unplanned pregnancies, abortions, single motherhood, infections or infertility.

Precisely. But with Gloria Steinem and Susan Faludi on FAIR's board, don't expect them to concede these points any time soon.

The elites have far too often dismissed fact for their ideological fiction. More and more Americans are beginning to awaken to this reality, and are looking to me for a second opinion. I give them the other side, which is based on common sense and traditional morality rather than academic hypotheses. And I am right (as I like to say on the air) "97.9 percent of the time." On radio for six years and more than 4,000 hours, I have of course made mistakes along the way. But I make every attempt to prominently correct every such error as soon as I discover it. Here's an example of what FAIR considers a "fabrication": In one of my books, I attributed to James Madison a quote that he did not make. (People have been misattributing this quote to Madison as far back as Harold K. Lane's 1939 book, *Liberty, Cry, Liberty.*) This is a mistake—not a lie. And I have yet to publicly promise a middle-class tax cut I privately dismiss as "intellectually dishonest," and which I have no intention of keeping.

Third, liberals fear me because I'm validating the thoughts of the silent majority. Liberals seek to lull Americans to sleep with promises that government will take care of everything, if they will just fork over their money. I, on the other hand, challenge people to wake up. Millions already seriously question the wisdom of handing $1.5 trillion a year to the federal government when the post office cannot even deliver the mail on time—and actually throws away what it is too lazy to deliver. I provide the hard information, statistics, and specific details from the record to confirm many Americans' suspicions about government "efficiency." That is the sort of thing that infuriates liberals, who are wed to the idea that government is good, and the bigger the better.

New York Times columnist Anthony Lewis, in a revealing July article entitled "Where Power Lies," argued that "power does not reside only in the White House or government anymore." His worst nightmare, apparently. Instead, "those who seek to destroy faith in the American political system have considerable power now, power demanding attention." Lewis breathlessly explained that "Rush Limbaugh's game" is "to throw dirt on government and anyone who believes that society needs government. In his hateful talk about President and Mrs. Clinton and others in office, he is really trying to destroy public faith in our institutions."

The charge is preposterous. He admits he never listens to my program—"a pleasure I deny myself," as he puts it. As anyone in my audience will tell you, I defend the institutions and traditions which have made America great. But perhaps Mr. Lewis should go back and reread some of his old columns for a clue about why Americans are so upset with government today. In 1992 he wrote: "Hyperbole is to be expected of politicians. But deliberate lies? I think that kind of politics has brought this country close to disbelief in its political system." He was referring, unconvincingly, to George Bush—but a reader can be forgiven if our current president springs to mind. And that is just it. Official deception and dissembling are responsible for Americans' growing anger and frustration with government. I simply shine the light of truth on it.

Lewis asserts: "Indeed, it is especially important to watch, and hold accountable, those who seek power without responsibility." Lewis was erroneously referring to me; the sentence accurately describes, however, Mrs. Clinton—who, unelected and unaccountable, has sought to reorder one-seventh of the American economy.

Clinton's Snow Job

LIBERALS ARE NOT UPSET because I am wrong; they are upset because I am right. Every day, I expose the Clinton administration's real agenda: "How can we fool 'em today?" I ask, "Where is the soul of Bill Clinton?" I point out that under Clinton, achievement must be vilified; the rich must be punished. I warn people that liberals support government programs, because government money is the basis of their political power. These are things Americans suspect anyway, but they have trouble discerning the facts amid the fog created by the mainstream media. I sift through the morning's headlines, through miles of videotape, through books, articles, and speeches in a relentless pursuit of the truth. More often than not, I confirm their fears—the Clinton administration is engaged in a massive snow job. That is validation.

The question, of course, is what people will do with truth once they have it. Liberals are absolutely convinced that I am always telling people to call Congress to complain about this issue or that (another erroneous FAIR charge). I did so once, simply to prove to a skeptical reporter what would happen if I actually did it. The calls shut down the Capitol Hill switchboard. The truth is, I don't need to urge people to call Congress. They are thoughtful, informed, serious people. That's why they listen to me. It is up to them to decide what to do with the truth. Some, I am sure, do call Congress. Others subscribe to conservative periodicals and read classic conservative books, teach their children at home, write letters to the editor, run for school boards, and volunteer to work on local political campaigns or with a local charity. The possibilities for action and involvement are as unlimited as well-informed, optimistic citizens make them.

"I don't understand: Why does anyone take Rush Limbaugh seriously?" asked *USA Today* columnist Michael Gartner, proceeding to attack me for producing "a stew of half-truths and non-truths." It is not surprising that this former president of NBC is so baffled. He is, after all, a charter member of the media elite, kicked out of NBC after *Dateline* staged an explosion of a General Motors truck, and after a *Nightly News* report on environmental abuses ran footage of "dead" fish that turned out not to be dead. The answer to his question, however, is simple. People take me seriously because I am effective. I celebrate an America made great because of the extraordinary accomplishments of ordinary people—unlike the media, who promote the mistaken premise that the country's success stems from government programs. What I express is called belief in the American people, not contempt for them.

Fourth and finally, liberals fear me because I am not running for political office, and thus I am invulnerable to the political attacks of liberals. "Demagogues . . . fizzle out because people weary of the act or because the political equation changes or because they face a real political challenge," insisted the *Nation*'s Alexander Cockburn in a July *Los Angeles Times* column. "There's almost no one out there fighting the political battles with Limbaugh in language ordinary people can understand and enjoy." The same month, leftist columnist Lars-Erik Nelson lamented in the *Washington Post,* "There is no leftist equivalent to Rush Limbaugh."

Liberals treat me as if I were the Republican presidential candidate. But I have no interest in running for office. Why should I? I am setting the agenda right where I am—with something very simple: The truth. Liberals, who for so long have dominated the nation's institutions and who have tried so hard to dominate the nation's political agenda, flounder helplessly as a result. They understand how to fight a political challenge—war rooms, bus tours, direct mail, editorials, protests. They do not know how to fight a cultural challenge—the explosion of talk radio—except to try to regulate it out of existence (as in their attempts to revive the Fairness Doctrine, dubbed the "Hush Rush Bill" by the *Wall Street Journal*).

What is actually happening now is a threat to liberal control of America's institutions. And this phenomenon is not a political one. The American people are discovering once again what the Founders always intended—that the country's future is in their hands. It depends on parents raising their children; it depends on teachers pushing these children to excellence; it depends on grandparents teaching these children the traditional lessons of morality and virtue; it depends on pastors, priests, and rabbis pointing these children to the God who loves them.

The Most Dangerous Man in America

THAT IS NOT TO SAY politics or the presidency is not important; it is. Washington takes too much of our money and our liberties and reinforces the dangerous myth that government can provide security and happiness and success. Yes, Americans need to send men and women of character to Washington and state capitals. But politics is not everything.

That is my message, and that is why I am dangerous. Neither the 1994 nor 1996 election results will serve as the sole indicators of the impact of my programs, because the battle is not simply for political control; it is for reestablishing control of America's institutions. And because I am affecting the debate on how that can be achieved, liberals are apoplectic.

Many times I get calls on my show from people who rail against one liberal outrage or another and complain that the country is going down the tubes. That was certainly the reaction this summer as liberals fired their salvos at me and my audience. But actually, the liberal extremists may well be on their last legs. Their power source, the Democratic party and its leadership, is woefully out of touch. They simply cannot extricate themselves from bondage; their power base is a constituency of victimhood. The shrill tone and apocalyptic hyperbole that characterize liberal attacks on me are instructive, speaking volumes about their fear of becoming irrelevant.

Historians will remember 1994 as a watershed year in American politics. This was the year that modern liberalism, the ideology dominating nearly every important cultural and political institution in the country, tipped its hand, revealing its deep insecurity. The summer of 1994 will be remembered as the season that liberals, acutely aware of the seismic rumbles just below the surface of American politics and society, unleashed their fury against a man who is neither a politician nor a candidate for political office. This was the summer all hell broke loose against the "most dangerous man in America."

Liberals are terrified of me. As well they should be.

The Revolution of 1994

John H. Fund

THE BELTWAY FINALLY ACCEPTED THE FACT that a political revolution is heading its way only last Thursday, October 13. On that day, a Times Mirror poll reported that 52 percent of registered voters plan to vote Republican for Congress, and only 40 percent Democratic. Charlie Cook, a respected Democratic-leaning political handicapper, said he now believed the GOP would win a Senate majority. But the most astonishing acknowledgment of the coming revolution came from the Clinton White House itself.

At a conference of liberal activists organized by *Mother Jones* magazine, Bill Galston, the president's deputy assistant for domestic policy, sketched a "dark picture indeed" of the political landscape. He said the Clinton administration has been "a qualified policy success, and an almost unqualified political failure." He admitted that "the weight of populist energy is not in our favor," and urged liberals to begin their analysis "from where the people actually are."

He warned that the national mood is not "some temporary wave of discontent" but represents "a generalized withdrawal of trust and confidence from governing structures." He urged liberals to recognize the public's criticism of centralized power and to think about a possible "devolution of power and responsibility" away from Washington.

Mr. Galston was largely met with silence by an audience that appeared to be divided between uncomprehending true believers and shell-shocked realists. Liberals may not have liked what Mr. Galston told them, but no one challenged him.

The United States is on the verge of a political earthquake similar to those that have rocked many nations since the end of the cold war. Voters in Italy, France, Sweden, Japan, and Canada all revolted against entrenched parties and tossed them out of power. Absent a communist threat, voters will no longer put up with the corruption, shoddy services, and arrogance that have characterized their ruling elites.

In America, the conventional wisdom until this month was that the midterm elections would be "anti-incumbent" and a pox on both parties. Yes, a few old GOP bulls may lose, but the incumbents in trouble now are all Democrats. Why?

A good place to turn for answers is a new study of America's political attitudes by the Times Mirror Center. Since 1987, Times Mirror has conducted surveys of what are huge groups of voters for its polls: 3,800 versus a conventional sample of 1,000. Their latest poll finds that Americans are increasingly negative about government, with 66 percent saying it's almost always wasteful and inefficient. However, Americans make a distinction in their feelings between the government and the nation itself. A surprising 68 percent say Americans can always find a way to solve problems, and 62 percent don't believe there are any real limits to growth in the future.

The Times Mirror survey indicates the nation has changed in fundamental ways. In the words of CNN political analyst William Schneider, the United States has become "ideologically populist, and operationally libertarian." Most people no longer believe Washington is relevant to their lives. A striking 69 percent say dealing with a federal agency is "often not worth the trouble," up from 58 percent in 1987. The number of people who don't think it's the responsibility of government to take care of those who can't care for themselves has climbed to 41 percent, up from 24 percent in 1987. That explains the growing interest in private charities.

Liberal Democrats have not caught this shift. Their mental radio receivers just do not pick up certain stations. They don't realize how many voters believe that anything tainted with Washington is tainted with poison. A Hudson Institute study to be released on Friday finds that 55 percent of Americans think Congress is the most powerful institution of government, but only 29 percent want it to be. People want more control at the state and local level, but most liberals—Mr. Galston excepted—don't get it.

Ironically, Ronald Reagan restored some public faith in Washington—66 percent now view Mr. Reagan positively—but the perception that Presidents Bush and Clinton didn't govern as they promised has ushered in a further decline in confidence. "Bill Clinton was elected as a Reagan Democrat, but has governed as a liberal," says Democratic consultant Brian Lunde. "It's the philosophy, stupid."

Bill Clinton has also educated many voters about which party has sole control of the federal government. In 1992, after two GOP presidents, only 52 percent knew Democrats had a majority in the House. Today, 60 percent do, and some even know it's been forty years since Republicans were in charge, before the events depicted in the recent movie *Quiz Show* occurred.

After examining many polls and talking with dozens of voters, I'm convinced there is an emerging political consensus in America. It includes some 70 percent of voters and centers on three core issues: political accountability, efficiency in government, and values. The Democrats will lose next month because they pursued a Washington-based ideological agenda that didn't address those core concerns. Republicans will win because they haven't yet shown that they too may fail to do so.

The first issue centers on accountability to voters. People are fed up with politicians who say one thing to get votes and then do something else in office. Doubters can look to what happened to George Bush and New Jersey Gov. Jim Florio after they said they wouldn't raise taxes and then did. Both lost to weak challengers, but Gov. Christie Whitman is now very popular in New Jersey after starting to deliver on tax cuts; while Mr. Clinton is dogged by the fact that millions of Americans believe nothing he says.

Public frustration with candidates who play games of "Surprise!" once in office has cemented support for term limits, which would reduce the number of career office-seekers who will say and do anything to gain political promotion. Colorado and Washington have passed laws requiring a vote of the people to raise taxes, and Oregon,

Missouri, and Montana will vote on the concept next month. I predict that at least one presidential contender—and maybe more—will make a call for voter approval of taxes at the national level a part of his 1996 campaign.

The second issue around which a consensus is forming is that few people see government as "a good buy." If it were a consumer product on a store shelf, it would be removed for being defective and sued for false advertising. With government taking more than 40 percent of national income, voters are demanding value for their tax dollars. They want to be treated as customers, not constituents. As political analyst Michael Barone points out, business went through a painful restructuring in the 1980s: downsizing, reorganizing, becoming lean and mean. America is now more competitive in world markets than ever before. But one major sector of American life is viewed as remote, bloated, and resistant to reform: public bureaucracies. We will soon have a twenty-first-century private sector traveling an information superhighway, while a nineteenth-century government pokes along on the equivalent of a stagecoach line.

Voters are demanding that officials practice performance-based politics and deliver value for money. "If we Democrats don't reduce taxes and spending, our party is going to be extinct," says Rep. Rob Andrews (Democrat, New Jersey). "The issue before Democrats today is whether we change or die."

The last issue concerns values. In the Hudson Institute survey, people believed the single greatest threat to future generations was the decline of morals and ethical standards. That explains why Bill Bennett's *Book of Virtues* has sold 1.5 million copies. Americans are generally tolerant and increasingly accept people who differ from them. But a clear majority are appalled by a cult of victimology whose adherents always blame someone else for their difficulties.

America was founded on the premise that so long as citizens accepted the consequences of their actions, it was their right to be reversed. Too many people shun personal responsibility, and think those who are irresponsible or foolish should be subsidized by others. At the same time, some want to ban everything from politically incorrect speech to toy guns and the wearing of fur.

Americans don't agree on abortion, the regulation of pornography, or many other values. But a growing number believe requiring more personal responsibility would help halt the fraying of our moral fabric. It might even result in less sin. The Times Mirror survey asked respondents if success in life is pretty much determined by forces outside a person's control. A total of 39 percent agreed and 59 percent disagreed. Interestingly, 26 percent completely disagreed with the statement, and 14 percent completely agreed; in 1987 a total of only 24 percent held such firm views.

The political party or leaders that tackle these three issues head-on will be entrusted with power. Right now, the failure of Democrats to recognize the public's anger with Washington solutions has opened up a wide opportunity for Republicans. However, if the GOP is handed power—in part in 1994 or in whole in 1996—it will have to deliver.

Should the GOP fail, increasingly independent voters will first turn on it and then question the relevance of the two-party system itself. They may even harness new technologies and look to Switzerland's solution—one in which voters themselves make key policy decisions through referendums and local governments. Switzerland's president can be identified by only a minority of voters. America's parties will either tame the revolution seething below them, or the voters will seek their own radical reforms by reinventing the government themselves.

About the Contributors

Fred Barnes is executive editor of *The Standard*.

Robert L. Bartley is editor of the *Wall Street Journal*.

William J. Bennett, a fellow at the Hudson Institute and the Heritage Foundation, is codirector of Empower America.

Tom Bethell is a columnist for the *American Spectator* and a Media Fellow at the Hoover Institution.

James Bowman is American editor for the *Times Literary Supplement* of London and movie critic for the *American Spectator*.

Richard Brookhiser is a senior editor at *National Review*, a columnist for the *New York Observer*, and author of *The Way of the Wasp* and *Founding Father*.

David Brooks is a senior editor at the *Standard*.

Christopher Buckley is author of *The White House Mess* and *Thank You for Smoking* and is editor of "Forbes F.Y.I."

Christopher Clausen is professor of English at Pennsylvania State University and author of *The Place of Poetry* and *The Moral Imagination*.

Danielle Crittenden is editor of the *Independent Women's Quarterly*.

Andrew Ferguson is a senior editor at the *Standard*.

David Frum is the author of *Dead Right,* a book about the Republican party.

John H. Fund is an editorial writer for the *Wall Street Journal*.

Paul A. Gigot is a member of the editorial board and Washington columnist for the *Wall Street Journal* and a commentator on the *Mac-Neil/Lehrer NewsHour*.

George Gilder is a fellow at the Seattle Discovery Institute in Seattle and author of *Wealth and Poverty, Microcosm,* and other books.

Mark Helprin is author of *A Winter's Tale* and other novels and is a contributing editor to the *Wall Street Journal*.

Kay S. Hymowitz is a senior fellow at the Manhattan Institute.

Donald Kagan is Bass Professor of History, Classics, and Western Civilization at Yale University and the author of a four-volume history of the Peloponnesian War.

Florence King is the author of *With Charity toward None* and other books and a columnist for the *National Review.*

Charles Krauthammer is a syndicated columnist.

William Kristol is editor and publisher of the *Standard*.

Rush Limbaugh hosts radio and television talk shows.

Charles Murray, a fellow at the American Enterprise Institute, is author of *Losing Ground* and coauthor of *The Bell Curve.*

Peggy Noonan, a former presidential speechwriter, is author of *What I Saw at the Revolution* and *Life, Liberty and the Pursuit of Happiness.*

P. J. O'Rourke, author of *Republican Party Reptile, Parliament of Whores,* and other books, is a correspondent for *Rolling Stone.*

Clifford Orwin is professor of political science at the University of Toronto.

John Podhoretz is deputy editor of the *Standard.*

Joe Queenan is the author of *If You're Talking to Me, Your Career Must Be in Trouble* and is a frequent guest on the *Imus in the Morning* radio show.

Dorothy Rabinowitz is television critic and editorial writer for the *Wall Street Journal.*

Lisa Schiffren, a former speechwriter for Vice President Quayle, is a writer who lives in Brooklyn.

Roger Scruton is the author of *Sexual Desire: A Moral Philosophy of the Erotic,* among many other books, and a professor of philosophy at Boston University.

Dave Shiflett, former deputy editorial page editor of the *Rocky Mountain News,* is a writer who lives in Virginia.

Christina Hoff Sommers is professor of philosophy at Clark University.

Jeffrey R. Snyder is a lawyer in Washington, D.C.

James Q. Wilson is professor of management and public policy at UCLA.

Permissions Acknowledgments